JUSTICE

Hope for everyone
everywhere

ADAM LIVECCHI

JUSTICE
Hope for everyone everywhere.

ADAM LIVECCHI

JUSTICE: HOPE FOR EVERYONE EVERYWHERE

ISBN 978-0-9893101-5-4

Printed in the United States of America.

First Printing: March 2016

For more information on how to order this book or any of the other materials We See Jesus Ministries offers please contact:
We See Jesus Ministries
www.WeSeeJesusMinistries.com

DEDICATION

Steve & Christina Stewart : This book is dedicated to you because your relentless love for Jesus and the poor has inspired and challenged me. Your pure and selfless motives are always visible to those that know you. Steve, I can't thank you enough for telling me in India that "I had a home in Vancouver should I want to come." My life changed as a result of your lives. Being with you guys gave me a dream, a vision and direction for the rest of my life. You are heroes, and we love you both very much. Thank you both from the very bottom of my heart.

Nic & Rachael Billman : This book is dedicated to you because you represent what God is doing in our generation. You will be pillars in this generation and your work in Brazil will echo through history. Your friendship and worship is priceless. When I think of you guys I think of a raw beating heart that aches for the overlooked and abused. Thank you for who you are and for your friendship. We love you both very much!

Reginald & Johanne Célestin : This book is dedicated to you simply because of your dedication to love Jesus and your own (Haitian) people. You guys love until it hurts. In spite of the many challenges you face, together you overcome them. With love you serve and just spend yourself on Jesus and his Kingdom. You lead with wisdom. I am deeply honored to call you friends. Reginald, I will never forget our conversation by the pool in Kaliko Beach where we both came to the sobering conclusion that - if we don't succeed many people will suffer. I remember the fear of the Lord and the desire to be faithful that came upon us that evening. We love you guys!

ENDORSEMENTS

The Apostle Paul declared, *"For the Kingdom of God is not in word but in power"* (1 Corinthians 4:20). It is the power of God that gives us grace to speak on behalf of the unborn; it is the power of God to display the mind of Christ to end systemic poverty; it is the power of God over every sickness and disease; it is the power of God over all darkness and evil that exists in the earth. The kingdom of God is not devoid of practical demonstration and application. This is the message from the heart of God given through Adam LiVecchi's latest book, "Justice". This book is a wonderful combination of practicality, scripture and revelation. The message released through this book demands action!

Abner Suarez
Author *Creation Reborn*
For Such A Time As This, Inc.
Dunn, NC USA
www.AbnerSuarez.com

Adam has done it again! I believe this is his best book yet, most likely because justice has long been the heart cry of his life. The first time that I ever met Adam it was at a conference in Maryland and I had just sung one of our songs

"Shores of Grace" and he came up to me and asked me to come to an event that he was doing and then started "preaching" about justice. I was so blessed by the purity of his heart to see justice as simply one of the characteristics of our God. This book not only reveals that characteristic but teaches us biblical and practical theology in regards to God's desire for justice and how we, His people, are a part of that. Through Adam's many trips to some of the poorest places on earth he has seen first hand what injustice looks like, however I am thankful that he first knew who Justice was, and this book reveals that so beautifully. It's not simply a complaint or response to injustice, but a compassionate cry for Godly justice in our generation. I loved the book and I know that you will also!

Nic Billman
President, Shores of Grace Ministries
Recife, Brazil
www.ShoresofGrace.com

Adam is a great friend and a rising voice in our generation calling the Church to works of justice. His passion for the poor, the marginalized, and for those suffering injustice, reminds me of the heart of our Lord. Every time I'm in contact with Adam's ministry I feel connected with the love for justice our Father has for humanity. This book will challenge your faith, reveal deep truths of the Kingdom of God, uplift your spiritual walk and most of all encourage you to not tire in doing good! Highly recommend it!

Teofilo Hayashi
Founder of Dunamis
Sao Paulo, Brazil
www.iDunamis.org

In "Justice", Adam truly captures the heart of God. God has much work for us to do that goes way beyond attending Sunday morning services at a nice church. He wants us to get our hands dirty, to right the wrongs of society, and to be the hands and feet of Christ to a hurting world. We can't change everything, but we can each pray and work to change something. Christ came to make a difference in our lives and now sends us to make a difference in others. Justice will equip and encourage you to make a difference!

Jack Redmond
Pastor of Evangelism and Church Growth
Author of *INFUSION*
www.4thgen.org

It doesn't take long while reading this book to see that Adam's heart beats like that of his Lord's. God is a God who has always noticed and extended grace to the downtrodden of our world. Adam does a good job revealing that powerful truth in this book. It's a very relevant message for the day and age in which we live. Great job Adam.

Pastor Don James
Lead Pastor of Bethany Church
Wyckoff, New Jersey
www.BethanyChurch.tv

I encourage everyone to read it, but only if you are prepared to be challenged and to be made uncomfortable with truth. Filled with not only overarching principles, but with nuggets of gold, *Justice: Hope for Everyone Everywhere*" speaks to many issues of a bigger, more powerful and inclusive Gospel. Well done, Adam, I believe that this is your most powerful book yet.

Steve Stewart
President of Impact Nations
www.ImpactNations.com

Adam has not only captured the heart of God in his new book "Justice", he has been transformed into an agent on assignment to bring God's Kingdom to earth as it is in Heaven! Adam walks in practical revelation by simply doing what God reveals to him. "Justice" will empower you to do the same. You will be encouraged to walk in real time revelation right where you are and take full advantage of the soil you are already standing on, because that's where God currently is. God is raising up new generals who will lead an army hungry for souls and God's Kingdom. Adam is one of those generals and he is leading change agents of God's justice all over the world!

"I press toward the goal for the prize of the upward call of God in Christ Jesus. Therefore let us, as many as are mature, have this mind; and if in anything you think otherwise, God will reveal even this to you. Nevertheless, to the degree that we have already attained, let us walk by the same rule, let us be of the same mind." (Philippians 3:14-16 NKJV)

Pastor Clem Salerno
Senior Pastor of Calvary Tabernacle
Cranford, NJ
www.ctnj.org

TABLE OF CONTENTS

CHAPTER ONE

THE JOURNEY BEGINS

God had an only Son, and he was a missionary and a physician. [1]
- *David Livingstone*

Come follow me.
- *Jesus of Nazareth*

Imagine

Let's say you were eating food at a medical clinic in a nation (Haiti) devastated by an earthquake, and there were hungry people all around you. So as to not offend them you went in a back classroom of the church. Imagine while you were eating, a little girl threw little rocks and dirt that hit you in the back of the head. How would you feel? Would you connect the dots between hunger and anger? Would you think about how where there is hunger and starvation there is also violence? Would you be mad that someone threw rocks at you? Would you feel in danger that perhaps there are more rocks with your name on them? Or would you feel gut wrenching compassion for the little girl because she was hungry and you were eating? Rewind from 2012 back to 2005. That's where the journey began.

Bethany Church, Wyckoff New Jersey

For me my love for the nations and the poor began at the altar of Bethany Church in Wyckoff, New Jersey. Pastor Don James, the lead pastor of Bethany church, is a man who has an incredible love for the nations. At that time, Hillsong wrote and released a very popular song called "To the Ends of the Earth." God used this song to prepare my heart for the nations. I would be facedown at the altar and weep and weep and weep some more. This song touched me in a way that I don't have words for other than that song became the cry of my heart. There was something about that song that deeply connected to everything I was beginning to desire as I started to spend a lot of personal time in the presence of God both at home and at church. The common denominator was facedown time with Jesus, that song and a deep cry to go to the nations. In April of 2005, the young adult pastor at Bethany Church, Chris Colletti, was taking a young adult team to Honduras. As soon as I heard of the trip I wanted to go and immediately committed to going. I had no idea what I was in for. Now I know that God was positioning me to see something that would change me, and the whole entire direction of my life. Jesus is really smart; he's got it all figured out. It is a good idea to trust him. One of the things I want to say in and through this book is it is safe to trust and follow Jesus. It may cost your life, but it is still your best bet. To love him is to obey him and in obeying him we get to know him and his amazing personality! That is good news.

Honduras - April 11-17, 2005

When we landed in Honduras, I quickly realized that we were no longer in the United States. Things were drastically different. I just didn't know exactly how different just yet. As we got through customs and left the airport we then got into a huge school bus and drove through Tegucigalpa, which is the capital city of Honduras. I started to see urban poverty like I had never seen before in the United States. I grew up going to an inner city church so I know about the hood, but this was different—way different from anything I had ever seen before. Later on we arrived at the hotel/buffet/gas station. As I got off the bus, I looked up and saw two men standing on the roof. One of them had a handgun the other one had an ak-47 machine gun with a banana clip on it. I remember thinking that is crazy. Where are we? What is the machine gun all about? Now I know that a gas station/hotel/buffet place that has 10-15 Americans in it would be a nice place to rob should there not be two guys on the roof, one of them heavily armed with an automatic machine gun. This was only the beginning of the culture shock I was in for.

Eventually we left the hotel again in that huge bus that had loud speakers on it so the gospel could be preached while the bus was moving. As we journeyed along a country road, I saw another horrific sight. Off the road to the right of us was a horrible car accident with dead bodies just lying there. They were missing limbs; if my memory serves me correctly, there was also a decapitated body. What was even more disturbing is it didn't look like this just happened. It looked like it happened at least a day or so ago. I was thinking this is crazy. There are dead people on the side of the road. What the heck is up with this place? What is going on here? First the guy with a machine gun on the roof, now the dead people on the side of the road? I was almost bewildered but for some reason I felt at peace and a sense of joy not about the dead people but about being in Honduras. It was almost like I felt at home?

Later in the journey we ended up in a very, very poor rural village. As the team and I got off the bus I saw a man walking back into the village with a machete in his right hand. As I looked to the left of me, I saw two naked children walking barefoot in sewage. They were somewhere between 3-8 years old. Off the road was a shack with a woman in it. She had a dirt floor and there was virtually nothing in her house. When I saw this, something inside of me turned and I immediately began to weep. The words that came out of my mouth were "I never knew. I never knew." Literally, I had never seen anything like that in my whole entire life. When I saw this, I knew this was terribly wrong. There was something very wrong about this whole scene. The feelings of outrage and anger over injustice and compassion for the people just filled my emotions. When I saw abject poverty for the first time, I immediately knew that I was born to see this change. That day my only way to respond to what God was doing in my heart was for me to give away my favorite Diesel shoes. It just so happened that those were the shoes on my feet. I left that village with no shoes. There were tears in my eyes and I was gripped with compassion for these beautiful people who were living in circumstances that nobody on the planet should have to live in. That day God marked my life. In that little desperately poor village in Honduras, my life was changed. God set me up. He opened my eyes and broke my heart all in a moment for a mission that he had been preparing me for, for some time. Preparation is huge. It is a game changer. The difference between a winner and a loser in sports is generally preparation. Once a man asked Abraham Lincoln if he had eight hours to cut a tree down what would he do? Abe replied, "I would sharpen my axe for six hours." Abe's answer was about preparation. Wisdom is always prepared. Wisdom sees preparation as completely necessary. According to Jesus, "Wisdom is justified by her children." In God's divine wisdom, he was preparing me for about two years so that when he allowed me to see what he wanted to show me I would respond correctly. Whatever you may be going through today just know you are being prepared for tomorrow. For me what started on the altar of Bethany Church in a very wealthy neighborhood in North New Jersey was solidified in a terribly poor village in Honduras. The desire for the nations is what God used to get me to the nation of Honduras to see what God wanted to show me. God wasn't looking to show me some phenomenon. He was looking to show me what his Son Jesus bled for – people. Jesus had rescued my life from destruction. Now he was telling me others need rescuing too. So let's get er' done! He didn't say let's get er' done but that was really what he was saying. When God allows you to see something that you know bothers him, it's because he is inviting you to do something about it. God is inviting us to be part of the solution. Pray about it, give to the cause and then do something about it. Partner with God and be a part of the solution. To do nothing is to be part of the problem. There are too many Christians who are neutralized by fear, unbelief, compromise and complacency.

Get in the game. Be a part of the change that Jesus told us to pray for when he taught his disciples to pray, "Your Kingdom come, Your will be done on earth as it is in heaven." In our obedience to Jesus, we can be a part of the answer to his prayer. In case we didn't figure it out yet the world around us doesn't' really care what we believe, but they are forced to notice what we do. The world around us takes notice of actions. Our actions show them what we really believe. *"Let your light so shine before men, that they may see your good works and glorify your Father in heaven."* (Matthew 5:16 NKJV) According to Jesus our obedience reveals the Father. In a planet with more than 153,000,00 orphans (yes, you read that correctly 153 million) perhaps obedience is a good idea. If Jesus obeyed then obedience is not an option in the kingdom. It's the only choice.

Jesus Defines Evil

"There was a certain rich man who was clothed in purple and fine linen and fared sumptuously every day. But there was a certain beggar named Lazarus, full of sores, who was laid at his gate, desiring to be fed with the crumbs which fell from the rich man's table. Moreover the dogs came and licked his sores. So it was that the beggar died, and was carried by the

21

angels to Abraham's bosom. The rich man also died and was buried. And being in torments in Hades, he lifted up his eyes and saw Abraham afar off, and Lazarus in his bosom. "Then he cried and said, 'Father Abraham, have mercy on me, and send Lazarus that he may dip the tip of his finger in water and cool my tongue; for I am tormented in this flame.' **But Abraham said, 'Son, remember that in your lifetime you received your good things, and likewise Lazarus evil things; but now he is comforted and you are tormented.** *And besides all this, between us and you there is a great gulf fixed, so that those who want to pass from here to you cannot, nor can those from there pass to us."* (Luke 16:19-26 NKJV)

In Jesus' parable, Abraham was a voice of righteousness and justice. Jesus used Abraham in the parable to define sickness and hunger as evil. He also described the rich man's abundance as good things. Jesus said you received good things, not you earned them. Here Jesus used Abraham to hold the rich man accountable for not doing what was in his power to do for the poor man. God will only hold us accountable for what we know to do because he is just. If God would hold us accountable for what we don't know or don't have the power to do then he would not be just and he is just. This rich man could have been a good neighbor and shared with the man who was right in front of his mansion, but he

> God will only hold us accountable for what we know to do because he is just.

did not. Then the rich man wanted the poor man to serve him in hell and he found no comfort or help. Remember the words of Paul the Apostle, *"Do not be deceived. God is not mocked; for whatever a man sows, that he will also reap."* (Galatians 6:7 NKJV)) Later, the rich man who was in hades asked Abraham to send someone to talk to his family about the reality of hades. Abraham denied him. Here is the reality—people in hell believe in personal evangelism. The rich and the poor alike both need the gospel for it is the power of God unto salvation. If you would like to reap salvation in your family, sow the message of the gospel into other people's family. Spiritual warfare is not looking for demons on top of mountains or buildings, it's living in the opposite spirit and sowing seeds we ourselves would like to reap.

Tela, Honduras - April 13, 2005

Jose Roberto Mendoza Doblardo is a man who received Jesus on the Honduras trip I wrote about earlier. Here is what happened. The Bethany Church team was in a church on a Wednesday evening praying for people. I was praying for a man. I had my hands on the man like a good Pentecostal/Charismatic should. Then Jesus spoke to me in the spirit of my mind and said, "Take your hands off that man and look outside." So, I did and there was a man about fifty feet past the little church we were at. The Lord said to me, "that is one of my lost sheep. Tell him he walked away from Jesus but Jesus never walked away from him." So I spoke what I heard and he responded, "This is true." I then asked him if I could pray for him and he said yes. So, we anointed him with oil, prayed for him gave him a Spanish bible and invited him to the crusade on Friday.

Jose came that Friday night and gave his life to Jesus. We blessed him with $50.00 USD just like they tell you not to do on mission trips. We told him that God's arm is not short and that his pocket is not empty. We hugged him and rejoiced with him because he had just made the greatest decision of his life. Then Saturday night he showed up at the crusade. He was there praising God like a totally new creation. His countenance had changed. He had changed—salvation was at work. That night I was sitting by the pastors and Jesus told me to go sit by Jose. So, I did and when I did I began to experience how the Father felt because a son came home. It was so overwhelming. I must have wept for about two hours. This reality overtook my heart for those two hours, and I could feel the delight of God for this man but all I could do was weep. Later that night, Jose gave me two postcards. (Written on the postcard was "para mi amigo que lo recuerda siempre" - "for my friend who always remembers") People matter. Jesus bled for Jose. You matter. Jesus bled for you. The young girl who is being raped daily in Brazil matters. The malnourished boy in Haiti who lost a leg in the earthquake on January 12, 2010 matters. The children in Somalia who are dying of aids matter to God. The countless babies that are being aborted in America matter to God. The young women in Russia who by the age of 30 have had on average more than 10 abortions matter to God. He wants to restore their dignity and change their hearts, minds and lives. God cares. He hears their cries. The real question is do we? Will we respond? I believe most people with a heartbeat who call Jesus Lord will respond. I am writing this book in faith that you will respond to Jesus. I am hopeful that people will be rescued because of your response. People will come out of darkness because you will let your light shine.

CHAPTER TWO

TO THE ENDS OF THE EARTH

We ought not to ask, "Can I prove that I ought to go?" but, "Can I prove that I ought not to go? [1]
- *C.H. Spurgeon*

But you shall receive power when the Holy Spirit has come upon you; and you shall be witnesses to Me in Jerusalem, and in all Judea and Samaria, and to the end of the earth.
Acts 1:8 NKJV

Following Jesus

To follow Jesus means we have to actually go somewhere besides church on Sunday. Conferences are great. I attend some and speak at others but that is not quite what Jesus had in mind when he told his early disciples to deny themselves, take up their cross and follow him. Following Christ means we will be inconvenienced; it means we will be moved with compassion for people. As we are moved with compassion, God gives us courage to act on their behalf. Following Jesus involves risk, which is why he told his early followers to count the cost. The cost could be persecution, it could cost our life. There is no promise of protection from persecution but there is a blessing that comes from it in the age to come. There is an honor that God ascribes to those who will suffer for righteousness' sake. Jesus himself declared, "Great is your reward in heaven." When Jesus first called his disciples, he said to them, "Follow me." Jesus did not tell them to believe; he told them to follow him and then gave them a reason to believe. In John chapter two, Jesus gave his followers a reason to believe. Through obeying his commandment, water was turned into wine. His glory was manifested, and his disciples believed on him. We need to give people a reason to believe instead of just telling them to believe. The gospel we preach needs to involve showing and telling, not all telling, and not all showing. The gospel of the Kingdom comes either by demonstration and explanation or by proclamation and demonstration. We demonstrate what we believe by how we live.

The gospel that does not move us will not save or change the world. The gospel we preach should produce sacrificial love that causes people to be moved with compassion and take courage against injustice. The gospel of the kingdom is the message that Jesus preached. That is the message we should preach as well.

Since Jesus died, rose and ascended to the right hand of God, the way we follow him now is through obeying what he has commanded us to do. This is possible only through the Holy Spirit. To be led by the Holy Spirit is to follow Jesus and in doing so we please the Father. There is no greater reality than when we live in agreement with what Jesus has done on our behalf. The feeling of knowing the Father is pleased is the ultimate reality. Eternity, which begins now and will never end, will be saturated with this reality in ways that words cannot fully communicate.

> Since Jesus died, rose and ascended to the right hand of God the way we follow him now is through obeying what he has commanded us to do.

This is possible only through Jesus; it is not our performance, but it's through his perfect sacrifice once and for all on our behalf that we can live with the Father's pleasure at the forefront of our emotions here and now. That will change the way we think and live. The result will be radical obedience to Jesus because he is worthy.

"And He said to them, Go into all the world and preach the gospel to every creature." (Mark 16:15 NKJV) When Jesus said this he meant it. He has never changed his mind. This verse is a commandment not a suggestion.

Following Christ will take us next door, across the street and to the ends of the earth. The gospel is for everyone, everywhere. We need to be gripped once again that the gospel is for everyone, everywhere. When we are gripped by this reality we will be willing and obedient, and through our obedience people will see Jesus. When we follow the Lord, there are two amazing realities we experience. Here is the first one. In following the Lord, we increase in the knowledge of God. In less complicated terms we really get to know someone when we spend time with and share experiences with someone. The nearness of the Lord Jesus is incredible as we walk with him. It's almost like the more uncomfortable we are or the greater risk we take the closer he feels. It is incredible. The abiding presence of the Lord Jesus is what distinguishes us from any other people on earth. Truly we are not alone.

The second greatest thing we get to experience when we follow Christ is to meet his friends. The problem we have now is that not all of his friends are friends with or friendly toward one another. According to the scriptures we will see this change. The Spirit and the Bride (or church) will say come, meaning there will be a unified cry from the church to God. Right now there is not a unified cry because there is still a job to be done. Let me share with you some experiences I have had while doing some on the job training.

Beijing, China -
October 25 - November 9, 2005

Let me start by saying that I wasn't always a Christian. I was involved in the streets and dealt drugs for a short time. Let me share with you two things I learned while I was living in sin. One thing was I didn't see anything and I don't know anyone. The second thing I learned is how to get something from one place to another place without certain people finding out. To make a long story short God was very merciful to me. These skills became useful when I went to China, only God wasn't giving me mercy by not giving me what I deserve but he was giving me grace to do with him what I could not or would not do without him. Another gentlemen and I went to China. He and I both brought in Bibles. I had 76 New Testaments in total. As we were going through customs, the Holy Spirit said to me "preach the gospel to this man." I was like, God, this guy doesn't even speak English. Anyway I shared with him as the Holy Spirit commanded. While talking briefly with him, the still small voice of Holt Spirit said to me "give him a Bible." So I did as Holy Spirit told me to and gave the man stamping my passport a New Testament. He gladly took it, and we went through customs and were able to get the rest of the Bibles

31

in with no trouble. What is impossible and illogical with man is impossible and logical with God. As we follow the Lord, we learn to lean not on our own understanding. If you are trying to get Bibles into China illegally you obviously don't give the customs agent one right? God doesn't necessarily care about the rules. What he wants is our love, which means we trust Holy Spirit enough to obey him.

After we left the airport in Beijing we had dinner with a Pastor and then went to an underground house church on the 15th floor of an apartment building. As we walked down the dark hallway we could hear the church singing in Chinese. As we got closer to the church gathering, we could just feel the pleasure of God. From the outside of the door, it sounded like one voice of complete unity as praise was being offered to the Lord from sincere and humble people. It was amazing. The people were beautiful. The love and humility of Jesus radiated off of them all. It felt like I was in heaven, if that makes sense. I was in an atmosphere of love, no pretense, no competition, no suspicion just love and complete devotion to Jesus. The pastor of this church had already spent some time in prison. This gathering was illegal. It's stunning to think that in some places Jesus is illegal, but that is a very present reality in Africa, the Middle and Far East. Not always but very often the more pressure that is put on the church, the more it grows in number, maturity and purity. The pastor asked me to preach to his congregation that evening. I felt like Jesus was asking me to preach. The thoughts going through my mind were, "I should be listening to you and you want me to preach?" I shared as the Pastor had asked. When I was done speaking his wife gave me 300 Yuan, which at that time was about $38.00 USD. The people didn't see themselves as victims of oppression or tyranny; they saw themselves as blessed, so they gave. People who are blessed bless others. People who feel like victims think that the world owes them something. More often than not victims are takers, while real believers are contributors. We are not victims. Let's see the perspective of the early church.

> *"And they agreed with him, and when they had called for the apostles and beaten them, they commanded that they should not speak in the name of Jesus, and let them go. So they departed from the presence of the council, rejoicing that they were counted worthy to suffer shame for His name."* (Acts 5:40-41 NKJV)

The Apostles were imprisoned and beaten, but when they were released they thanked God that they were worthy to suffer for the name of Jesus. Even in suffering we are not victims! The renewed mind sees suffering for Jesus as a privilege. I am not asking to be beaten or tortured. However, I am saying that there are no victims in the Kingdom of God and even in suffering we are not victims. As Jesus said, *"Blessed are those who are persecuted for righteousness' sake, For theirs is the kingdom of heaven."* (Matthew 5:10 NKJV) Being persecuted for righteousness sake is proof that we belong to Jesus. Persecution is a proof that we possess the Kingdom of God. The Apostles in Acts 5:40-41 really knew they were blessed which is why they rejoiced because they were counted worthy to suffer for the name of Jesus. You may not be suffering physical persecution. Maybe you are being mocked by coworkers or even made fun of by family members because you are a lover of Jesus. In some way we are all going through something. In reality our faith is being tested. *"That the trial of your faith, being much more precious than of gold that perisheth, though it be tried with fire, might be found unto praise and honor and glory at the appearing of Jesus Christ:"* (1 Peter 1:7 KJV) As our faith passes through testing we are refined which is good but also when our faith is being tested it produces three things that Jesus is worthy of – praise, honor and glory. God allows pressure praise, honor and glory. God allows pressure on us because he is producing something in us. If you are going through something just know the Father is producing something in you that is worthy of his Son Jesus so just keep pursing the Kingdom.

We left Beijing and went to a University in another city. We ministered to many of the University students as well as some of the faculty. It was an absolutely amazing time. I watched people get born again everyday. Everyday as we gathered students were added to the church Jesus is building. It was incredible. Sometimes words don't do justice to an experience but I am trying my best. The Chinese college students who we ministered with were very unique. They were humble and full of love willing to risk their freedom for Jesus. They were also very sharp in the word of God and had very keen discernment, which only comes by the Holy Spirit. The young college believers who were saved for less than a year already knew all the false doctrine that the western English teachers / missionaries were teaching. What I felt from them was a perfect mixture of love, humility and discernment. It was like Paul the Apostle's prayer for the Philippian church passed through time and space and fell on these young Chinese believers. *"And this I pray, that your love may abound still more and more in knowledge and all discernment, that you may approve the things that are excellent, that you may be sincere and without offense till the day of Christ,"* (Philippians 1:9-10 NKJV)

I think the purest discernment I have ever encountered was from those young people in China. You could tell they were grateful for the missionaries coming, but knew some of their teachings were off. They weren't malicious, but they weren't blind either. They could see and love. They were truly Christ-like for Jesus sees all that we are and all that we are not and still loves us.

When we are pure in heart we see God. We see his possibilities in the impossibilities of life. But we also see circumstances and people for who they are and not just how they are. In other words, we don't just see problems we see opportunities. We can walk in love and walk in discernment. Love isn't blind. We can have eyes that see and still look at people for who God is making them to be. When we have discernment, we can partner with God in what he is doing because God reached down and out to us when we were down and out. For us to do justice means we need to reach out to others and lift them up. The words of Revivalist John Wesley still echo through history now, "Do all the good you can, by all the means you can, in all the ways you can, in all the places you can, at all the times you can, to all the people you can, as long as ever you can."

CHAPTER THREE

INJUSTICE

Injustice anywhere is a threat to
justice everywhere.[2]
- *Martin Luther King, Jr*

Justice is the foundations of
kingdoms.[3]
- *Latin Proverb*

Where there is injustice there
is an invitation to do justice. All
around us there is a gross amount of
injustice. All you have to do is turn
your phone on and check a news
app. For those of you who are a bit
more old school, turn the radio on
during your commute to work and
just listen. Most of the news is either
about corruption or injustice. All
of these injustices are an invitation
for us to move beyond fear and
complacency and do something. To
be perfectly clear, I will name several
huge injustices. You don't have to go
to Africa to find injustice. Injustice
has been legislated (Roe vs. Wade) as
law in America for more than 30 years
now. The church must do something
about injustice, or we will become
irrelevant in this generation. Injustice
should activate compassion, and
compassion should lead us to Christ-

like action. Let me be clear—everyone can't do everything but everyone can do something.

Abortion is Murder

In my opinion, it is still the greatest injustice simply because a child in the womb has nowhere to go. The child can't run, or fight back. He or she is destroyed by the "choice" of the person who is supposed to nurture and care for him or her. Mother Theresa even said, "I feel the greatest destroyer of peace today is "Abortion." With that being said abortion is a Kingdom issue. If the most vulnerable are not safe, no one is. Having compassion for a hungry child in Africa is trendy and cool even in Hollywood. But what about the unborn right next door? If we are going to talk kingdom and justice, then we can't leave out abortion and just talk about the poor, or those who are being trafficked. Abortion is what it is because men are not men. In this generation, men seek pleasure without commitment and what you get is abortion. Most women would not have an abortion if the man would stand up and say I made that baby, now I will man up and take care of him or her. I deeply feel for women who have had abortions. I even feel for the men who have seduced

> I feel the greatest destroyer of peace today is "Abortion".
> - Mother Theresa

women into killing their own child. Before I was married, I had a girlfriend who had an abortion before she and I dated. The effect that the abortion had on her soul was very deep almost like what an open wound would be to the skin. The good news is that with Jesus we can find forgiveness and redemption. Through the cities of refuge in the Old Testament, God shows us his value system. He would rather a guilty person go free than an innocent person be condemned. Stay with me for a moment. Here is a thought I had recently pertaining to God being totally good – Because God is just he doesn't condemn the innocent. Because satan is deceived, he deceives people into aborting babies. What he is doing is actually populating heaven. Even in unspeakable tragedy Jesus still wins!

Bonded Physical Labor

According to antislavery.org this is what bonded labor is.

> "Bonded [labor] is the most widely used method of enslaving people around the world. A person becomes a bonded [laborer] when their [labor] is demanded as a means of repayment for a loan. The person is then tricked or trapped into working for very little or no pay, often for seven days

> a week. The value of their work becomes invariably greater than the original sum of money borrowed. Often the debts are passed on to next generations."[5]

This is almost slavery, but not exactly. It is economic slavery, which happens physically because of someone's bad circumstances or because of a bad choice to work for a corrupt and greedy landowner. This takes place in Africa, India, South East Asia and in the Caribbean. I have witnessed this injustice first hand in Bulera, Uganda. Bulera is a small rural town full of beautiful people. Across the street from a growing Spirit filled church, there was a tea planation. The people on the tea plantation are bonded laborers. They live on the land and are fed and housed by the landowner. It costs more money to live on the land than they get to work on it, so they have a perpetual debt that is growing. Instead of looking elsewhere for work, the people often stay and work in the tea fields completely hopeless. They are breathing but not really alive. They are enslaved by their own choice that they felt forced to make due to poverty. The hard part is that often they are not forced to work there. I am not making light of poverty or highlighting the greed of the landowner. I am simply sharing with you another way of how bonded labor happens.

Slavery according to the Oxford dictionary is - the state of being a slave: thousands had been sold into slavery. Slaves are people who are bought and sold against their will. To my liberal friends if you are against slavery and are pro-choice you are actually unaware of reality because slavery violates a person's free will just like abortion. There I had to say it. Anyway slaves are used and abused both physically and sexually. In the world today, there are more than 28 million slaves worldwide. 80 % of them are women and children. That by far exceeds the number of slaves during the transatlantic slave trade of the 1800's. These numbers include children who are sold 10 times a night to all different Western men in South East Asia. These numbers include young woman as young as 10 years old on the streets of Recife, Brazil. These numbers also represent men, women and children in India who make bricks all day and even into the night. These numbers also include young men and children who were forced to dig in Sierra Leone, West Africa. These numbers also include children in Northern Uganda who are stolen from their parents and then forced to be child soldiers who later sometimes even end up executing their own parents or families. Can you imagine turning a 9 year old into a terrorist? Well, it happens in the world we live in. Isolating ourselves from injustice doesn't stop; it only prolongs the suffering of the innocent. Going to church more and praying more as great as that is won't stop it either.

All of these oppressed innocent people suffering are our neighbors, what will we do about their plight? Can we hear their cries for help or is our worship music too loud? Are we too busy being entertained to care deeply for others? Are we selfish? Are we fearful? What is it that is neutralizing the most wealthy church that ever existed on planet earth from doing more about these unspeakable atrocities? Slavery exists today in America; this is not just a developing world problem. The color of slavery today is not black and white. It's green. Now slavery is about money and a gross lust for power that is always exercised to control those who are weak and vulnerable and unprotected by the law because of their poverty. Even yesterday (2/10/2014), while my parents were in Little Ferry, New Jersey at the Municipal court paying a ticket for parking on their own lawn in this wonderful free country called America they ran into a pimp and a prostitute. My point is that injustice is everywhere and more than ever it's becoming a threat that we need to be aware of and do something about. Let's remember the words of Martin Luther King, Jr. that still echo through history, "Injustice anywhere is a threat to justice everywhere." Again, I will repeat that we can't do everything, but everyone can do something even if it's just engaging in one of these injustices, we must get involved. Now is the time! It's time for the church to get off the bench and get into the game. "The world is tired of hearing the gospel preached by the church. They want to see it practiced by the church."[6]

If we are passionate or becoming passionate about Justice, we must be very careful. First, we can't get mad at the church as a whole for its complacency because we have all procrastinated about something. Therefore we must keep an attitude of love and patience with the church because the church belongs to Jesus and how we treat the church reveals how much we love Jesus. Remember when Jesus encountered Saul on the road to Damascus? He asked Saul *"why are you persecuting me?"* (Acts 9:4) In other words, Jesus doesn't just identify himself with the least of these, he also identifies himself with the church which is his body. It's not only about how we treat the poor, but it is also about how we treat the body of Christ. The best thing we can do is lead by example. Preaching out of frustration will not change anyone's heart, mind or life. My second caution is we must maintain a bold compassion towards the oppressor as well. Praying for both the oppressed and the oppressors tenderizes our hearts enough to share the love of Christ should we run into a man who is using or abusing a woman and or child. These men are all around us; some of them are even in our churches. It's not enough to have compassion only for the oppressed. Anyone with a heartbeat can have compassion for the oppressed. But it takes the Spirit of God to put love and compassion in our heart for the oppressor. When you see Jesus in Acts 9 encountering Saul of Tarsus on the road to Damascus remember he was trafficking innocent people from place to place, having some arrested and others killed. While he was on his way to do more evil against the innocent Jesus shows up shining like the sun at noonday and puts Saul's retinas out of commission for three days. What are we seeing here? Glad you asked. We are seeing the compassion of Jesus for the oppressor. Jesus knows full well what will happen to the oppressor should they not repent, therefore he has compassion even for them, and so should we. Let's keep in mind that hell is still really hot and forever. Here Jesus is physically embodying Isaiah's prophecy about the Messiah. *"The Spirit of the Lord GOD is upon Me, Because the LORD has anointed Me To preach good tidings to the poor; He has sent Me to heal the brokenhearted, To proclaim liberty to the captives, And the opening of the prison to those who are bound;"* (Isaiah 61:1 NKJV) We must remember that the gospel is for the captives (the oppressed) and the prisoner (the oppressor). The gospel is good news to all as long as they can believe it and obey it.

Water / Clean water

"But let justice run down like water, And righteousness like a mighty stream." (Amos 5:24 NKJV) In this verse both justice and righteousness is likened unto moving water. This is pretty ironic to me especially when;

> "Half of the world's hospital beds are occupied by people with an easily preventable waterborne disease. Every 20 seconds a child under five years of age dies from waterborne illnesses. More than one-third of Africa's population lacks access to safe drinking water. 75 percent of the people in Latin America and the Caribbean suffer from chronic dehydration because of poor water quality. According to the World Health Organization 80 percent of all sickness and disease worldwide is related to contaminated water. Dirty water kills more children than war, malaria, HIV/AIDS and traffic accidents combined."[7]

According to wateroneworldsolutions.org it is estimated that 5.3 billion people, two-thirds of the world's population, will suffer from water shortages by 2025. Now is the time to do something about the water issue as a whole.

The water / clean water issue is something that perhaps can be solved in our generation if we would only care enough to do something about it. David Bornstein author of a blog post entitled "The Real Future of Clean Water" for the New York Times estimates that it would take 535 billion dollars to solve the problem.[8] When you break 535 billion dollars down into 315 million American citizens you will come to know that America alone could solve this problem if each of its citizens gave 1.18 cents a day which is 35.38 a month for 4 years. Each individual would willfully contribute $1698.41. If you multiply 1698.41 by 315 million you would get 535 billion dollars. Let me be clear I don't think America is the Savior of the world or the world police. I was just illustrating that this problem could easily be solved especially if you include some other wealthy nations. America is not anointed to care for the poor, the body of Christ is. Good news to the poor is the gospel, but it is also clean water. It's not one or the other it is both. For justice to roll down and righteousness to be like a mighty stream perhaps the church as a whole might want to do something about the water / clean water issue. In fact it's even Biblical.

> *"So he cried out to the LORD, and the LORD showed him a tree. When he cast it into the waters, the waters were made sweet. There He made*

a statute and an ordinance for them, and there He tested them, and said, If you diligently heed the voice of the LORD your God and do what is right in His sight, give ear to His commandments and keep all His statutes, I will put none of the diseases on you which I have brought on the Egyptians. For I am the LORD who heals you." (Exodus 15:25-26 NKJV)

Here as Moses obeyed the Lord a miracle was performed. The results were clean drinking water for Israel and a promise of health by God himself for Israel if they would diligently obey God. As much as God wants people to obey him is as much as he wants people to have clean water and be healthy. It is interesting how both clean water and diseases are mentioned in this scripture. As we have seen earlier there is clearly a connection between clean water and health. Every human who is created in the image and likeness of God should have access to clean drinking water. This can be accomplished in our generation. Will you be a part of the solution?

The Hunger and Anger Connection

On Saturday, December 22, 2012 We See Jesus Ministries conducted our very first medical clinic in Bertin, Haiti. Bertin is about 45 minutes outside of Port Au Prince, Haiti's capital. The clinic was in a church in a poor neighborhood. We saw about 125 people. The clinic was fairly smooth. Some people were healed, a few were saved and all around it was pretty smooth for the first one. We took some teams to the streets to do evangelism and pray for the sick. It was a good time. When we came back from the streets we took a break to have lunch. Pastor Reginald Celestin's wife Johanne cooked lunch and it was amazing as usual. Eating at medical clinics where you are serving the very poor is always a pretty challenging event. It feels weird eating when you know how hungry people are around you. To be honest it is down right uncomfortable and often you have to push the feeling of guilt out of your mind so you can eat. Sometimes some team members don't eat. It's complicated; sometimes you just have to be there. This would be one of those times. Any way the team went into a back room of the church to eat discretely so as not to offend people. Everything was going fine until small pebbles with a few little rocks and a large handful of dust flies through the window and hits me in the head. A little girl got me with a direct hit to the head and neck. There went my lunch. Why did she do it? Because she didn't have lunch. It was then when I learned the hunger and anger connection. Hunger truly does give birth to anger. I always kind of figured that but on December 22, 2012 in Haiti it was revealed to me and to my chicken sandwich. I was irritated for a very brief moment. After the irritation, I truly felt bad for the child. I felt really bad because she was hungry. It broke my heart that such a young little girl was so hungry that she was angry— so angry that she would act out like that. This experienced reminded me why we are working in Haiti. Now I am really feeling encouraged knowlng we are working exactly where God is sending us. Please pray for this ministry and its work in Haiti. Pray about partnering with us or coming on a trip to Haiti or somewhere else in the world to share the love of Christ with those in need. This young girl is not an isolated issue at all. In fact she is not an issue; she is my neighbor; she is a person to be loved and cared for not a problem to be solved. In fact, according to globalpost.com, Haiti is as of November 27, 2013 the 5th hungriest nation in the whole world. Please keep in mind that Haiti is only about 3 hours from Miami, Florida.[9]

There are too many injustices in the world to fit into one chapter. Here are a few other ones that would be good to know about so that you can help those who are in need: widows, orphans, domestic violence, persecuted religious minorities, homelessness (especially in cold weather climates), disabled veterans, people with disabilities, and senior citizens who have little to no family who visit them. These are just a few. The list could go on for way too long, so let's do something about what we know. It would help us to see these circumstances as an opportunity for the Kingdom of God to come instead of just seeing these circumstances as just problems. Together in Jesus' name, we can change the world.

CHAPTER FOUR

GOD LOVES JUSTICE

Righteousness and justice are the foundation of Your throne.
Psalm 89:14a NKJV

For I, the LORD, love justice;
Isaiah 61:8a NKJV

It doesn't get any clearer than that. God loves Justice. God is just therefore God loves justice. When we love God, we love what he loves. As we mature, we begin to hate what he hates. Often when the world accuses the church of hate it is actually a compliment. They are actually saying that our feelings are aligned with God's. Unbelievers often accuse God and Christians of being hateful, but the reality is they are sinful and so they can't see clearly. Flip Benham said, "Truth is hate to those who hate the truth." While it is good to hate what God hates we need to first make sure that we love what he loves. The Apostle Paul told us to pursue love in the book of 1st Corinthians. If we are to pursue love, we will have to pursue justice because God loves justice. Justice for the poor, needy oppressed and persecuted is an expression of God's love. In fact, there are only two people the Lord gets off his throne for and it's not the rich and powerful but it is the poor and persecuted, see Psalm 12:5, Acts 7:56. We need to stop talking about God's love and start showing God's love.

When we show people the love of God, we are saying to those who don't know Jesus that they can trust him. The followers of Jesus shape how the world sees the true and living God. Are we showing the world a clear picture of Jesus or a distorted picture of him? Eventually we are going to have to be honest with ourselves. Eventually we are going to have to align our priorities with God's. Jesus had a bone to pick with the religious system of his day. Here is what he said,

> "Woe to you, scribes and Pharisees, hypocrites! For you pay tithe of mint and anise and cummin, and have neglected the weightier matters of the law: justice and mercy and faith. These you ought to have done, without leaving the others undone. Blind guides, who strain out a gnat and swallow a camel!" (Matthew 23:23-24 NKJV)

Jesus rebuked them for majoring on the minors. I must be honest with you, if we look at our own spending or most church budgets, we would see the same reality present: we major on the minors. We are in desperate need of God's help. I would imagine that 95% of the people reading this book don't pray to statues, which is idolatry. But when our priorities are out of order that is just as much idolatry as is bowing down to a false god or a statue of Mary.

Jesus deserves more than a nice carpet in our church or an amazing sound system. He deserves people out of every tribe, tongue, kindred and nation because he paid for them with his very own blood. All through the Bible and human history God has acted on his people's behalf. Now is the time for his people to act on his behalf and finish what he called us to do. We are called to preach the gospel everywhere and to literally disciple nations. This can happen through generosity. In other words we do justice and the people of the world see the mercy of God. Our actions show the world his heart, and then people and nations change the way they think about God. It's the kindness of God that leads men to repentance. Generosity is a very clear expression of kindness. Remember Peter was fishing all night and couldn't catch anything. Jesus tells him where to throw the nets; he does; the net breaks and Peter says to Jesus "depart from me for I am a sinful man." Jesus never mentioned his sin. He was generous to him in a supernatural way and the result was Peter changing the way he thinks. Often our gospel is too small and too complicated. We need a simpler and bigger gospel. The good news is that God is very generous and he gave his Son. Jesus is our advocate with the Father. We need to be an advocate for the poor and oppressed. When the society we live in sees that we care about what God cares about, they will begin to actually listen to what we are saying instead of viewing us as weird and irrelevant. When we value human life more than our own comfort then we will have the attention of the world around us. Doing good for those who can do nothing for us in return shows the world our motives and gives them a reason to believe in the Jesus we speak about. Jesus gave the people of his day a reason to believe in him. We need to give the world around us a reason to believe in him. *"Let your light so shine before men, that they may see your good works and glorify your Father in heaven."* (Matthew 5:16 NKJV) Our light shining before men is the good works we do for them. The Father's Glory is directly attached to our good works, so we might as well do something for the world around us. If

> Doing good for those who can do nothing for us in return shows the world our motives and gives them a reason to believe in the Jesus we speak about.

we really want the Father to be glorified, we will obey his Son Jesus and do things for those around us. It is just that simple.

The more we know and love God, the more his interests become our interests. This last section of this chapter is written to encourage you in a very specific area. I am endeavoring to show you through several different parts of scripture that God will act on behalf of his people. God is a just Judge, and he will execute justice for his people. We see this reality in both the Old and New Testament. Sometimes justice for his people is judgment for their enemies. To fully partner with God in his redemptive plan for humanity, we need to have confidence in him. To fully obey Jesus, we will need more than self-confidence, we will need confidence in a God who acts on behalf of his people. Without understanding deeply that God is just, we will never believe him to execute justice from heaven towards earth. Satan always lies to us. His intention is that we would accuse God. Satan accuses us so that we will accuse God. If or when we buy into any of these lies, we immediately begin to question God's integrity. When we do that, we are actually saying that God is not just and that he is not true. The results of this are most believers do not step out in faith because they are not deeply sure that they can fully trust God. Evidence of this would be the 2.9 billion people on planet earth who have never heard the gospel before. I am writing this because we all need to grow in faith. According to Paul the Apostle, we are growing from faith to faith. The more faith we have the more we will be persuaded that God will do what he said he will do especially when it comes to acting on behalf of his people.

> "Throughout the biblical text, the theme of justice remains a constant presence. In some contexts, the pursuit of justice may require punishment for misdeeds or inaction that remind the people of God of their responsibilities to the covenant relationship. In other contexts, the notion of justice may require that the marginalized receive equitable treatment in the community. Whatever the case, it is undeniably clear that God is just and requires justice of His people." - Sally Holt

God speaks to Abraham. *"Then He said to Abram: "Know certainly that your descendants will be strangers in a land that is not theirs, and will serve them, and they will afflict them four hundred years. And also the nation whom they serve I will judge; afterward they shall come out with great possessions."* (Genesis 15:13-14 NKJV) God gave Abram (Abraham) a prophetic word about what would happen when the Children of Israel come out Egypt. He said they will be afflicted for four hundred years and then he will judge them (Egypt) and then they (Israel) will come out with great possessions. Fast-forward about four hundred years.

"And the Egyptians urged the people, that they might send them out of the land in haste. For they said, "We shall all be dead." So the people took their dough before it was leavened, having their kneading bowls bound up in their clothes on their shoulders. Now the children of Israel had done according to the word of Moses, and they had asked from the Egyptians articles of silver, articles of gold, and clothing. And the LORD had given the people favor in the sight of the Egyptians, so that they granted them what they requested. Thus they plundered the Egyptians." (Exodus 12:33-36 NKJV)

God's judgment on Egypt was his justice for Israel. What God said to Abraham came to pass just when and how God said it would. The justice of God for his people demanded that because they were exploited for so long they would have to come out with great substance. It's like they were getting a pay out for their work, not a hand out. The gold and the silver that they taken out of Egypt was most likely mined by their very own hands. There are several things we learn about God through this story. The first one being that God keeps his word, the second being that God will act on the behalf of his people. Third we learn that God will administer justice to those who are oppressed. God took the Egyptians who at the time were the most powerful nation in the world and slapped them around and dismantled their army in moments. The justice of God will bring nations to their knees in a moment. I have seen him bring a nation to its knees in a moment. When the earthquake struck Haiti on January 12, 2010, Voodoo priests were crying out to Jesus. They were not crying out to their demons or false gods or dumb statues. They immediately began to cry out to Jesus who is the living God. When the shaking comes, the desire of the nations comes next. As the people of God, we must have a burning conviction that God knows, cares, hears, feels, sees and will act for his people.

Israel's sin and idolatry always led them into captivity. We must also know that our sin and idolatry will lead us into captivity as well. Let me modernize that statement by saying that sin and Idolatry lead to spiritual complacency. Many years after Israel came out of Egypt, it found itself in bondage yet again now to

Persia. From this place of captivity, God raises up Nehemiah to do something about Israel's peril. God allows Nehemiah's heart to be broken and his eyes to be opened. Nehemiah sees the condition of the walls and gates of Jerusalem and he begins to weep, mourn, fast and pray.

Nehemiah continues going about his normal business as King Artaxerxes' cup bearer. But the King notices something different about Nehemiah; he notices sadness on his face and asks him what's wrong. Nehemiah responds and tells the King what is bothering him exactly. King Artaxerxes then responds, "What do you want me to do for you?" Nehemiah sneaks in a quick prayer and then requests that the King send him to Jerusalem to fix the walls and gates. Nehemiah continues by asking the King to authorize the restoration to his governors and also pay for it. The King responded with a yes. What I want you to see is that Israel was under Persian captivity meaning they were slaves to Persia. Now you have the King of Persia authorizing and paying for the rebuilding of Jerusalem's wall and gates. This is nothing but the Justice of God. Because Persia was exploiting Israel's work force, Persia must pay for Jerusalem's walls and gates to be fixed. I just want you to leave this chapter with a renewed confidence in God. Just know that God will act on behalf of his people.

Previously in this chapter you have seen some Old Testament examples of God acting on the behalf of his people. Now you will see some New Testament examples of God acting on behalf of his people. The greatest thing that God did for someone he did for everyone. The Father sent his only Son to save us from our sins and rescue us from death and hell. He didn't die for some he died for all. Because God is good and just he offers everyone, everywhere throughout all times Jesus his Son. After Jesus rose from the dead and ascended to the right hand of God, we see some great examples of God acting on behalf of his people. In Acts 5, the Apostles are imprisoned unjustly for healing the sick and the Angel of the Lord lets them out of prison. Here we see the Justice of God clearly. They did nothing wrong in the sight of God and he himself lets them out of prison. The justice of God reveals the Supremacy of Jesus Christ. In Acts 12, Herod kills James the brother of John with a sword. In that same chapter, Peter is released from prison again by the angel of the Lord. At the end of Acts 12, Herod is executed by the Angel of the Lord in front of a large crowd of people. He is left there and worms ate his body. I am not sure how you feel about capital punishment but God obviously believes in it. What you see in Acts 12 is the Justice of God. God releases his justice to show us that prison bars and politicians will not stop his plans. The

Gospel will be preached and the Kingdom of God will only increase.

In Acts 16, we see that Paul and Silas go to prison because Paul cast the devil out of a girl. So in Jesus' name, he gets the girl out of spiritual prison and they get thrown into prison. At midnight Paul and Silas were singing praises to God and an earthquake hits only the prison and they are set free. But instead of running, they preach the gospel to the jailer and his household and they were all saved and baptized. The people that put stripes on their back were the ones to clean their wounds. Here we see that the justice of God brought salvation to a whole family. The Philippian church was birthed through these events. What the enemy meant for evil God turned for God. What they enemy thought would be Paul and Silas' limitation was really the church's multiplication. God's plans for your life will not be hindered if you like Paul and Silas remain thankful in all things. Thanksgiving will bring about the miraculous in your life. We can remain thankful in all things because we know that God is good and he is Just. Remember Jesus wins and he will act on behalf of his people.

CHAPTER FIVE

THE FAST THAT FREES

The cry of the poor must either be heard by us, or it will ascend up against us into the ears of the Lord of Sabaoth. [10] - *F.D. Maurice*

Feel for others – in your pocket. [11] - *C.H. Spurgeon*

The fast that God is looking for is not the one where we starve ourselves, but the one where we feed others. Pure religion is not to pray for the widows and orphans; it's to visit them. Pure religion is when we take action and help those who cannot do anything for us in return. That is exactly what Jesus did for us. He died for us while we were yet sinners. He didn't need anything, but he wanted us and so he gave himself for us so that he might have us and that we might have him.

The Prophet Isaiah receives a strong word from the Lord with a lot of promise for God's people "if" they will respond correctly. Scripture is timeless and these words echo through time and space and are very relevant to the people of God today. Isaiah 58 begins with a rebuke and ends with a promise but in the middle we find instruction.

> *"Cry aloud, spare not; Lift up your voice like a trumpet; Tell My people their transgression, And the house of Jacob their sins. Yet they seek Me daily, And delight to know My ways, As a nation that did righteousness, And did not forsake the ordinance of their God. They ask of Me the ordinances of justice; They take delight in approaching God."* (Isaiah 58:1-2 NKJV)

Here we find a God that is not seeker friendly. He actually wants his people to know their sins— interesting. Anyway, he finishes verse two with *"they take delight in approaching me."* If you read only the beginning of the chapter taking delight in approaching God doesn't sound bad. Being happy about going to church isn't a bad thing. If you continue to read the whole chapter you will find out that God is saying that his people take delight in religious activity. That is not a good thing. The good news is there is hope. *"Then you shall delight yourself in the LORD; And I will cause you to ride on the high hills of the earth, And feed you with the heritage of Jacob your father. The mouth of the LORD has spoken."* (Isaiah 58:14 NKJV) Here we see the promise of great blessing both inwardly and outwardly. The people of God go from taking delight in approaching God to taking delight in God. If the people will adhere to the word of the Lord spoken by Isaiah, there will be a dramatic shift. Through obedience to God's word, the people go from taking delight in religious activity to delighting in God himself. God promises to elevate their position in the earth and feed them a meal called inheritance. Not bad!

The beginning rebuke is rough; the end promise is awesome and the instructions in the middle are simple. There is no need to complicate what God has made simple. Often the reason people try to complicate what God has made simple is because they have no intention of doing what God has said. Here is the middle where we find keys that unlock heaven.

"Is it a fast that I have chosen, A day for a man to afflict his soul? Is it to bow down his head like a bulrush, And to spread out sackcloth and ashes? Would you call this a fast, And an acceptable day to the LORD? "Is this not the fast that I have chosen: To loose the bonds of wickedness, To undo the heavy burdens, To let the oppressed go free, And that you break every yoke? Is it not to share

your bread with the hungry, And that you bring to your house the poor who are cast out; When you see the naked, that you cover him, And not hide yourself from your own flesh? Then your light shall break forth like the morning, Your healing shall spring forth speedily, And your righteousness shall go before you; The glory of the LORD shall be your rear guard. Then you shall call, and the LORD will answer; You shall cry, and He will say, 'Here I am.' If you take away the yoke from your midst, The pointing of the finger, and speaking wickedness, If you extend your soul to the hungry And satisfy the afflicted soul, Then your light shall dawn in the darkness, And your darkness shall be as the noonday. The LORD will guide you continually, And satisfy your soul in drought, And strengthen your bones; You shall be like a watered garden, And like a spring of water, whose waters do not fail." (Isaiah 58:6-11 NKJV)

I will repeat - The fast that God is looking for is not the one where we starve ourselves, but the one where we feed others. According to Isaiah, God was not looking for his people to be in sackcloth and ashes. He was looking for them to stop oppressing their workers. God was (is) interested in the hungry being fed, the naked being clothed and the outcast being embraced. It seems that religious activity doesn't impress God too much. In the passage above God tells them to let the oppressed go free. Obviously, God doesn't like slavery. He continues by telling them to share their bread with the hungry. As he continues he mentions these very words, *"Your healing shall spring forth speedily."* What he is actually telling them is that they are sick, and their healing will come as they care for others. Bam, Jesus hits them with an uppercut! Go figure. Start caring for others and you will be healed— sounds therapeutic. Take you eyes off yourself, and you will get well. Isaiah continues by saying if you do all this justice stuff "then your light will break forth." What he was saying is that darkness is when we don't love our neighbor and you guys are in darkness. Isaiah was suggesting that if they care for the poor, let the oppressed go free and take in the outcast then they (Israel) would be healed and then their light would break forth. He even mentioned that God's glory would be their rearguard, meaning in plain language that God himself will watch their back. Not a bad deal huh? Our light shining before men is directly correlated to our good works. The glory the Father receives is also directly attached to what we do, not to what we believe or pray. Believing, praying and starving ourselves is simply not enough according to scripture. We must take action on the behalf of others – period. Often we are waiting for God to move, but in reality he is waiting for us to move.

> "Now in those days, when the number of the disciples was multiplying, there arose a complaint against the Hebrews by the Hellenists, because their widows were neglected in the daily distribution. Then the twelve summoned the multitude of the disciples and said, 'It is not desirable that we should leave the word of God and serve tables. Therefore, brethren, seek out from among you seven men of good reputation, full of the Holy Spirit and wisdom, whom we may appoint over this business; but we will give ourselves continually to prayer and to the ministry of the word.' And the saying pleased the whole multitude. And they chose Stephen, a man full of faith and the Holy Spirit, and Philip, Prochorus, Nicanor, Timon, Parmenas, and Nicolas, a proselyte from Antioch, whom they set before the apostles; and when they had prayed, they laid hands on them. Then the word of God spread, and the number of

the disciples multiplied greatly in Jerusalem, and a great many of the priests were obedient to the faith." (Acts 6:1-7 NKJV)

This passage of scripture begins by showing us one of the challenges of growth. The Hellenists (Greek) widows were being neglected in the

> If the gospel is not tangible it's not good news.

daily administration of food, which means the society brought this problem to the church because the church was doing something about the problem. So, the twelve Apostles tell the larger group of disciples to select seven men full of the Holy Spirit and wisdom. In other words, the Apostles don't' select these men they delegate the disciples to select leaders to lead the feeding effort. The Apostles then lay hands on them and commission these men to overseer the feeding of the Greek and Hebrew widows. The results were that word of God spread, the disciples multiplied and a great many of the priests became obedient to the faith. Action begets obedience. The priests have a reason to believe because they see something tangible enough to believe and obey and that was the feeding of both the Hebrew and Greek the widows. At this point, the Hebrew priests were perhaps moved by the Hebrew Christians that actually cared enough to feed the Greek widows. The cross of Christ slayed cultural enmity and produced spiritual unity that was expressed through the Greek and Hebrew widows being feed. A gospel of action and demonstration produces obedience. The good news for those hungry poor widows were they were getting fed daily. If the gospel is not tangible, it's not good news. The gospel must be preached and demonstrated if we expect people to believe it enough to obey it. The gospel is not to be simply believed, it is to be obeyed. *"In flaming fire taking vengeance on them that know not God, and that obey not the gospel of our Lord Jesus Christ:"* (2 Thessalonians 2:18 KJV) Let me say it this way the gospel that is really believed is obeyed.

CHAPTER SIX

PHILANTHROPY

Think of giving not only as a duty
but as a privilege. [12]
- *John D Rockefeller*

*It is more blessed to give than to
receive.* - Jesus of Nazareth

Jesus is both generosity and hospitality personified. He generously gave his life and he freely gives us all things withholding no good thing from those who walk uprightly. He also welcomed us into his Kingdom and gave his Kingdom to us. *"Blessed are the poor in spirit, For theirs is the kingdom of heaven."* (Matthew 5:3) The poor in Spirit possess what money cannot buy. The Kingdom of God is not earned or bought it is given and received. Jesus makes this possible. He is so generous he gives us himself and his Kingdom. Which means we possess another reality that at any given time (kairos) can break through the world (kosmos) and come into the earth. The Kingdom comes to the earth to reveal that Jesus is Lord of both heaven and earth. As we obey Jesus his Kingdom comes and reveals what he is really like. When that happens people want him. Bill Johnson said, "Everyone wants a King like Jesus." The Prophet Haggai refers to Jesus as the Desire of the Nations, and he is, and he knows he is.

By faith we become a vital part of something a lot bigger than us. God made a promise to Abraham that was manifested in Jesus Christ, who is that promise, and keeps his word to Abraham by blessing all the families of the earth. This happens when we share the love and power of Jesus to the world that he loves and died for. The brutal death of Christ shows the Father's great value for people created in his image and likeness. The Father is in the people business. Therefore we must be about his business just as Jesus was.

God's Promise to Abraham

Now the Lord had said to Abram: "Get out of your country, From your family And from your father's house, To a land that I will show you. I will make you a great nation; I will bless you And make your name great; And you shall be a blessing. I will bless those who bless you, And I will curse him who curses you; And in you all the families of the earth shall be blessed." (Genesis 12:1-3 NKJV)

One of the most common things about people of faith is they are generous. God promised that through Abraham all the families of the earth shall be blessed. This means that God was speaking both prosperity and generosity over Abraham. This is a prophecy, a command and a promise directly from a God whose only limitation is that he can't lie. Abraham didn't waste any time. Look what happens in the very next chapter.

> "And there was a strife between the herdmen of Abram's cattle and the herdmen of Lot's cattle: and the Canaanite and the Perizzite dwelled then in the land. And **Abram said** unto Lot, Let there be no strife, I pray thee, between me and thee, and between my herdmen and thy herdmen; for we be brethren. Is not the whole land before thee? **separate thyself, I pray thee, from me: if thou wilt take the left hand, then I will go to the right; or if thou depart to the right hand, then I will go to the left.** And Lot lifted up his eyes, and beheld all the plain of Jordan, that it was well watered every where, before the LORD destroyed Sodom and Gomorrah, even as the garden of the LORD, like the land of Egypt, as thou comest unto Zoar.

Then Lot chose him all the plain of Jordan; and Lot journeyed east: and they separated themselves the one from the other. Abram dwelled in the land of Canaan, and Lot dwelled in the cities of the plain, and pitched his tent toward Sodom. But the men of Sodom were wicked and sinners before the LORD exceedingly. **And the LORD said unto Abram, after that Lot was separated from him, Lift up now thine eyes, and look from the place where thou art northward, and southward, and eastward, and westward: For all the land which thou seest, to thee will I give it, and to thy seed for ever. And I will make thy seed as the dust of the earth: so that if a man can number the dust of the earth, then shall thy seed also be numbered. Arise, walk through the land in the length of it and in the breadth of it; for I will give it unto thee.** *Then Abram removed his tent, and came and dwelt in the plain of Mamre, which is in Hebron, and built there an altar unto the LORD."* (Genesis 13:7-18 KJV) (Emphasis on the bold words.)

Here we see that Abram preferred Lot and was generous to him giving him the choice of prime real estate. God immediately responded to Abram's generosity and promises him more land and an innumerable amount of descendants. God commands Abram to walk the length and the breadth or width of the land. From Heaven's perspective Abram is walking the land that God promised him in the pattern of the cross. I am not sure if Abram knew that one of his descendants was going to die on a cross, rise on the third day and be the person who makes all the families of the earth to be blessed. I am not sure what Abram knew, but I do know that God knew all of this from before the foundation of the world and was working all things together after the counsel of his own will. God is intentional about what he does. The scriptures tell us that God requires us to do justly, or to do justice, which requires us also to be intentional about what we do. If we are going to do justly and be generous, we will have to be intentional about it. People don't prosper or become generous by accident. Doing justice and being generous takes great responsibility and intentionality. It takes discipline and self-control. Almost all generosity is a result of discipline and self-control.

Adam LiVecchi

God's promise to Abram is spiritual but it is also about philanthropy, generosity and hospitality. Doing good for others, being generous with your home and resources shows people what the Father and his Kingdom are really like. Generosity is the clearest expression of good will. The Father loved the world so he gave Jesus. That was the single most generous act of all time. We love the people of the world, so we give them Jesus, our time, and our money; we do good so that they will see the Father and give him the glory he deserves. Let's see a biblical end result of philanthropy. In John 4, Jesus meets a Samaritan woman at a well. *"Are You greater than our father Jacob, who gave us the well, and drank from it himself, as well as his sons and his livestock?"* (John 4:12 NKJV) Here we learn that this well was a gift from Jacob who was Abraham's grandson. God is fulfilling his promise to Abraham in and with Christ at a well that Abraham's grandson Jacob gave to the people of Samaria. Here we see natural generosity and spiritual revelation taking place in the same place. It is no coincidence that Jesus met that woman at the well. The result of Jesus meeting this woman at the well was that Jesus revealed himself to her plainly saying to her that he was the Messiah.

> Generosity is the clearest expression of good will.

"And many of the Samaritans of that city believed in Him because of the word of the woman who testified, He told me all that I ever did. So when the Samaritans had come to Him, they urged Him to stay with them; and He stayed there two days. And many more believed because of His own word. Then they said to the woman, Now we believe, not because of what you said, for we ourselves have heard Him and we know that this is indeed the Christ, the Savior of the world." (John 4:39-42 NKJV)

A city was touched by what started as Jacob giving a well to people who obviously needed it. Jesus shows up and reveals himself to a woman. He gets invited to a city and the consensus in the city was that he was the Savior of the world. A natural gift initiated the process of a spiritual discovery. Often God meets a natural need to reveal a spiritual truth. Whether we give a gift or have a need both realities are an invitation for God to invade. We just need to have faith and do what he tells us to do. The only real expression of faith is obedience. Jesus did only what he saw the Father doing and he said only what he heard the Father saying. The Father was revealing Jesus to the Samaritan woman at a well Jacob gave to her forefathers in the land God promised Abraham. It's almost like philanthropy led to eternity. The practical temporal things we do for people matter in eternity.

Jesus' Earthly Identity

"The book of the genealogy of Jesus Christ, the Son of David, the Son of Abraham:" (Matthew 1:1) Here we see Jesus' natural roots in Abraham. Jesus was descended from Abraham but also Jesus said, "before Abraham was I am." Jesus who is fully God was also fully man.

What Jesus did while on the Earth

"How God anointed Jesus of Nazareth with the Holy Spirit and with power, who went about doing good and healing all who were oppressed by the devil, for God was with Him." (Acts 10:38) Doing good here means to be philanthropic. Jesus was a supernatural philanthropist who brought heaven to earth displaying to the world that the Father cares. Jesus was a walking, breathing, physical manifestation of God's promise to Abraham to bless all of the families of the earth. Jesus was a philanthropist and so are you. A philanthropist is someone who sees a need and meets it. A philanthropist sees problems as opportunities. Where there is hunger we bring food or teach

people how to farm or even buy them land to farm. Where there is unclean drinking water we dig wells or bring water filters. Where there is sickness we bring healing and medical clinics. The point is that we are agents of hope and justice. We are instruments of love. Our love for God is seen in how well we love people who can do nothing for us in return. That is the love that Jesus demonstrated all through out the gospels. The justice of God is about Jesus getting what he paid for not about people getting what they deserve. God's vision is people redeemed out of every tribe tongue and nation. The Father's vision cost him his only begotten son. He is very serious about this vision. His vision happens when his sons and daughters take their place. As we bless the nations God fulfills his promise to his friend Abraham. Our obedience is directly attached to God's integrity. The Father really trusts us. We are loved and trusted so that we bring hope to the hopeless and justice to the oppressed.

Jesus Led by Example

In the Kingdom, all leadership is demonstrated by example.. If Jesus is really our Lord then we need to follow his example. The book of Acts says that Jesus went around doing good, healing all who were oppressed of the devil for God was with him. The book of Acts can record that reality because that is exactly what Jesus did in the gospels. Jesus' death and resurrection give us eternal life, but his life shows us what life could be like if we would live fully yielded to the Father. Jesus was not just a philanthropist, he was a supernatural philanthropist. Jesus was the walking, talking manifestation of God's promise to Abraham. Jesus is the Father's good will towards men.

Here are some examples of Supernatural Philanthropy:
- Jesus turned water into wine. (John 2)
- Jesus fed the 5,000. (Mark 6)
- Jesus cleansed the leper. (Mark 1)
- Jesus caused the lame to walk. (Mark 2)
- Jesus raised the dead. (John 11)
- Jesus cast demons out of people. (Matthew 8)

It wasn't enough for Jesus to be supernatural; he actually commanded his followers to be supernatural also. Christ in us is now the hope of glory for the world around us. Jesus can supernaturally visit someone in dreams and in visions and even in person, but his primary way of reaching people is through you and I. Jesus made this very clear. Let's keep in mind that Jesus is a King and when he speaks, it's a commandment not a suggestion.

Jesus Commanded Us

• *"And Jesus came and spoke to them, saying, All authority has been given to Me in heaven and on earth. Go therefore and make disciples of all the nations, baptizing them in the name of the Father and of the Son and of the Holy Spirit, teaching them to observe all things that I have commanded you; and lo, I am with you always, even to the end of the age."* Amen. (Matthew 28:18-20 NKJV)

• *And He said to them, "Go into all the world and preach the gospel to every creature. He who believes and Is baptized will be saved; but he who does not believe will be condemned. And these signs will follow those who believe: In My name they will cast out demons; they will speak with new tongues; they will take up serpents; and if they drink anything deadly, it will by no means hurt them; they will lay hands on the sick, and they will recover."* (Mark 16:15-18 NKJV)

The passages above are often referred to as the Great Commission. Jesus is commanding his disciples to manifest the promise God gave to Abraham. Matthew's gospel is telling us to make disciples of all nations teaching them complete obedience to Jesus. Mark's gospel is telling us to preach the gospel to everyone everywhere and that there will be miracles when we obey what Jesus commanded. These two passages are very complementary. You can't disciple someone who hasn't first received the gospel. (Summarized) So preach the gospel to everyone, everywhere and miracles will happen. Baptize these new believers and then you can teach them to obey all things Jesus commanded. God put the desire of the nations inside of us and told us to disciple the nations. Jesus would not tell us to disciple the nations if they could not or would not be discipled. We need to change the way we see. We need to see the world in the context of obedience to Jesus. God's law should be the apple of our eye, meaning we should look at everything in the context of obedience to Jesus. We should look at circumstances with the desire to obey and honor Christ in all things. My good friend Abner Suarez says, "Friends of God have made obedience to God a settled issue." Our disobedience and complacency is the biggest injustice to the world around us. To not preach the gospel to those who have not heard it is the greatest injustice. If we value the body and the blood of Jesus, we will preach the gospel. People perish because we let them, not because God wills them to perish.

> *"How then shall they call on Him in whom they have not believed? And how shall they believe in Him of whom they have not heard? And how*

*shall they hear without a preacher?
And how shall they preach unless
they are sent? As it is written: How
beautiful are the feet of those who
preach the gospel of peace, Who
bring glad tidings of good things!"*
(Romans 10:14-15 NKJV)

In this scripture Paul clearly appropriates
the responsibility of preaching the gospel
to believers in Jesus. You and I are called
to preach the gospel. We don't have to feel
called we are. It's not just the job of pastors
and evangelists; it is the assignment of all
who believe. To ignore that commandment is
to ignore Jesus himself. Jesus said, "If we are
ashamed of him he will be ashamed of us."
Just a reminder that Jesus said what he meant
and meant what he said. He has not changed
his mind. The scriptures are clear God is not
willing that any should perish. So Jesus tasted
death for every man. Jesus tasted death for
everyone because there is room in the Fathers
house for everyone everywhere. The love and
resources of Father God cannot be exhausted
they can only be rejected. One day the church
is going to get God's vision, there will be a
generation gripped with God's vision enough
to do something about it.

The Promise Fully Manifested.

"Now when He had taken the scroll, the four living creatures and the twenty-four elders fell down before the Lamb, each having a harp, and golden bowls full of incense, which are the prayers of the saints. And they sang a new song, saying: You are worthy to take the scroll, And to open its seals; For You were slain, And have redeemed us to God by Your blood Out of every tribe and tongue and people and nation, And have made us kings and priests to our God; And we shall reign on the earth." (Revelation 5:8-10)

Here we see people redeemed out of every tribe, tongue and nation. Today on planet earth there are still 2.9 billion people who have never heard the gospel. These people stand in the way of this vision being fully manifested. The truth is the scripture will be manifested. My question is what part will you play in God's story of redemption? Will you give? Will you go? Where will you go? When will you go? Will you preach? Will you disciple? What is God asking you to do? I know you will respond in fact I acknowledge everything good that God put in you in Christ. *"That the sharing of your faith may become effective by the acknowledgment of every good thing which is in you in Christ Jesus."* (Philemon 1:6 NKJV) According to Paul the Apostle, when you acknowledge or recognize the gifts God gives other, you are activating their gifts. Here is a promise we can be a part of, *"For the earth will be filled with the knowledge of the glory of the LORD, as the waters cover the sea."* (Habakkuk 2:14 NKJV) The whole earth will experience God's manifested presence. This scripture in different words is communicating the same massage as Joel 2:28 when God said through the mouth of Joel that he would pour out his Spirit upon all flesh. However Habakkuk uses a very fascinating metaphor that you have to think about to really understand. *"For the earth will be filled with the knowledge of the glory of the LORD, **as the waters cover the sea.**"* That is a dominant metaphor as waters cover the sea dominantly. Can you image the presence of the Lord being the most dominating reality about planet earth? It can happen and according to Habakkuk it will. When it will happen is not for me to say, but it will. How it will happen is not for me to say, but in all of God's wisdom he has invited us and commanded us to be a part of everything he is doing. So we might as well respond to his love and love him back. We love him through obeying him, it is just that simple.

CHAPTER SEVEN

FACETIME

He who has pity on the poor lends to the LORD, And He will pay back what he has given.
Proverbs 19:17 NKJV

He who oppresses the poor reproaches his Maker, But he who honors Him has mercy on the needy.
Proverbs 14:31 NKJV

Jesus had three very close friends. By his sovereign grace and divine wisdom, he allowed these three men to experience things that the other nine disciples did not experience. These experiences are as follows: a girl being raised from the dead and Jesus' Glorification on the mountaintop before his resurrection, see Mark 5:35-43, 9:1-9. These three men played very significant roles of leadership in the early church. James was the pastor of the church in Jerusalem, Peter was given apostleship to the Jews, and John was the prophet to the seven churches in Asia and the author of what would be the last book of the Bible. All three of these men are contributing authors to the Bible. These men were very close with Jesus, and he entrusted them with more leadership than the other nine disciples

Saul of Tarsus was converted by seeing Jesus on the road to Damascus. Several years after that he met up with Peter, James and John and they had only one thing they wanted to say to him.

> *"But on the contrary, when they saw that the gospel for the uncircumcised had been committed to me, as the gospel for the circumcised was to Peter (for He who worked effectively in Peter for the apostleship to the circumcised also worked effectively in me toward the Gentiles), and when James, Cephas, and John, who seemed to be pillars, perceived the grace that had been given to me, they gave me and Barnabas the right hand of fellowship, that we should go to the Gentiles and they to the circumcised. **They desired only that we should remember the poor,** the very thing which I also was eager to do."* (Galatians 2:7-10)

These powerful men who arguably were Jesus' best friends only told Paul to remember the poor. They didn't give him a church planting strategy, or ask him is he still suffering emotionally from the people he had killed before he was a believer. They didn't even take him to a church growth conference or an inner healing weekend. They simply were concerned about the less fortunate— the least of these. Perhaps the words of Jesus never left their minds or hearts, *"whatever you have done to the least of these you have done to me"*. Of all the things they could have said to him they only desired that he remember the poor, which he was already eager to do because he truly knew Jesus.

These experiences that follow are real living encounters with Jesus in the face of the poor. If you have read my book "Sitting at His Feet" these stories will be familiar to you.

In February of 2008 while I was with Impact Nations in **Andhra Pradesh, India** God spoke to me in a profound way. I was at a medical clinic in south India. It was hot, humid and pouring rain. I was standing in line with an elderly man. I was being friendly with him so I gave him a hug as an act of love because I could not speak his language. When I hugged him, immediately Jesus spoke to me. He said, *"I was sick and you came to me."* When I heard this, I began to weep like a baby. Jesus had just spoken to me from the least of these. He said whatever you do unto the least of these you do to me, and so he spoke from the person he identifies himself with in Matthew 25:35-36 which says, *"for I was hungry and you gave Me food; I was thirsty and you gave Me drink; I was a stranger and you took Me in; I was naked and you clothed Me; I was sick and you visited Me; I was in prison and you came to Me."* I knew this was Jesus speaking to me because he said, "I was sick and you came to me." This rocked my world. After that I lost the ability to function for a while; this had such a traumatic effect on my soul. For the rest of the day, I was totally messed up and full of joy unspeakable as I worked in the medical clinic.

As the journey continued in September of 2009, I was in **Montevideo, Uruguay**. In the beginning of the trip, my friend Teofilo Hayashi and I prayed for a woman with a tumor, and it instantly disappeared. Later on this same trip, we were walking to church on Sunday morning. I saw a street boy who looked hungry so I invited him in to have coffee and breakfast with me. It was him and I sitting at the table. As he was sitting there with me eating, I was telling him that Jesus loved him in Spanish. I stopped and said to the Lord, "He really smells, Lord." Immediately Jesus responded to me, "What, Adam, you do not like the way I smell? I was hungry and you gave me food." Here again Jesus was speaking in the face of the least of these. As I was sitting with this young man who is way too young to be homeless, I was weeping because of what Jesus just said. This really blew me away. I felt like I got saved all over again when the Lord spoke to me about the boy's smell. The boy then comes with us to church and sits in the front row with my friend Teofilo and me. Later in the service he gets saved. As I sat by the homeless, I learned more about the fragrance of Christ than in any church service. This experience had a profound effect on my heart because I cannot forget the stench of that boy, which was really the fragrance of Christ in the face of the least of these.

About a month later, in **New Jersey** in October of 2009, I hosted our first Prophetic Conference called "Awake to Righteousness." I had some food prepared in the back for the speakers. When service was over and the speakers and I went back to eat some amazing Cuban sandwiches, I noticed there were several people back there that were not invited. Usually I have no problem being strong with people but that time I did not for some reason. Several "down and outers" were back there eating with the speakers and me. So later that night I said, "Lord do these people just not respect my authority because I am young or something? Is that why they were back there?" Jesus said, "No you prayed to be like me and these are the kind of people I attract." Well, out come the tears and confession and repentance all over again. Now, Jesus is speaking on behalf of the down and outers. Religious hierarchies and boundaries mean nothing to King Jesus. Quite frankly, he would probably rather eat with the "down and outers" than the conference speakers or Bishop so and so. We must learn to calibrate our hearts to hear what Jesus is saying even if it goes beyond our religious thinking of how something should be.

Carrefour, Haiti - January 12, 2010

An earthquake shook Haiti and brought a nation to its knees in thirty seconds. I happened to be there during the quake. I was in the epicenter of the quake and God miraculously spared my life. I was able to come out and return in February of 2010 and then three other times that year. The Lord allowed me to experience what he said in his word. *"Whose voice then shook the earth: but now he hath promised, saying, Yet once more I shake not the earth only, but also heaven."* (Hebrews 12:26) I love this scripture; it has become flesh in me because I lived through this experience of God's voice. That same voice that called my name twice and scared the hell out of me literally shook the earth.

When I came back from Haiti that February, I stayed in **Bavaro, Dominican Republic** for a few days to relax and also preach. One day I was walking back from the Internet cafe. As I was walking back to the church, I saw a Haitian eating from the garbage. So I grunted at him and signaled for him to get out of the trash and so he did. I walked over to him and gave him enough money for a decent meal because he was obviously hungry. His shirt was shredded, so I took my tank top off and gave it to him. As I walked away discouraged about this poor man's condition, I took my golf shirt out of my book bag and put it on. Then suddenly the Lord spoke to me and said, "That is how you feel about me, you gave me the cheaper shirt and you kept the nice one for yourself." So I asked Jesus to forgive me for giving him the cheaper shirt. Jesus needed to be clothed In the face of the needy, but I was more concerned about me. When Jesus speaks to you, it will cause you to see yourself, people and life for what they really are. This messed me up and showed me I am messed up. I was honored that he would even say something like this to me. He trusted that I would know it was him, and not try to bind the devil when it was actually Jesus speaking. The sharpness of Jesus' word cut into my heart and made me aware of its hardness. Then he was able to come in and touch it and heal it and make it tender to his voice. A heart that is tender to his voice will be generous toward others, even at the expense of self. It is a good thing when the Lord brings correction into our life. It may not feel good but the long-term results are worth a little temporary pain, and besides Jesus gave us the comforter to help us through the rough times.

Carrefour, Haiti - August 8, 2010

It was a humid night, and I was doing an open-air crusade in a poor and fairly dangerous neighborhood. There were roughly 1500 people there. It began to pour and pour as I was preaching so I got off the stage and told the people that since they were wet I was going to get wet with them and pray for anyone and everyone who needed prayer. So a huge crowd of people came forward for prayer. So the prayer team went down to pray for the sick and demonized. People were getting healed and demons were being cast out. Roughly one thousand people stayed in the rain to dance and praise Jesus; it was beyond words. In the rain that night I truly experienced joy unspeakable. After I had finished praying for the people who were in line, I began to dance and sing and scream Jesus. Then a few moments later I stopped and looked into the crowd. When I focused on the crowd, I began to weep. It was then when Jesus spoke to me and said, "This is why I said blessed are the poor for theirs is the kingdom." I fell apart and started crying and dancing and thanking Jesus for speaking and allowing me to be around people who love him so much. Remember to listen for Jesus because you never know when he will say something that will change your life forever. I was there to minister to the people, but in reality Jesus was ministering to me through them.

Mityana, Uganda - May of 2011

May of 2011 I had the privilege of helping to lead a team for Impact Nations. My Spiritual Father Steve Stewart had a heart attack so he sent me in his place. It was terribly unfortunate that he had a heart attack, but a great honor to stand in for him while he was recovering. My job description was to preach the gospel and heal the sick. I was doing that two ways. One was in open-air meetings in the evenings after their medical clinics. The second was taking teams into the villages to pray for the sick and preach the gospel while the medical clinics were going on. Impact Nations is an organization that mixes the supernatural with the practical, the results are amazing. On this particular trip we saw many miracles including the deaf hearing, and the lame walking. The gospel was preached to the poor; Muslims came into the Kingdom of God. Hundreds and hundreds of desperately poor people received free medical treatment. In fact, I personally watched my friend Heidi Dunbar who is a nurse practitioner take several bugs out of an elderly woman's ears. Yes, you read that correctly several bugs out of an elderly woman's ears. Having bugs in your ear is an injustice! No human being created in the image of God should have bugs living in their head because they don't have access to a doctor or medicine. We should see injustice and respond with compassion. Real compassion leads to action.

On May 13, 2011 my world got turned upside down again. We were in Mityana Uganda visiting a very small local hospital. To give you an idea of the type of place I am talking about, the building was a one story brick building. The mattresses were stained with blood. Some mattresses had no sheets and if the family members of the patient didn't bring the patient food he or she did not eat. To say that animals in America receive cleaner care is not an understatement; it shouldn't be true but it is. This book is meant to make you want to do something about it. *"For it is God who works in you both to will and to do for His good pleasure."* (Philippians 2:13 NKJV) God gives us both the desire and the power to do what is right.

The AIDS Wing - May 13, 2011

As we went through the hospital, we prayed for the sick and shared the gospel with people. As we continued, we found our way into the AIDS wing, which consisted of two large rooms perhaps 20 x 20 with about roughly eight people total in each room. My friend Josh and I met a man named Fred. He was 33 years old and was dying of aids and tuberculosis. Fred weighed 60 pounds; he had open wounds on his arms, and his bones were coming out if his face. As we were praying for Fred his Father just stood there and watched us. While we were praying Fred grabbed my hand with what little strength he had left. He then began to touch my arm and finally put his arm around my neck. At that moment I just began to weep. Then with what little breath he had in him he asked Josh how he was? Josh also began to weep. When we finished our prayer, his family thanked us for praying for him. We were praying for his healing; we were speaking life in Jesus' name. To be honest, I don't know if he lived or died, but I do know he got loved. Randy Clark said, "Everyone may not get healed, but everyone must get loved." The Father mentioned to me that he was familiar with the pain that this Father had in his heart because he outlived his Son. There are too many Fred's dying unnecessarily. The only difference between him and say Magic Johnson is money. If this man had money, he may be alive today. I may never know what happened to Fred or his family, but I knew that as I looked into his eyes I could see Jesus. What I do know is by visiting Fred we were really visiting Jesus. Jesus said, *"I was sick and you came to me"* and he really meant it. Not only does Jesus identify with the sick, his stripes have paid for their healing. It is important to know and remember that humility and compassion should always lead to faith. Faith gives us access to God's power and resources so that we can help make a difference in the lives of others.

Jesus and the Poor

The connection between Jesus and the poor in the scriptures is inseparable. Jesus is profoundly humble. God is self-existent and self-sufficient. He has no needs outside of himself, yet he chose to identify himself with the poorest and most needy people. *"He who has pity on the poor lends to the LORD, And He will pay back what he has given."* (Proverbs 19:17 NKJV) To give to the poor is actually giving to a God who has no needs. It is stunning to think that we can actually lend God something simply by helping those who cannot return the favor. Lending to God is simply a great idea. He is the only one who is guaranteed to never go bankrupt. Giving to the poor is actually investing in the incorruptible. There are no recessions in the Kingdom of God. Remember the words of the Prophet Haggai, *"The silver is Mine, and the gold is Mine, says the LORD of hosts."* (Haggai 2:8 NKJV) Not only is it right to give to the poor, it is also smart. Wise investors are those who

> Giving to the poor is actually investing in the incorruptible.

know when to take risks. Giving to the poor is a non-risk investment that is guaranteed a return by a God who is completely incapable of lying. Not only is it right and smart Jesus himself commanded us to give to the poor.

> "Take heed that you do not do your charitable deeds before men, to be seen by them. Otherwise you have no reward from your Father in heaven. Therefore, when you do a charitable deed, do not sound a trumpet before you as the hypocrites do in the synagogues and in the streets, that they may have glory from men. Assuredly, I say to you, they have their reward. But when you do a charitable deed, do not let your left hand know what your right hand is doing, that your charitable deed may be in secret; and your Father who sees in secret will Himself reward you openly." (Matthew 6:1-4 NKJV)

Jesus didn't say **if** you give to the poor he said **when**. What is interesting about this passage is that before Jesus taught his disciples how to pray he taught them how to give, whom to give to and who would reward their giving if their motives were correct. The purest expression of love is to help those who cannot help us in return.

CHAPTER EIGHT

INVISIBLE

What are Christians put into
the world for except to do the
impossible in the strength of God.[13]
- *General S.C. Armstrong*

God loves with a great love the
man whose heart is bursting with a
passion for the impossible. [13]
- *William Booth*

God commands us to do that
which we cannot do without him so
that we never try. Jesus said, "*With
God all things are possible.*" We
need to believe this more than ever
and live from that place. Once we
start to believe we begin to see. Oral
Roberts said, "If you see the invisible
you can do the impossible." "*Faith is
the substance of things hope for and
the evidence of things unseen.*" Faith
sees the invisible. Jesus saw the faith
of several men who brought their
lame friend to him; the result was the
lame man walked. Let me make this
simple, Jesus saw their faith by their
actions. Biblical faith leads to action
especially on behalf of those who
cannot help themselves. Jesus who is
the justice of God justified this man
and forgave his sins. He illustrated the

forgiveness of sins through the healing of the lame man's body. Here we see the goodness of God leading this man to repentance. He forgave a man who wasn't even saying he was sorry. Wow!

Jesus commanded the lame man to do what he could not do. Jesus said, *"Take up your bed and walk."* When the man obeyed Jesus the miracle was activated and everyone around them saw the power of God. The results were a multitude came to hear Jesus speak. What we need to understand is that when people see the power of God then they want to hear what we have to say. Jesus gave people a reason to believe and we are called to do just as he did in his name.

We can't do justice for people if we can't see them or their conditions and needs.

> *"Then Jesus went about all the cities and villages, teaching in their synagogues, preaching the gospel of the kingdom, and healing every sickness and every disease among the people. But when He saw the multitudes, He was moved with compassion for them, because they were weary and scattered, like sheep having no shepherd. Then He said to His disciples, "The harvest*

truly is plentiful, but the laborers are few. Therefore pray the Lord of the harvest to send out laborers into His harvest." (Matthew 9:35-38)

To see we must look. If we want to see in the Spirit, we will need to look in the natural. Jesus looked at the multitude and saw that they were like sheep without a shepherd and he did something about it. If we can see, we can feel and when we feel, we move. When Jesus saw the crowd, he saw their physical and spiritual conditions. He saw people that were tired (weary) and scattered (needed direction). Jesus responded by sending his disciples out to minister in the surrounding areas. Jesus' solution to the people being tired and lost was an outreach. Jesus knew that the gospel of the kingdom would give these tired and lost people strength and life, and so he sent his disciples to minister to them. Here we see that Jesus knew the people's condition. He was aware of what they needed and when and it began by him seeing. Seeing doesn't happen if we don't look. If we open our eyes and hearts, God will show us how to bring mercy and justice to those who need it. If we are sensitive, he will tell us when as well. We just need to be willing to look so that we can see.

"So they departed to a deserted place in the boat by themselves. But the multitudes saw them departing, and many knew Him and ran there on foot from all the cities. They arrived before them and came together to Him. And Jesus, when He came out, saw a great multitude and was moved with compassion for them, because they were like sheep not having a shepherd. So He began to teach them many things. When the day was now far spent, His disciples came to Him and said: "This is a deserted place, and already the hour is late. Send them away, that they may go into the surrounding country and villages and buy themselves bread; for they have nothing to eat. But He answered and said to them, You give them something to eat. And they said to Him, Shall we go and buy two hundred denarii worth of bread and give them something to eat? But He said to them, How many loaves do you have? Go and see. And when they found out they said, Five, and two fish. Then He commanded them to make them all sit down in groups on the green grass. So they sat down in ranks, in hundreds and in fifties. And when

He had taken the five loaves and the two fish, He looked up to heaven, blessed and broke the loaves, and gave them to His disciples to set before them; and the two fish He divided among them all. So they all ate and were filled. And they took up twelve baskets full of fragments and of the fish. Now those who had eaten the loaves were about five thousand men." (Mark 6:32-44 NKJV)

Can we see people or are we just too preoccupied with ourselves like the disciples were? To be totally honest, sometimes I am preoccupied with myself. How about you? Let's be honest. Liars don't inherit the kingdom of God. The disciples did not see the multitude the same way Jesus saw them. Jesus saw their condition and began to teach them. Jesus saw that the multitude was like a bunch of sheep without a shepherd. He saw that they were lacking direction and so he taught them. When the day was over, the disciples wanted to send everyone home but Jesus knew they needed to eat. The disciples saw a problem while Jesus saw an opportunity. Whether we are looking at poverty, hunger or injustice, we must learn to see with compassion so we can see an opportunity and size that opportunity. Leonard Ravenhill said, "The opportunity of a lifetime must be seized within the lifetime of the opportunity." Jesus was able to see both their physical and spiritual condition. If we are going to be moved with compassion towards the lost and poor, we must first see them as Jesus saw the crowd. Jesus didn't see the needs of the multitude as a problem to be managed; he saw their needs and did

> In the Kingdom of God there are no problems only opportunities.

something about it because of what he knew about his Father. We must allow our relationship with God to shift how we see problems. In the Kingdom of God, there are no problems. There are just opportunities for God to be glorified by him doing the impossible through us just as he did through Jesus. It's inconceivable to think that God doesn't have problems, and he doesn't. God has only solutions. Now do you see one of the reasons he wants us to hang out with him? If we are going to do justice, we need to have a renewed mind that sees solutions instead of just seeing the problem. It's not that Jesus didn't see a problem, he just saw behind the problem. Faith doesn't deny reality; it transcends it and brings God's reality to mankind so that He is glorified.

Lima, Peru - November 2008

In November of 2008, I went to Lima, Peru with Impact Nations. It was a great experience. There are several reasons that it was great one being that Starbucks was only a few blocks from our hotel. So we had the best of both worlds. We had a mission's trip with Starbucks. This was like heaven on earth for me. Another reason or a more important reason that it was a great experience was because of all the people we saw that were healed and saved. One man stuck out in particular. I will tell you what he said to me, and I will never forget it. It was in the early afternoon. We had left the rest of the team in the church while the medical clinic was going on. I was leading a small team up the side of a large mud hill to preach the gospel and heal the sick in Jesus' name. We were going door-to-door and shack-to-shack literally. As we approached the top of this hill, we knocked gently on a shack. The man apprehensively let us into his very humble abode. We shared the gospel with him and prayed for him. He gladly received Jesus. As we were getting ready to walk back down the hill, about 2000 steps, to the church the man said to us, "thank you no one has ever came to me before." I fell apart. It was like Jesus was talking to me through this man. I was sick and you came to me. I was deeply touched by his simple thank you. I thought to myself there is a church maybe 2000 feet away and no one ever spoke to him? As I reflect on this reality, wisdom tells me not to judge the church in his neighborhood. I just feel grateful to have been a part of God's plan for this man's life. This man was 45 minutes outside of the city of Lima Peru and about 2000 feet from a church, yet he was never visited by anyone of the church before. Often when people think of unreached people groups, we think of people in caves Afghanistan or very remote villages in India or Africa or even Buddhist monks in Tibet or Mongolia. But we must know there are many people in this hemisphere who also have never heard the gospel before. The question is can we see these people who seem to be invisible? Let's fast-forward four years.

Philadelphia, Pennsylvania - January 2012

In January of 2012 my wife and I found ourselves in yuppie-ville or skinny jeans land Philadelphia. The kind of neighborhood where there is a coffee shop and a violin store very close to each other. I know you are getting the picture. There are also several churches in this little neighborhood. We were in a violin shop because a generous soul decided to give my wife money for her to buy a new bow for her electric 5 string viola. These nice people recommended we go to a certain shop and so we did. After my wife picked out her new bow, we were paying for it and I asked the middle aged (white) woman if there was anything she needed prayer for. She immediately stopped me and said to me that "no one has ever asked me that before." This woman wa. years old. She lived in America in a p. there are churches everywhere, but ~ the church. Is this woman invisible? Can a. see her? Does she know there is a God ~ loves her and gave his Son for her? If I stop and think about this, it deeply bothers me. It bothers me enough that I am writing about it at 3:19 in the morning. I am not condemning the church in her area. I have not preached the gospel to every person I have ever seen or even all of my neighbors. All I am saying is that Jesus is worthy of so much more. He's worthy of more from my life and if you are honest with yourself he is worthy of more in your life. Injustice is when people in the world don't know that there is a God in heaven who loves them and gave his Son for them. The gospel is about Justice. Jesus paid for the redemption of all men. It's our job to tell them that their debt has been paid. If they reject it, at least we told them what Jesus has done. God is just and he sends no one to hell. People send themselves to hell when they choose to reject who Jesus is and what he has done for them. God is just. If people reject his Son, they are then held accountable for his blood, and they chose hell. God is not willing that any should perish, so he gave Jesus. Just remember that God is the most generous person ever! Let's fast-forward 22 months.

Stanhope, New Jersey - October 2013

My brother Aaron and I were coming back from a Prophetic school that we did in Eastlake, Ohio. It was a cold night, and we were driving for at least six hours. It was late at night and so we stopped for some coffee so we could get home alive. Unfortunately Starbucks was closed, so we had to settle for Dunkin Donuts. No one was in the store except us and the young man who was working. I began to preach about Jesus to the dude and after a minute or so I asked him if he knew who Jesus was. His exact response with a look of slight bewilderment was "Jesus who?" I explained to him that Jesus died on a cross for our sins, and then mentioned to him the crosses in front of church buildings and he then began to understand why there were crosses in front of the church buildings. Is Patel invisible? Is the church silent? What is going on? This town has about ten churches in it now according to the yellow pages website. Again where is the church? It's time for the church to come out of the closet and go public about Jesus' love for the world. I don't feel like a super Christian because I simply did what Jesus commanded his disciples to do. To be honest, there are times when I don't say anything to anyone. What I am saying is that we cannot assume everyone around us has heard the gospel and has rejected Jesus. There are 2.9 billion people who have never heard the gospel before. Let's make Jesus famous in this generation for the nations are his inheritance.

"The church doesn't have a mission the mission has a church." (Steve Stewart) We need to be possessed by mission not controlled by fear or silenced by shame. Fear and shame silence many in the church today. Now is not a time to be silent. Through faith in God and the faith of Jesus towards us we can reach the unreached, rescue the oppressed and love the forgotten into the Kingdom through the gospel being preached and lived. You were created for this. *"For we are His workmanship, created in Christ Jesus for good works, which God prepared beforehand that we should walk in them."* (Ephesians 2:10 NKJV) Because we are God's work, we might want to do some work. Because God is working in us, he also wants to work through us. Paul the Apostle is clear that God prepared us do specific works, and so to not do them is to actually disobey God. We quench and grieve the Holy Spirit when we don't do what God has prepared us to do. Apostolic Christianity is about action. The book of Acts is not called the prayers of the Apostles or the doctrine of the Apostles. It's called Acts because of the actions of the Apostles. It is very clear that without the Holy Spirit and prayer, these acts would not have happened. But they did have the Holy Spirit, and they did pray and obey and the acts did happen. Now it is our turn; we must move beyond prayerlessness and pray. We must move past complacency and obey Jesus so that others can taste and see that the Lord is good.

CHAPTER NINE

GOOD WORKS

For as the body without the spirit is dead, so faith without works is dead also.
James 2:26 NKJV

But whoever has this world's goods, and sees his brother in need, and shuts up his heart from him, how does the love of God abide in him?
1 John 3:17 NKJV

These scriptures show us that both faith and love are expressed by a corresponding action. Whether we are doing something for someone or giving something to someone both faith and love are expressed by action. *"By this we know love, because He laid down His life for us. And we also ought to lay down our lives for the brethren."* (1 John 3:16 NKJV) Jesus showed us his love by dying for us. What we really believe we live. Faith is more than a belief and love is more than a feeling. Let me be clear. We don't work for salvation, but we do workout our salvation. John Wimber said, "People who are saved act like it." Jesus came to save us from our sins and ourselves. Jesus didn't just die for us; he died as us so that we would not just live for ourselves. The most miserable existence is one of selfishness. I find it interesting how many Christian church going people are depressed and even medicated for depression. If you want to be cheerful listen to the timeless advice of Mark Twain who said, "The best way to cheer yourself up is to try to cheer somebody else up."[17] Please understand I am not judging anyone. What I am simply saying is, if we lived our lives by focusing less on ourselves, we would probably be a lot less depressed.

Healthy people love themselves because they understand that God has chosen to love them. They understand that they are loved by God and a lot of their life is spent on trying to love others because they know that they are loved. If you really experience the love of God, it is impossible to not give it away. When people don't really know or feel that they are loved by God and others, they will often spend a lot of their time focusing on themselves trying to get their love deficit met by self-gratification and entertainment. I think entertainment is just as big of a problem in the church as pornography is.

In America especially, Christianity has become a subculture and often that keeps us from reaching the culture. In the West, for the last several hundred years Christianity has been mainly about gathering together. For example, if I mention the word church, most people will immediately think of a congregation of people gathered together in a building somewhere. Imagine if the word church was mentioned and immediately we thought of immoveable strong loving people who care for the poor and heal the sick. I am believing for the church to be thought of as a living organism instead of a static gathering that is for the most part very predictable. I am hoping that for the next at least 100 years that Christianity will once again become more about obeying Christ. I am not saying that we should not gather together weekly. I am simply saying that it's time to be the church and not just go to church. Church is not a place or an event; it's a people who call Jesus Lord and live like it.

Now is the time to act on what we believe. I wrote this book with the intention of calling the readers into a place of obedience to God, which will mean both hope and justice for others. Most believers when led by example usually respond very well to doing something about what they believe. We were created in Christ Jesus for good works. *"Who gave Himself for us, that He might redeem us from every lawless deed and purify for Himself His own special people, zealous for good works."* (Titus 2:14 NKJV) We are not a peculiar people because we shake rattle and roll. We are not a peculiar people because we anoint things with oil and blow the shofar. Doing good works for others out of a pure heart is actually what makes us a peculiar people. We are fisher of men and not just fishing for our own bellies. We are called to be different, to live a life that is always benefiting others and that is what sets us apart and makes us peculiar. We are peculiar because we do good for those who would do no such thing for us, we bless those who curse us, and give to those who can never repay us. This is who we are; this is how we are called to live. When we begin to embody the gospel, the world will coming running into the Kingdom and not a moment sooner.

> Doing good works for others out of a pure heart is actually what makes us a peculiar people.

The Apostle Paul profoundly embodied the truth of the gospel. Listen to these words to see just how much he agreed with the truth. *"From now on let no one trouble me, for I bear in my body the marks of the Lord Jesus."* (Galatians 6:17 NKJV) His physical body was a reflection of the truth of the gospel. Not everyone will be counted worthy to suffer in this manner but all of us should absolutely embody the truth of the gospel. Our lives should show the world around us God's value system. In

Paul's personal handwritten letter to Philemon, there are several great truths' we need to see. This short letter has three main characters: Paul the writer, Philemon the recipient and Onesimus the subject. Onesimus used to be a slave of Philemon until he ran away. In those days Onesimus was actually a criminal who had a debt to pay to Philemon. So what happens is that Onesimus meets Paul the Apostle while Paul is in prison. Paul preaches the gospel to him and he gets saved. .

> "I appeal to you for my son Onesimus, whom I have begotten while in my chains, who once was unprofitable to you, but now is profitable to you and to me. I am sending him back. You therefore receive him, that is, my own heart, whom I wished to keep with me, that on your behalf he might minister to me in my chains for the gospel. But without your consent I wanted to do nothing, that your good deed might not be by compulsion, as it were, but voluntary. For perhaps he departed for a while for this purpose, that you might receive him forever, no longer as a slave but more than a slave—a beloved brother, especially to me but how much more to you, both in the flesh and in the Lord. If then you

> *count me as a partner, receive him as you would me. But if he has wronged you or owes anything, put that on my account. I, Paul, am writing with my own hand. I will repay—not to mention to you that you owe me even your own self besides."* (Philemon 1:10-19 NKJV)

In this text, Paul the Apostle is embodying the doctrine of both redemption and justification. Here Paul puts his money where his mouth is. The imprisoned Apostle is so concerned with the restoration and placement of Onesimus he is willing to pay his debt. Paul is telling Philemon to receive him as a brother and not as a slave. The name Onesimus means profitable. Onesiums did not live up to his name until he met Jesus. In fact he was unprofitable. The gospel transformed him and then and only then was he able to live up to his God given identity.

Throughout history, people have tried to use Paul the Apostles writings to justify slavery. Deceived sinful people are always looking to see if they can justify their sin. Here we see Paul willing to use his own money to have someone reinstated back into the Christian community as a brother instead of a slave. Here Paul is embodying the gospel and showing us he is not for slavery. In fact, here we see clearly that

Paul is clearly against slavery. Slavery is not God's will for anyone anywhere, ever.

Isaiah 61 clearly shows us that the gospel is preached so that the oppressed go free. Jesus taught us to pray God's Kingdom come on earth as it is in heaven. In heaven there are no slaves, therefore God's intention for earth is that slavery would be abolished. For slavery to be abolished poverty must be abolished because slavery is a byproduct of poverty. In fact poverty creates an atmosphere that slavery can thrive in.

CHAPTER TEN

THE END OF POVERTY

Poverty is no virtue; wealth is no sin.
- *C.H. Spurgeon* [14]

Most poverty is a lack of opportunity.
- *Adam LiVecchi*

Poverty does not exist in the Kingdom of God. Jesus said, "Blessed are the poor for there is the Kingdom of God." The poor are blessed because generally they are rich in faith, see James 2:5. The scriptures do not say blessed is poverty. When God created Adam and Eve before sin, there was not a trace of poverty. Sin creates an environment that is conducive to poverty. Let me be clear. Being poor is not a sin and being wealthy does not mean you are godly. Money is neutral. If you have money, money will do what you tell it to do. If money has you, you will do what it tells you to do. It's that simple. As a Father, I would never want or will my children to be sick or broke. I am not a better Father than God. To be clear, God doesn't want you to be broke or sick because He is not sick or broke. Any father that would want his or her child to be broke or sick is simply not right in the head or heart. In fact, Jesus desires us to be with him where he is, and where he is (heaven) there is no lack or sickness in heaven.

For almost ten years now I have seen the affects of abject poverty on different societies, and it is really ugly! The lack of daily necessities claims the lives of thousands of people every day. This should not be. The good news is we can do something about it. Not only can we do something, God commands us to do something about it therefore we must. We can do what I would call poverty intervention and poverty prevention. Often you will hear people with good intentions say something like this, "I don't want to give a man a fish, I want to teach him how to fish." That is noble and I understand what this well-meaning person is saying, but some people on planet earth may just die if they wait until they learn how to fish to eat. For many people, the time of their next meal will determine if they live or die. Don't feel guilty if you have a stainless steal refrigerator full of food— just share. This is not about guilt; it's about compassion that leads to action. Action releases healing and hope which then brings about real sustainable change.

The generation of people who Moses led out of the promised land experienced divine protection, divine health and supernatural sustainability. The heavens rained bread daily. How is that for daily bread? (Exodus 16:4) On top of that their sandals didn't wear out and they were walking for 40 years, see Deuteronomy 29:5. Also there was no sickness among them, see Psalm 105:37. When they began to build the temple Moses had to tell the people to stop giving because the people gave above and beyond what was needed, see (Exodus 36:1-7.) God promised them a land with milk and honey and he delivered. Milk and honey means a land of prosperity and sustainability. In fact God is so generous he intended for them (Israel) to live in homes they didn't build and drink from vineyards that they didn't plant.

Prevention

If you remember any thing from this book, remember this - God is generous! Because God is generous, we give. When God gave Moses the law, he made provision for the poor and the stranger. *"And when ye reap the harvest of your land, thou shalt not wholly reap the corners of thy field, neither shalt thou gather the gleanings of thy harvest. And thou shalt not glean thy vineyard, neither shalt thou gather every grape of thy vineyard; thou shalt leave them for the*

> Because God promised prosperity, he commanded generosity.

poor and stranger: I am the Lord your God." (Leviticus 19:9-10 KJV) Because God promised prosperity, he commanded generosity. Prosperity is for generosity. Prosperity is not simply for our comfort and security. Israel was taught to live conscious of the poor and the stranger because God loves the poor and the stranger and he commanded Israel to care about whom he cares about. Let me say something really simple: giving prevents stealing. Also, the more generosity we express, the less envy others will have toward us. We can't live in reaction to how others feel about us, but we must understand that we have been blessed to be a blessing.

Intervention

*"At the end of every seven years thou shalt make a release. And this is the manner of the release: Every creditor that lendeth ought unto his neighbor shall release it; he shall not exact it of his neighbor, or of his brother; because it is called the LORD'S release. Of a foreigner thou mayest exact it again: but that which is thine with thy brother thine hand shall release; Save when there shall be **no poor among you**; for the LORD shall greatly bless thee in the land which the LORD thy*

God giveth thee for an inheritance to possess it: Only if thou carefully hearken unto the voice of the LORD thy God, to observe to do all these commandments which I command thee this day. For the LORD thy God blesseth thee, as he promised thee: and thou shalt lend unto many nations, but thou shalt not borrow; and thou shalt reign over many nations, but they shall not reign over thee." (Deuteronomy 15:1-6 KJV)

God's intention is that none of his people would be poor. Lack is not a part of God's economy, and he doesn't want it to be a part of his children's economy either. Every seven years, debts were erased. This created a culture of forgiveness and also prevented systemic poverty. God also instituted the year of Jubilee, which according to Leviticus 25 was to occur every 50 years. This too was created to prevent generational or systemic poverty. We don't have to love money to hate poverty. All we have to do is love people to hate poverty. To love people is to hate poverty. Poverty steals dignity, and people die prematurely because of abject poverty. I am going to go out on a limb and share what I really think in my book. If we the church did more to help the impoverished, perhaps we would have a stronger voice in the moral conversation that is going on in the Western world. As I write this, the US department of World Vision has just began to hire homosexuals. This should not be. Compassion doesn't go against the scriptures. We must be careful when working with victims of suffering, oppression and poverty that we don't take on the mentality of a victim. In God's economy sin is still sin, and Jesus died to free us from our sin, not comfort us in it. The good news is the very next day World Vision apologized and returned to the biblical standard of marriage, which is one man and one woman till death do them part.

The New Testament gives a glimpse of the age to come where poverty will be completely done away with. Here Peter is preaching.

> *"And with many other words he testified and exhorted them, saying, Be saved from this perverse generation. Then those who gladly received his word were baptized; and that day about three thousand souls were added to them. And they continued steadfastly in the apostles' doctrine and fellowship, in the breaking of bread, and in prayers. Then fear came upon every soul, and many wonders and signs were done through the apostles. **Now all***

who believed were together, and had all things in common, and sold their possessions and goods, and divided them among all, as anyone had need. So continuing daily with one accord in the temple, and breaking bread from house to house, they ate their food with gladness and simplicity of heart, praising God and having favor with all the people. And the Lord added to the church daily those who were being saved." (Acts 2:40-47 NKJV)

There is so much going on in this passage. In this text the believers were willing to subtract from what they had and God was willing to add to the church daily. When we are willing to subtract what we have, God is willing to add to who we are. The believers sold their possessions so that no one was needy among them. Not everyone was rich, but no one was poor. I am not advocating socialism or communism because that is a forced redistribution of wealth. Here we see believers giving out of their own free will, seeing a need and meeting it. This text shows us a little piece of heaven. Within this community of believers, poverty was abolished! Poverty can be abolished in our churches and communities. If people weren't broke or sick in our churches, they wouldn't be able to build buildings fast enough to contain the church growth. Some would say are you preaching a health wealth gospel? My response would be—would you like to be sick and broke? If you are sick, you can't really serve God well because you are not feeling well. If you are broke, how much can you really give to those in need? I am not saying that money and health are the ultimate goals of the gospel because they are not. What I am saying is that God is a good Father and he doesn't want you poor or sick. The gospel being preached to everyone everywhere opens up the doors of opportunity for everyone everywhere to thrive in what God created them to be. No one anywhere can ever be all that God intended him or her to be unless they are first made a new creation. Without the creator, we can't be or do what were created to be and do. Without Jesus we can do nothing, especially anything of eternal significance. To Jesus we are valuable; in Jesus we are powerful. Through Christ, we can do all things because he strengthens us. Jesus takes us from being able to nothing without him, to being able to do everything with him.

The gospel really is good news. More than ever we need to believe that and live like we believe it. Remember this the Kingdom of God is an invitation to a feast, not an invitation to a fast. That is good news in a hungry world where thousands of people starve to death everyday. The gospel of the Kingdom is still good news. Good news means justice for today and hope for tomorrow. When the Kingdom comes justice is established and hope is given. The Kingdom of God only increases therefore hopelessness is not an option in the Kingdom of God. Be filled with hope because God has a plan for your future.

CHAPTER ELEVEN

RESCUE AND REBUILD

Born-again Christians were in the forefront off every major social reform in America during the 1830s. They spear-headed the abolitionist movement, the temperance movement, the peace movement, and the early feminist movement.[18]
- *Charles G. Finney*

The words above are both historic and epic. They need to be read today. Believers must understand God's call to rescue lives and rebuild cities. We know bodies can be healed, even modern medicine can tell us that. We know lives can be changed; we even know families can be restored. My question to us is do we know that cities can be rebuilt, and nations can be healed and discipled? If we don't know and believe this now would be a good time to challenge our unbelief and allow God to magnify our vision of Jesus and what Jesus will do before his physical feet touch down on Mount Zion.

Rescuing Lives

Biblically speaking rescuing lives is what we have been commanded to do. We may not feel called to it, but we are. It's that simple. Living a life of faith means we live beyond our feelings. Obedience to what God has called us to do will always require that we live above our feelings. Just know that feelings make a great friend, but a terrible boss. Steve Stewart mentored me. Steve has a ministry called Impact Nations. Their theme is "rescuing lives." For the rest of my life, I want to rescue lives. I know that is what God wants me to do. I would dare to say that he wants you to do the same simply because that is what Jesus did. He came to seek and to save that which was lost. To be honest, I must give you a bit of a disclaimer. Rescuing lives releases supernatural goodness in your life, so just be careful!

Job explains why he was the man!

"Moreover Job continued his parable, and said, Oh that I were as in months past, as in the days when God preserved me; When his candle shined upon my head, and when by his light I walked through darkness; As I was in the days of my youth, when the secret of God was upon my tabernacle; When the Almighty

was yet with me, when my children were about me; When I washed my steps with butter, and the rock poured me out rivers of oil; When I went out to the gate through the city, when I prepared my seat in the street! The young men saw me, and hid themselves: and the aged arose, and stood up. The princes refrained talking, and laid their hand on their mouth. The nobles held their peace, and their tongue cleaved to the roof of their mouth. When the ear heard me, then it blessed me; and when the eye saw me, it gave witness to me: **Because** *I delivered the poor that cried, and the fatherless, and him that had none to help him." (Job 29:1-12 KJV)*

I love Job's bluntness. He explains all that he had and why. He had the protection of God and revelation from God. The secret or intimacy of God rested upon his home. His children were with him. He had a rock that poured out rivers of oil, which is pretty supernatural. Moses' rock only gave him water—not bad! The community respected Job. Older people even stood for him which is, culturally, a great sign of honor. Even princes or politicians were quiet when he was there. Now you know that is just as supernatural as a rock pouring out rivers of oil.

He was honored and known to be wise. You could say he was deeply respected. According to Job he had all of that - "*Because I delivered the poor that cried, and the fatherless, and him that had none to help him.*" Giving to the poor is really lending to the Lord and when Jesus repays, he repays very generously! Job rescued those who had no one to help them. The key to a significant and blessed life is to help those who no one is helping and those who cannot repay you. If you do that with the intention of Jesus being glorified and people being blessed, you will be truly blessed in ways that you could not fully imagine until it happens.

> The key to a significant and blessed life is to help those who no one is helping and those who cannot repay you.

Cities Being Rebuilt.

Over the years I have had the privilege of watching Impact Nations go from rescuing lives to now rebuilding a city in Uganda. Several years ago, Steve Stewart had a heart attack and he asked me to fulfill his preaching engagements in Uganda with a team of more than 30 people from four different nations. It was an amazing time, and it was my first time in Africa. Impact Nations conducted a medical clinic in a town called Kalonga. The locals told me that they were the first white people (International Team) to ever do a medical clinic there. During the day, powerful healing took place as the medical clinic was going on. Muslims were healed and came to Jesus. I would call that a good day in the Kingdom. I left the medical clinic with a translator to pray for some sick people and take some pictures. As I walked through this small village, a cute little girl with a big smile came up to me barefoot and in rags. She smiled and presented me with two hard-boiled eggs. I almost fell apart, literally. Here this little girl saw me as a guest and instead of her feeling bad for herself because she was very poor and had no shoes, she was willing to joyfully give what she had. This wrecked me. It was like I was looking at Jesus as I looked at her. I wept again as I was writing this because I revisited the pictures of her. Honestly, I have learned so much about Jesus by being with the poor. If you want to go to Bible school and don't really care about credentials go spend some time with the poor. You will look Jesus in the face and learn enough to change your life in just a few weeks. Anyway that evening I preached at a small open air meeting across the street from the church where the medical clinic was earlier that day. Here is a link to the video in case you would like to watch it. In fact if you go to 20:29 you will see a small village (Kalonga) of people invite Jesus and the kingdom of God into their village. (https://www.youtube.

com/watch?v=OyZ6uiaw00E) Before the prayer of salvation, they invited Jesus and His kingdom into their little city. I am not sure what to make of this but now a few years later Kalonga is literally being transformed. God is using the church that the medical clinic was at and Impact Nations to literally transform this little city. If you would like to see what God is up to in Kalonga, Uganda through Impact Nations check it out on their website - www.impactnations.com. To be clear I am not trying to make this about me. What I am showing you is that when a group of desperate people in faith invite Jesus and His Kingdom into their city He comes. Just know that what began as lives being rescued is resulting in a city being rebuilt.

> *"The Spirit of the Lord GOD is upon Me, Because the LORD has anointed Me To preach good tidings to the poor; He has sent Me to heal the brokenhearted, To proclaim liberty to the captives, And the opening of the prison to those who are bound; To proclaim the acceptable year of the LORD, And the day of vengeance of our God; To comfort all who mourn, To console those who mourn in Zion, To give them beauty for ashes, The oil of joy for mourning, The garment of praise for the spirit of heaviness;*

That they may be called trees of righteousness, The planting of the LORD, that He may be glorified. And they shall rebuild the old ruins, They shall raise up the former desolations, And they shall repair the ruined cities, The desolations of many generations." (Isaiah 61:1-4 NKJV)

The Gospel of the kingdom is about the salvation of individuals and the rebuilding of cities. In the gospel of Luke, Jesus makes a profound statement concerning cities being changed. *"Woe to you, Chorazin! Woe to you, Bethsaida! For it the mighty works which were done in you had been done in Tyre and Sidon, they would have repented long ago, sitting in sackcloth and ashes."* (Luke 10:13 NKJV) Here Jesus is showing us that signs and wonders have the ability to change the way a city thinks. Signs and wonders in Jesus name and rebuilding the city will definitely help change the way a city thinks. We need to believe this. If we don't believe this can happen why would we work towards it? What we believe about God often determines what we will receive from him. Isaiah 61 begins with me and ends with we. Jesus is the specific "Me" in verse one, see Luke 4:18-21. He begins preaching to the poor and healing the broken hearted and the sick it. When he comforts the mourning and gives them beauty for ashes and the oil of joy and the garment of praise, the language goes from "Me" to "we." Jesus plants healthy people and they become fruitful. The fruitfulness is described in several ways. Remember that their fruitfulness is God's glory. *"And they shall rebuild the old ruins, They shall raise up the former desolations, And they shall repair the ruined cities, The desolations of many generations."* (Isaiah 61:4 NKJV) The end result is this *"For as the earth brings forth its bud, As the garden causes the things that are sown in it to spring forth, So the Lord GOD will cause righteousness and praise to spring forth before all the nations."* (Isaiah 61:11 NKJV) It's good to know that it is the Lord who *will cause righteousness and praise to spring forth before all the nations.* He will do it through us, but to know he is doing it takes the pressure off us. Jesus has a yoke; it is easy, and his burden is light. However, he does have a yoke and a burden which is to say there is a work to be done that he cares about and let's partner with him in it. The word righteousness in the verse above means moral virtue or justice. Justice and praise will spring forth in all nations. Justice and praise are evidence that the gospel is bearing fruit in the lives of people.

Justice and praise are springing forth in the nation of Brazil. My good friends Nic and Rachael Billman and the Shores of Grace Ministries team are doing the gospel in the

streets of Recife, Brazil. According to .
annual report by the Mexico Citizens Council
for Public Security[19], 21 out of the 50 cities in
the world with the highest murder rate per
capita are in Brazil. Recife ranked 32 on the list.
I share these statistics with you so you know
the sacrifices and the risk involved in what the
Billman's are doing. The truth is they are not
afraid but the facts are what they are doing is
dangerous and very expensive. They are taking
people (street children and prostitutes) out of
the lion's mouth and the lion bites. Please pray
for their safety and effectiveness in the gospel.
Following Jesus and doing Justice is risky but
Jesus is worth it. When they sing *worthy is the
Lamb*, they really mean it. And that is what
Jesus is worthy of.

The Shores of Grace team minister to
prostitutes and street children weekly. In fact,
we have been there with them. We literally
brought Domino's pizza to prostitutes. As we
ministered to the girls everyone of them had
the same dream. That dream was simply to
come off the streets! Here is my journal entry
after being with them on the streets in July of
2013.

urch - Words cannot express what we
..ered this night but I will try. We were
in the center of Recife, Brazil. We were
loca.ed underneath was a side an overhang of
a bank where the people took refuge from the
rain. Some of the people were sleeping on make
shift beds with blankets over them. There were
used condoms and unopened condoms on the
ground. There were also small children with no
shoes on. The killer part of this was that 75 %
of the people were sniffing glue out of plastic
bottles while we were singing and worshipping.
It was one of the most surreal evenings of my
life. In the beginning, I was playing soccer
with a young boy. Then I took a broom from
a woman in her mid 40's and began to sweep
the place where the people were living. I was
literally sweeping used condoms off the tile
floor where the people were sleeping on their
thin dirty foam mattresses. Then I prayed for a
woman with some eye trouble and her vision
improved a little. Then a man came and got
Pastor Siméa De Souza Meldrum. The man
then took us across the street to where he
was living. The man was 43 years old and had
lived on the streets for 13 years. We spoke
with him and preached to another young man
who was 24 and living on the streets. He had
not seen his family in years. He told me he
needed clothes so he could get a job. He only

had the pair of shorts that he had on. I told him that Jesus had not forgotten about him. In just a few minutes, people from the spiritualist community brought him clothes. He was so happy; he smiled at me and said see look God has not forgotten about me. It was powerful. This story perfectly illustrates that demons are subject to us in Jesus' name. Even demonic people must cooperate with Jesus!

At the end of the night four young children were rescued from homelessness and sexual torture. Two young girls were taken from the streets of Recife, Brazil to project Bethany, which is the Shores of Grace rescue home. Two young boys one of whom had painted fingernails and would be raped on the streets for money were taken to the Father's House, which is a rescue home for young boys. The feelings that I had tonight were literally inexpressible with words so tears were definitely part of the equation. As the street boys and girls were splitting up to go to separate houses in different parts of the city one of the young girls said unforgettable words. Here is the link to the short video in case you would like to watch the story - https://www.youtube.com/watch?v=WwGvo-a29rM

Every time the Billman's and the Shores of Grace team rescue a life from sexual slavery, poverty or drug addiction they are rebuilding their city. We cannot rebuild a city simply by building new buildings. God is in the people business, not the building business. When we start rebuilding cities and buildings, we must keep the people in mind instead of our own egos. We must be compelled by love and moved with compassion, not by a desire that is self-seeking. I trust that if you got this far in the book that you want to do something about it. The next section is dedicated to how you can practically do something about it.

CHAPTER TWELVE

JUST DO IT

Talk doesn't cook rice. [15]
- Chinese proverb

He does much who loves much. [16]
- Thomas Kempis

Reading about what is wrong with the world doesn't make anything right. In fact, reading about how to change the world doesn't change the world. All it does is give us hope that the world can and should change. If we act in faith and obey what Jesus commanded and live with his value system, the world most certainly will change. I will not devalue prayer in the name of action. Growing in Jesus through reading and praying God's word (the Bible) is the first step toward having Holy Spirit led direction toward anything meaningful or significant. Pray about the injustices in the world and simply ask Holy Spirit what would he like you to engage with? Jesus came to destroy the works of the devil, which is our assignment. Jesus did only what he saw the Father doing. If Jesus destroyed the works of the devil, it's because that is what the Father willed. The results of sin are the works of the devil. In this book, you read enough about the issues facing our world today for you to know what they are. If you need any reminding just turn on the radio, TV or go to a news app on your phone, tablet or computer. Now that you are spending time with Jesus in his word and in prayer, let's move to some more practical things that can be done to change the world and bring justice and hope to the nations and our neighborhoods.

Give what you don't use, want or need to those who do need or want what you have. It can be as simple as passing things like baby clothes or winter jackets on to those who can't afford what you may not even need. Learning to live conscious of others is a process. It will take some time to have a paradigm shift in how you approach people. If we value people, we will give to them. It's very simple, so let's keep it simple and do something for those who are in need. You never know one day you or I may be that person in need. So plant good seeds and you will reap a good harvest. Also, don't assume that someone is poor because they are lazy. There are poor people who are lazy and they deserve to be poor and all your giving won't do anything for them except maybe keep them alive. However there are those who have genuinely caught the raw end of the deal or have been given the short end of the stick. So give with compassion and seek to understand the dynamics of the person you are trying to bless. If the opportunity arises or is appropriate, form a relationship. People are not projects; they are people. What we may do for them may be a project, but you don't want them to ever feel like they are a project.

Volunteer your time with your church or at a local feeding program in your area. If you don't know where one is just Google it; Google knows! Don't make a commitment that you can't keep. You will only discourage yourself and disappoint others. Start slowly and increase your efforts overtime. Don't start out in fifth gear and then drop it down to second. Don't despise small or slow beginnings. Before we can change the world, we must change.

Share on social media. Social media has already changed the world and it will continue to change the world at least for the foreseeable future. When someone posts a blog, video, fundraiser or project share it, retweet it, or reblog it. If you are really committed to the person, project or message send it to your e-mail list. The only thing better than social sharing is – cash! Sometimes the end result of sharing things on social media is a financial contribution or transaction. I cannot stress how important it is to share what you believe in.

Buy things that are not made by slave labor. One day Steve Stewart was with me in New Jersey and he asked me to take him to a place where he could get some nice comfortable shoes. So I took him to Nordstrom's Rack. He found a nice pair of Clarks. Steve would not buy the shoes until he found out that they were not made in a sweatshop or by slaves. So we found out that they were not via their website and then and only then did he buy the shoes. That man is serious about Justice and he lives what he preaches. I will never forget that day as long as I live! Fair-trade coffee is another item that is used all the time that can be purchased that assures the workers are getting a fair living wage. Also buying this book and other books like – *When Everything Changes* by Steve Stewart and *Between the Flowers and the Broken* by Nic Billman and giving them away to others helps spread the message of hope and justice.

Fast a dinner out or even your coffee allowance for a week and give the money to an organization that you believe in that is giving hope, preaching the gospel and doing justice for the poor and marginalized. It wouldn't hurt us to deny our self for the benefit of someone else once in a while. In fact it would help us build self-control.

Start up a small business. *"Dishonest scales are an abomination to the LORD, But a just weight is His delight."* (Proverbs 11:1 NKJV) God delights in fair-trade. God loves justice; doing business in a fair and honest way is something God delights in. We know God delights in prayer, but do we know that God delights in fair-trade business? Where someone receives a product or service, someone is employed, someone is served and there is a profit involved. Did you know that God delights in that process? Well he does. Also consider hiring the elderly or even a disabled person who is able to perform tasks that help your business. Consider giving a job to someone who may not be your first choice in hiring. Give a job to someone who is of a different color skin than you.

Partner monthly with a ministry or organization that you believe in and trust. Here are three – Shores of Grace, Impact Nations and We See Jesus Ministries.

Go on missions trip with Impact Nations or We See Jesus Ministries, or visit the Shores of Grace mission's base in Recife Brazil and see what they do firsthand.

Commit to see a project through from beginning to end. Attach your heart and finances to a specific goal that a ministry or organization you trust is working towards and see the project through. Pray

> "Do not let what you cannot do interfere with what you can do."
> - *John Wooden*

about it, give to it and share the project with others. Get involved, stay involved and then celebrate its completion.

Invite a speaker who specializes in justice to come speak in your church or at your event. Also we can have a consultation about works of justice for your church, ministry or business. We can customize a plan for you, so that you can reach whom God is giving you a burden for. Our contact info is in the back of the book.

Do what you do for the glory of God, in the name of Jesus through the power of the Holy Spirit. Finally "Do not let what you cannot do interfere with what you can do." (John Wooden)

RECOMMENDED READING

Stewart, Steve. *When Everything Changes.* Abbotsford: Fresh Wind Press, 2012.

Billman, Nic. *Between the Flowers and the Broken:Stories, Songs, and Lessons from the Streets of Brazil.* Joelton; Shores of Grace, 2013.

Stearns, Richard. *The Hole in our Gospel.* Nashville; Thomas Nelson, 2009.

Stearns, Richard. *Unfinished.* Nashville; Thomas Nelson, 2013.

Gibbons, Dave. *The Monkey and the Fish: Liquid Leadership for a Third-Culture Church.* Grand Rapids; Zondervan, 2009.

Walker, Daniel. *God in a Brothel: An Undercover Journey into Sex Trafficking and Rescue.* Downers Grove; InterVarsity Press, 2011.

Clark, Randy. *Supernatural Missions : The Impact of the Supernatural on World Missions.* Mechanicsburg; Apostolic Network of Global Awkening, 2012.

Baker, Heidi. *There is Always Enough.* Ada; Chosen Books, 2003.

Baker, Heidi. *Compelled by Love*. Lake Mary; Charisma House, 2008.

LiVecchi, Adam. *Go.Preach.Heal.* Little Ferry; We See Jesus Ministries, 2011.

ENDNOTES

[1]Waters, Mark. *The New Encyclopedia of Christian Quotations.* (Hampshire; John Hunt Publishing, 2000), p.674.

[2]Waters, Mark. *The New Encyclopedia of Christian Quotations.* p.531.

[3]Waters, Mark. *The New Encyclopedia of Christian Quotations.* p.541.

[4]http://www.life-changing-inspirational-quotes.com/mother-teresa-quotes.html#Abortion

[5]http://www.antislavery.org/english/slavery_today/bonded_labour.aspx

[6] Gibbons, Dave. *The Monkey and the Fish: Liquid Leadership for a Third-Culture Church.* (Grand Rapids; Zondervan, 2009), p.143.

[7]https://www.foodandwaterwatch.org/water/interesting-water-facts/

[8]Bornstein, David. (2013, August 21). "The Real Future of Clean Water". [Web Blog]. Retrieved from http://opinionator.blogs.nytimes.com.

[9]McGrath, Timothy (2013). The Hungriest Places on Earth. *Global Post.* Retrieved from

http://www.globalpost.com/dispatch/news/
politics/131127/thanksgiving-the-hungriest-
places-earth

[10]Waters, Mark. *The New Encyclopedia of Christian Quotations.* p.733.

[11]Waters, Mark. *The New Encyclopedia of Christian Quotations.* p.402.

[12]http://www.nptrust.org/history-of-giving/
philanthropic-quotes/

[13]Waters, Mark. *The New Encyclopedia of Christian Quotations.* p.526.

[14]Waters, Mark. *The New Encyclopedia of Christian Quotations.* p.735.

[15]Waters, Mark. *The New Encyclopedia of Christian Quotations.* p.13.

[16]Waters, Mark. *The New Encyclopedia of Christian Quotations.* p.14.

[17]Waters, Mark. *The New Encyclopedia of Christian Quotations.* p.164.

[18]Waters, Mark. *The New Encyclopedia of Christian Quotations.* p.967.

[19] http://www.seguridadjusticiaypaz.org.mx

NOTES

NOTES

NOTES

NOTES

NOTES

Connect with the Author

 Facebook/AdamJLiVecchi

 @AdamLiVecchi

 @AdamLiVecchi

 AdamLiVecchi.tumblr.com

 www.AdamLiVecchi.com

—————— www.WeSeeJesusMinistries.com ——————

Connect with the Ministry

 Facebook/WeSeeJesusMinistries

 @WeSeeJesus

 @WeSeeJesusMinistries

 Channel : WSJMinc

 SoundCloud/WeSeeJesusMinistries

 (201) 562-6335

Connect with the Church

 facebook.com/RescueChurchtv

 @RescueChurchtv

 @RescueChurch.tv

 (201) 562-6335

www.RescueChurch.tv

Recent books by Adam LiVecchi

REDISCOVERING THE PROPHETIC

"Revelation comes into manifestation through perseverance. God builds us through what he reveals to us."

FOLLOW *Lead* MENTOR

"Authority to lead is birthed from the ability to follow. We cannot skip any part of the process if we want to live out our full potentional."

CPSIA information can be obtained at www.ICGtesting.com
Printed in the USA
BVOW08*1303060716

454635BV00003B/5/P

Animal Fakes & Frauds

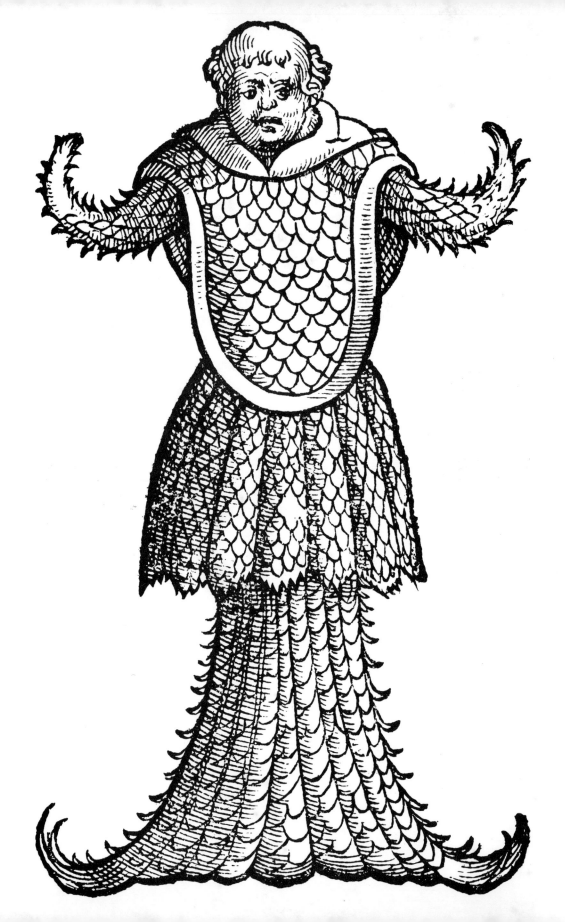

Animal Fakes & Frauds

Peter Dance

SAMPSON
LOW

First published in 1976 by
Sampson Low, Berkshire House,
Queen Street, Maidenhead,
Berkshire SL6 1NF

© S.P. Dance 1975
All rights reserved
SBN 562 00045 3

Printed in Great Britain by Purnell & Sons Ltd.,
Paulton, Avon

Contents

Acknowledgements

For helping me in various ways, often at short notice, I am grateful to the following persons.

From the British Museum (Natural History): Dr.P.Freeman, Mr.L.G.Howarth, Mr.A.Watson, Mr.P.E.S.Whalley and Dr.W.T.Tams (insects); Mr.A.Currant (fossils); Mr.I.C.J.Galbraith (birds); Miss D.Hills (jackalope, yeti); Dr.J.Jewell (Roman dogs); Mr.M.J.Rowlands and Mr.R.Banks (literature); Mr.D.L.F.Sealey (literature, fossils). From the National Museum of Wales, Cardiff: Dr.D.Bassett and Dr.R.M.Owens (fossils). Mr.D.Heppell of the Royal Scottish Museum, Edinburgh (birds, fur-bearing trout, literature); Dr.Bengt Hubendick, Director of the Göteborg Museum (White Russian shore muddler); Mr.G.Hopkins of the sub-department of Veterinary Anatomy, University of Cambridge (Cambridge centaur); Mr.G.P.Whitley of Sydney, Australia (jenny hanivers); Mr.Philip Cambridge of Huntingdon (jenny hanivers); Mr.P.J.van der Feen of Domburg, Holland (jenny hanivers, orang pendek); Mr.D.A.E.Spalding of the Provincial Museum of Alberta, Canada (mermaids); Dr. Boeseman of the Rijksmuseum van Natuurlijke Historie, Leiden (mermaids); Mr.R.Knapp of Martinez, California (mermaids); Mr.R.Whittington-Egan of London (mermaids); Mr.L.Goodson of Tring (insects); Mr.J.M.Chalmers-Hunt of West Wickham (insects); Mr.M.J.Hulswit of New York (snouters); Mr.K.Denham of Sampson Low, publishers (for enthusiastic support at all times); and my wife Una (for putting up with me and my monsters for so long).

Introduction

The seeds of this book, one of the more unlikely fruits of a long flirtation with a specialised branch of zoology, were sown about a decade ago. Inevitably, my duties as a conchologist at the British Museum (Natural History) involved delving into many obscure books and manuscripts on natural history, and being of an inquiring and undisciplined disposition, I could not resist the temptation to stray from the straight and narrow path of my speciality whenever I came across anything unusual

One day, when idly flipping the pages of Seba's *Thesaurus,* an enormous folio work in four volumes, my attention was arrested by the representation of a seven-headed hydra–the same hydra which features so prominently in the third chapter of this book–and from that moment I opened my file on man-made monsters. Gradually, I unearthed a succession of weird and wonderful monsters which never walked, flew or swam on this or any other planet. Like Seba's hydra they were all conceived and contrived by man.

I discovered that human ingenuity in the art of monster making had been frequently exercised to fabricate butterflies, fossils, birds, mermaids, dragons and basilisks. It had also produced a winged cat, a pygmy bison, a sea-spider and a fur-bearing trout. With his Nondescript, Charles Waterton had succeeded in transforming the lineaments of a monkey into those of a human being. Buckland's Nondescript, on the other hand, was unlike anything which ever drew breath this side of the infernal regions of Hades. Here, indeed, was a collection as fantastic as that in any mediaeval bestiary and one, moreover, which had never been assembled in book form. Having decided to assemble them for a book I found that there were plenty of references to them in literature but very few artefacts seem to have survived the ravages of time and man's changing attitudes. I have certainly overlooked some but I doubt that those still to be exhumed from museum cellars, attics of baronial halls, church vaults and curio shops, where such esoteric rubbish sometimes accumulates, will alter the overall picture fundamentally.

Reluctantly, I have decided not to discuss a class of objects commonly listed in the inventories of collections stored in churches, palaces and similar depositories many years ago. Typical examples are griffins' eggs, rocs' feathers, phoenix tails and dragons' eggs. Most of them are identifiable as parts of animals such as the elephant, the rhinoceros and the narwhal, which, though familiar to us now, were once rarely if ever seen in their entirety by Europeans. These objects were merely assumed to be parts of mythical beasts and were not artefacts or composite. I have also bypassed ephemeral monsters and fakes created by photomontage, these being usually devised for advertising products or amenities.

A few readers may be disappointed that I have written nothing about the Iceman, the monster sensation of 1969. This bulky anthropoid object, resembling a primitive human, was said to have been found in a block of ice floating in the Bering Sea. It was supposedly purchased in Hong Kong by an enterprising American, who exhibited it widely in the United States. The Iceman was described as a new species of the genus *Homo* by Bernard Heuvelmans; was brought to the attention of the FBI because foul play with a high-calibre rifle was suspected; was investigated by skilled anthropologists –and then mysteriously disappeared off the scene. Fascinating and enter-

taining though the story undoubtedly is, it lacks, for me anyway, one vital ingredient: the body. No investigator, as far as I know, ever had a close look at the object except through a thick wall of ice and it is still impossible to say what it was. I must know what my monsters are before I can discuss them. I have no doubt that the Iceman was a hoax from first to last and the object in the ice was probably a dummy. But, until I know for sure what it was, I prefer to pass it over in silence. Those who want to know more about the Iceman should read John Napier's *Bigfoot* (1972) which gives an excellent review of the known facts and a plausible reconstruction of the sequence of events involving it.

Trying to categorise monsters can be very frustrating because one may be the archetype or derivative of another, and some seem to have been given more than one name while others have been misnamed from time to time. This is especially true of mythical monsters. Several differently named monsters, for instance, can be grouped generically as dragons; others, such as the griffin and harpy, can only be grouped as composites, their bodies being compounded of parts of different animals. For this reason the arrangement of monsters, fakes and frauds in this book should not be taken too literally.

A fabricated monster is only one step removed from an imagined one, but I have tried to avoid trespassing into the land of mythical monsters more than was absolutely necessary, that territory having been investigated very fully by others. But there is a kind of no-man's-land, a land inhabited by sophisticated and unsubstantial creatures, which I have explored in some detail. Here live the Snouters, the Hoodwink, Hardy's Swift and the Dog-collared Sombre Blackbird, light-hearted inventions of men who have thought them up as a brief respite from more serious studies. The future of the man-made monster or animal fake or zoological hoax, call it what you will, is probably in the hands (or rather the heads) of such men rather than in the hands of the taxidermist. We are, after all, too wise these days to be misled by any more-substantial inventions. Or are we? Perhaps this book indicates that we can still be taken in. I hope so.

Overleaf: An Assyrian bas-relief depicting lion headed guardians with maces and daggers.

Chapter 1
Fact into myth

If the Arab could wave a magic wand over the camel, he might instantly change it into something totally different; a winged horse perhaps, or a dragon. It is inconceivable that, given the opportunity he would have invented an animal so devoid of grace and beauty as the camel. The only way that the Arab, or anyone else, can improve the camel's uninspiring appearance is by using his imagination. He may then describe the imagined improvements in spoken or written words, pictures, or sculptures. At this point, myth begins to take over from fact.

To a considerable extent, any imaginary improvements to the camel, or any other creature, would be likely to flatter the men whose imaginations furnished them. It is natural for us to want to be associated with things which excite admiration or fear. It is also natural for us to want to reach out, in our imaginations, for that which is beyond experience and often beyond reality. Although unable to sprout wings, we have always yearned to fly like a bird. Our imagination, which can put wings on anything, has put them on humanoid creatures known as angels. The large number of representations of imaginary creatures provided with wings may also signify, in part, the unconscious desire of those who drew or carved them to be able to fly.

One way of coping with something unknown is to make an imaginary representation of it so that it may be identified and may, through familiarity, become less frightening. Today we are bombarded with representations of so many monstrous creations, from Frankenstein's monster to the Wombles, that we are no longer frightened by any of them. We are now more inclined to laugh than to scream at such terrors. Perhaps the only ones which can still effectively frighten us are those which are of fearsome aspect *and* have wings. Their winged nature makes them harder to escape from. The pterodactyl which suddenly swoops into view on a cinema or television screen may or may not bear a close resemblance to the creature which lived on earth aeons ago. But it is on the screen, not just because the moviemaker wants to present us with an approximation of the truth but because he wants to present us with a very satisfying monster. As fossil evidence of the pterodactyl was not uncovered until the nineteenth century we should not expect to find representations of living ones before then, and indeed we do not. But we do find representations of several creatures, unknown living or fossil, which could be used as stand-ins for the pterodactyl. The public would hardly notice the difference if, instead of a pterodactyl, a griffin or a dragon descended from its inaccessible mountain lair and carried off the heroine. Had palaeontologists not unearthed the remains of dinosaurs and other large prehistoric creatures, moviemakers and producers of horror comics would have invented them, or they may have dug into the accumulated strata of man's earlier imaginings, and resuscitated griffins, dragons, harpies and hydras for our delectation. Human imagination is an almost bottomless reservoir of

'Dragons and griffins and monsters dire
Born of water, or air, or fire'.

The literature dealing with mythical monsters is very extensive and much of it very ancient. Most of the printed accounts are derived from sources predating the invention of the printing press. Because of the nature of the subject matter, the accounts become more and more embroidered as they are related by successive writers who

Above: The harpy, a predatory female monster which features in Greek mythology. Below: A griffin, after a pen drawing from a medieval German manuscript. The legendary griffin was compounded of the rear part of a lion and the head, feet and wings of an eagle.

could not resist the temptation to add material of their own invention. The eastern Mediterranean region seems to have given birth to many of the legendary monsters which are familiar to us today. One of the earliest to appear must have been the griffin, originally compounded of an eagle's head and wings, and the body of a lion. A tiny golden effigy of one was found in the royal tombs of Crete. This gives the griffin concept a pedigree of 3000 years at least. It is the literature of early Greek mythology, however, which is the apparent source of most of the monsters which have come down to us from classical antiquity. Homer's *Iliad* tells of the invincible chimera having the head of a lion, the body of a she-goat and the rear of a dragon. The concept of the dragon itself is often traced back to Homer. The centaur, in

An interpretation, by Aldrovandi, of the two-headed Chimera. Aldrovandi's illustration may have been copied from an Etruscan bronze (see Encyclopaedia of Mythology (Larousse), *p. 163).*

which the upper part of a human form merges into the rear half of a horse, may have been an invention of the ancient Greeks, and the winged horse, typified by Pegasus, may also have originated with them. These, and some of the other monsters which are found in the literature of early Greece, will appear elsewhere in this book.

It would be incorrect, however, to assume that the monsters associated with the ancient Greeks all originated in their fertile minds. There were, after all, other civilisations contemporary with, or earlier than, theirs which could have furnished material on which to base at least some of their mythical monsters. The Assyro-Babylonian culture, which flourished in the valley between the rivers Tigris and Euphrates from the beginning of the third millennium B.C., could have inspired several of the so-called Greek myths in which monsters are incorporated. Bas-reliefs depicting winged dragons, winged bulls with human heads, eagle-headed human forms with wings, lion-headed genii and many other monsters had been a prominent feature of Assyrian and Babylonian architecture long before the *Iliad* and the *Odyssey* were written down. There is no reason why the Greeks should not have known about these representations of monsters and it is difficult to escape the conclusion that their own monsters were, to a considerable extent, adaptations of them. Similarly the early Egyptian civilisation could be another source from which the Greeks derived inspiration. There was a profusion of animal-headed human forms to choose from, either in the shape of statuettes or wall carvings. Minoan Crete almost certainly contributed to the Greeks' treasury of monsters. The Sumerians, Chaldeans, Scythians, Syrians and Indo-Iranians also left behind evidence, in the form of artefacts or carvings, which show that fabulous monsters formed an integral part of their mythologies.

Many of the monsters of classical

Left: Nisroch, the eagle-headed god of Assyrian mythology. Right: Shedu, the Assyrian-Babylonian winged bull with human head.

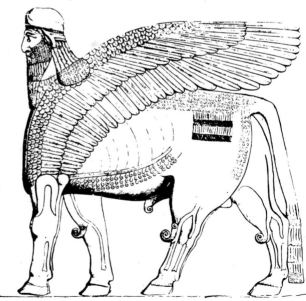

Left: The Babylonian Pegasus, from a wall carving in ancient Nineveh. Below: In Greek mythology, the centaurs were fierce monsters, half man and half horse, who lived in Thessaly.

15

antiquity were incorporated into manuscripts and published works produced in Europe from the Middle Ages onwards, and it was through these writings that knowledge of most of the monsters was transmitted to our own civilisation. The amazing archaeological discoveries made at Ur, Nineveh, Babylon and elsewhere in the Near East and Middle East are all of comparatively recent date. It is to these that we should turn if we want to understand the monsters of the ancients. Trying to understand them through the writings of men who lived at any time from the beginning of the Christian era up to the Renaissance, or even later, is an almost hopeless task. Centuries of religious dogma and superstitious fear, and the prolonged popularity of uncritical writings on natural history, such as those spawned by the credulous Pliny and the motley collection of animal stories known collectively as the *Physiologus,* adulterated

the mythical lore of the ancients and gave rise to a host of new monsters.

The fabrication of life-like monsters is a phenomenon characteristic of the sixteenth to the eighteenth centuries though it is not exclusive to that period. The sculptured monsters of antiquity, such as those on the walls of Assyro-Babylonian palaces, may have been almost as real and as frightening as the creatures they supposedly represented. They were always obviously artificial, however, and were never intended to deceive the beholder into thinking otherwise. If the ancients did fabricate monsters out of animate and inanimate objects, we have no record of their having done so. Even if they had done so, nothing would now remain of their handiwork. Consequently, the following chapters deal mostly with artefacts of comparatively recent date although the inspiration for some of them is as old as the beginnings of recorded history[1-4].

Chapter 2
Basilisk and jenny haniver

Among the most popular of all monsters fabricated by man is the jenny haniver. And what, you may well ask, is a jenny haniver? A recent definition tells us that it is the body of a real animal which human skill and ingenuity has changed into something resembling an imaginary or legendary creature[1]. If we were to accept this definition literally, it could be applied to almost everything discussed in this book. For our purposes the definition is too broad. We need to define it more precisely. A distinguished Australian ichthyologist, Gilbert P. Whitley, considers jenny hanivers to be fishes of the skate or ray tribe which have been distorted by hand, dried and varnished. This makes them look like miniature shrivelled-up dragons with wings and tails and usually with demoniacal faces. Whitley tells us how to make a jenny haniver. It is done 'by taking a small dead skate, curling its side fins over its back, and twisting its tail into any required position. A piece of string is tied round the head behind the jaws to form a neck and the skate is dried in the sun. During the subsequent shrinkage, the jaws project to form a snout and a hitherto concealed arch of cartilage protrudes so as to resemble folded arms. The nostrils, situated a little above the jaws, are transformed into a quaint pair of eyes, the olfactory *laminae* resembling eyelashes. The result of this simple process, preserved with a coat of varnish and perhaps ornamented with a few dabs of paint, is a jenny haniver, well calculated to excite wonder in anyone interested in marine curios. The front aspect of the finished article is really the under surface of the skate, whose back and true eyes are hidden by the curled pectoral fins'[2].

That, as far as we are concerned, is what a jenny haniver is although the

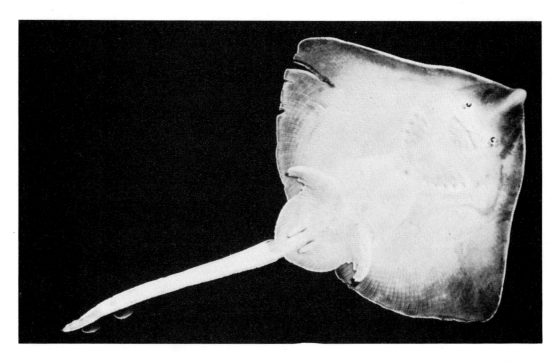

The underside of the thorn-back ray, Raja clavata. *The evil 'face' of this fish has inspired generations of hoaxers and monster-makers.*

manipulation of the various parts admits of considerable variation. But how did it get its unusual name? The standard dictionaries seem to have overlooked the name altogether so they cannot help us. The word *jenny* usually denotes a female creature but *haniver* has no obvious meaning or derivation. In a letter sent to G. P. Whitley, Dr. Rivis Mead (who had once owned a jenny haniver) explained that it had been purchased by him in a shop in Whitby, Yorkshire, England 'where the saleswoman had a long story about their capture on the coasts of Belgium and Holland. The name as given to me sounded like Jeanie Hanvers, so maybe it has something to do with "Anvers", the French name for Antwerp–a probable place of their origin. Possibly they are made there by fishermen or sailors'[3]. No-one has yet come up with a more plausible, or even an alternative explanation of the name. As far as

I know its first published appearance was in 1928 in the article by Whitley quoted above, so it may have been current only since then.

There are two principal reasons why jenny hanivers should have been made originally: because a skate or ray has a suggestive appearance and can be easily manipulated, and because it gave substance to or was a suitable substitute for a legend. As Willy Ley has pointed out[4], the appearance of a ray swimming in an upright position near the glass of a large aquarium is rather frightening. The observer has the unpleasant feeling that he is staring at an evil-looking mask out of which two baleful eyes stare back at him. The 'eyes' are actually the animal's nostrils, so the imagination already sees what is not there, even before the creature is manipulated. But why should anyone want to manipulate it so that it assumes a very different appearance? What is

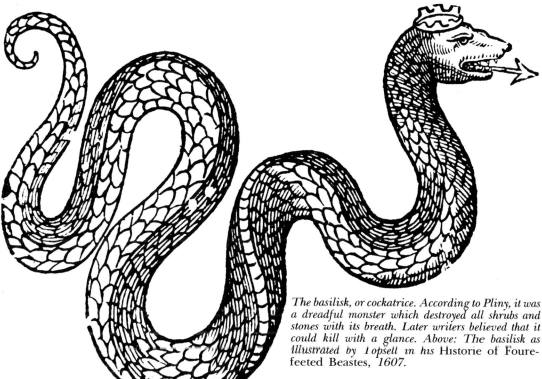

The basilisk, or cockatrice. According to Pliny, it was a dreadful monster which destroyed all shrubs and stones with its breath. Later writers believed that it could kill with a glance. Above: The basilisk as illustrated by Topsell in his Historie of Fourefeeted Beastes, 1607.

Below: The basilisk as represented in Johann Stabius' De Labyrintho, printed by W. Huber, Nuremburg, 1510.

the legend requiring substance?

Here we are thrown straight into the realms of myth, superstition and irrational fear, for the jenny haniver is a manifestation of that terrible monster, the basilisk or cockatrice. To the early commentators on natural history the basilisk was just a snake, a king among snakes and extremely venomous, but it still looked like a snake. From at least the time of Pliny onwards it was said to be the death of any living thing that it breathed upon and later on even its glance was said to be lethal. By about the thirteenth century, however, it had become a frightful monster and had acquired several more equally absurd attributes. It had to be born of an egg laid by a seven-year-old cock bird during the days of Sirius the dog star. The egg it sprang from was said to be spherical, not ovoid, had no shell and had to be hatched by a toad. Obviously the birth of a basilisk must have been a

19

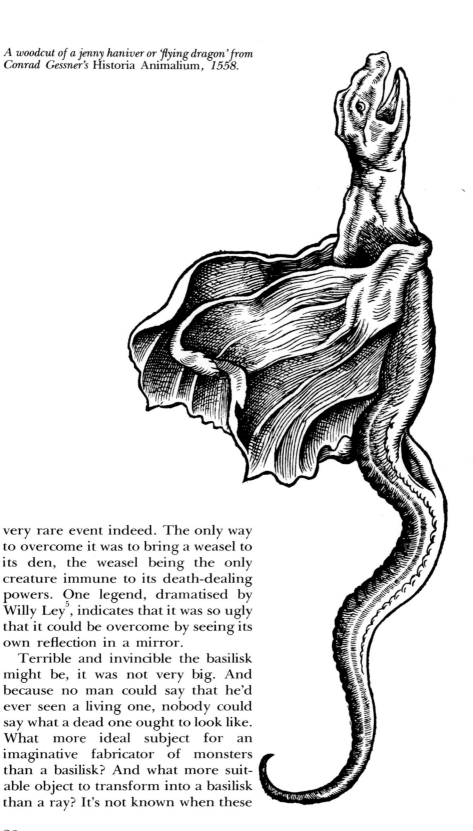

very rare event indeed. The only way to overcome it was to bring a weasel to its den, the weasel being the only creature immune to its death-dealing powers. One legend, dramatised by Willy Ley[5], indicates that it was so ugly that it could be overcome by seeing its own reflection in a mirror.

Terrible and invincible the basilisk might be, it was not very big. And because no man could say that he'd ever seen a living one, nobody could say what a dead one ought to look like. What more ideal subject for an imaginative fabricator of monsters than a basilisk? And what more suitable object to transform into a basilisk than a ray? It's not known when these

20

artefacts were first made but they were certainly around in some numbers in the sixteenth century. In 1558 Conrad Gessner printed a woodcut of a jenny haniver and reveals in his accompanying text what it is. 'The vendors of [quack] medicines and certain others [of that ilk] are accustomed to dry rays and fashion their skeletons into varied and wonderful shapes for [exhibition to] the multitude. They also exhibit others which resemble the serpent or the winged dragon. [To make these] they bend the body [of a ray], distort the head and mouth, and cut away other parts. They take away the forward parts of the sides [the fins or wings] and raise up the remainders that they may simulate wings, and other parts they modify as they wish. I depict here such a specimen as was once brought to me'.[6] Gessner even went so far as to say that his reason for illustrating a specimen was to warn people about such things masquerading as basilisks, winged serpents or young dragons. Over a century later F.M. Misson, in the course of a visit to Italy, saw how the basilisk was made there. 'The invention is prettily contrived', he says, 'and has deceiv'd many; for they take a small *Ray*, and having turn'd it after a certain manner, and rais'd up the fins in the form of wings, they fit a little tongue to it, shap'd like a dart, and add claws and eyes of enamel, with other little knacks dexterously piec'd together; and this is the whole secrecy of making basilisks'[7]. It appears from these extracts that the making of jenny hanivers must have been widely practised in the sixteenth and seventeenth centuries. Probably as many were made in Italy as in Belgium and France.

Gessner was not the first to publish a picture of a jenny haniver but he was the first to say correctly what he was

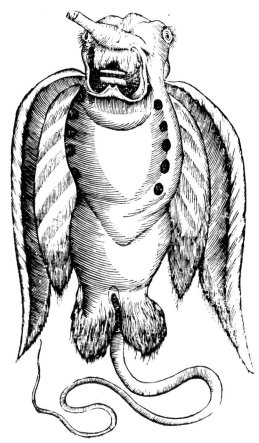

Ulyssi Aldrovandi's monstrous 'sea eagle', an illustration of a jenny haniver which appears in his book De Piscibus, *1613.*

illustrating. In 1553 Pierre Belon, in the first published treatise on fishes, published what is almost certainly the first picture of a jenny haniver. His woodcut certainly depicts the European eagle ray but the specimen shows signs of having been tampered with. It has an open mouth, pendent upper lip, and paired nostrils resembling eyes. The snout is so distorted that it stands out unnaturally from the head and the twisted aspect of the upper side of the head are surely evidence of human interference, albeit unskilful interference[8].

A more sophisticated version of Belon's 'sea eagle' is illustrated by Ulyssi Aldrovandi, a writer no monster

21

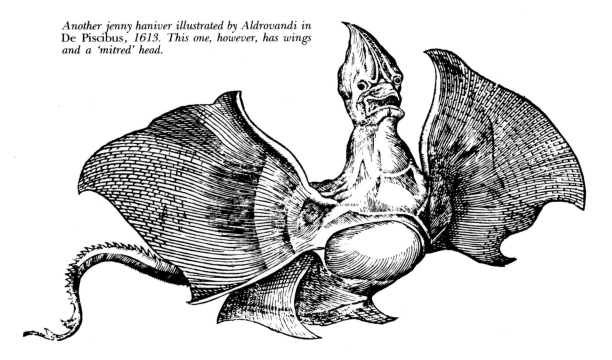

hunter can ignore, in his *De piscibus*[9]. Aldrovandi's 'sea eagle' has no tail spine, has two wings on each side, a much more expressive face with the snout protruding at right angles to it, more prominent eyes and other improved features. Belon seems to have been unaware that he was illustrating a fake but Aldrovandi was not so easily misled, the caption to his drawing indicating clearly the monstrous nature of his subject. There is little doubt that Aldrovandi's drawing is largely based on Belon's but Aldrovandi got his description of it from the 1579 edition of the works of Ambroise Paré[10], the illustrious French surgeon. With this exception Aldrovandi may have seen and handled all the jenny hanivers he illustrated in his books. It is known that he had several of them in his own museum. Those he illustrated are of various shapes which indicates that their fabricators did not necessarily have the basilisk in mind when making them. He illustrates one,

for instance, which is very different to, and much more artistically fashioned than, the 'sea eagle' but which cannot be considered 'basilisk orientated'. It is a flying dragon, the wings (actually the pectoral fins) having been separated from the head and manipulated to appear capable of flight. The mouth has been much distorted, the nostrils drawn to represent eyes and the snout produced upwards and backwards to resemble a horn or crest. Another specimen, less artistic in conception but probably more accurately drawn, has widely gaping jaws. This bears a striking resemblance to a well-preserved jenny haniver housed in the Rijksmuseum of Natural History at Leiden in Holland. The form, particularly the widely gaping jaws, and general appearance of the Leiden specimen suggest that it is of considerable antiquity and may even be contemporary with that illustrated by Aldrovandi. The drawing shows that a crude attempt was made to give Aldrovandi's

22

Right: A photograph of a well-preserved jenny haniver housed in the Rijksmuseum. Leiden. It is 14.5 cms. in length. Reproduced by permission of Dr. M. Boeseman of the Rijksmuseum, Leiden.

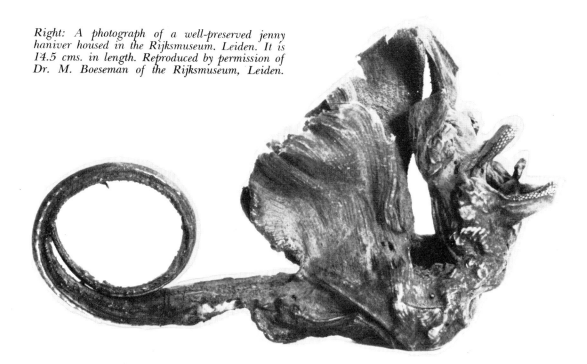

Below: Drawing from Aldrovandi's De Piscibus *of a 'Draco effictus ex raia'—a dragon made from a ray. Aldrovandi's drawing and the photograph are so similar that they may represent the same specimen. If this is the case, then the Leiden specimen is over 350 years old.*

23

specimen simulated hind feet by manipulating the rear fins. The coiling of the tail in the drawing is also a characteristic of the Leiden specimen.

Up to this time no writer had described a jenny haniver as a representative of a basilisk, but in his *Serpentum et draconum*, a posthumous book which appeared in 1640, Aldrovandi illustrates one in two positions. He says it was fashioned out of a ray and was seen by 'the renowned Mercurialis' in the treasure house (or museum) of the Emperor Maximilian. As can be seen, the specimen is exceptionally contorted. Apparently the basilisk was of protean form because Aldrovandi himself reproduces from earlier works representations of two basilisks, one of which has a crown and four pairs of legs and the other a crown and no legs. Very different again is the one portrayed in 1716 by J. H. Lochner von Hummelstein from

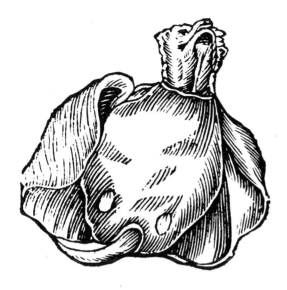

Above: Two views of a basilisk illustrated by Aldrovandi in his Serpentum et Draconum Historiae, *1640. Below: A very different basilisk, also illustrated by Aldrovandi, this one having a crown and four pairs of legs.*

the collection of curiosities formed by Basil Besler and his nephew Michael Rupert Besler[11]. In this one, a much more imaginatively constructed and better drawn object than Aldrovandi's, the head parts have been even more distorted and the pectoral fins have been separated from the head and split so as to form a pair of front legs as well as wings. The rear legs seem to have been made from the clasping organs of what was evidently a male ray, possibly a thornback *(Raja clavata)*.

In Duhamel du Monceau's treatise on fishes[12] there is an illustration of another jenny haniver which, though similar to Aldrovandi's and Lochner's, shows several important modifications. Instead of a pair of pectoral-fin front legs it has lion-like fore-paws set at the base of the pectoral fins, these paws being almost certainly additional items formed from some easily worked substance, possibly wax, cemented on to

the fish. The snout is twisted downwards and forwards and the wings have been strengthened to make them splay out like fans. Duhamel had several similar specimens which he said were made and offered for sale as *'poissons singuliers'* at various seaports. What seems to have been an almost identical specimen, in the museum of Athanasius Kircher in Rome, was described by P. Buonanni in 1709[13]. This implies a seventeenth- rather than an eighteenth-century origin for these more sophisticated models.

Perhaps the smallest jenny haniver on record was the one which reposed in Tradescant's Ark at Lambeth in London. In the published catalogue of this collection, formed by John Tradescant and his son of the same name during the seventeenth century, there is listed 'A natural Dragon above two inches long'[14]. London was able to show off another jenny haniver (of

One of the curiosities collected by Basil and Rupert Besler, illustrated by H. Lochner von Hummelstein in 1716. This 'dragon', constructed from a dried ray, has four legs as well as a pair of wings.

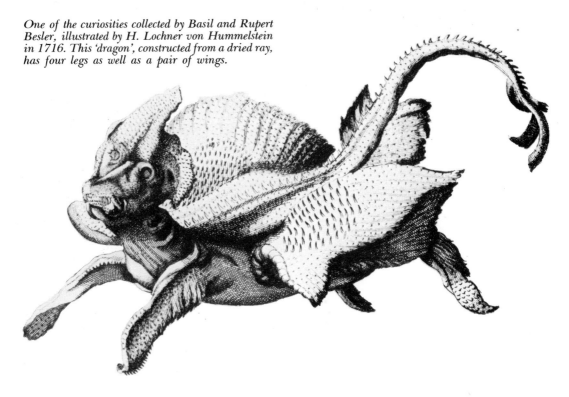

unknown dimensions) early in the eighteenth century. The Chelsea coffee house of Don Saltero (James Salter) was famous for its remarkable collection of 'rarities'. Not a few of these were spurious, such as 'A piece of Queen Catherine's Skin', 'Petrified Rain' and 'Pontius Pilate's wife's grandmother's hat', so it is not surprising to find that it contained 'The Basilisk, supposed to kill with his eyes'[15].

Much later, in 1797, George Humphrey, a London dealer in shells and curios, listed a jenny haniver in his catalogue of the collection of natural (and unnatural) objects brought to England by the exiled Minister of Finance for France, Charles Alexandre Duke of Calonne[16]. The catalogue entry reads: 'Thornback – a. Young – Maid – Normandy – *Raia clavata* Linnaeus. This has been bent so as to represent a dragon, and has even, in this state, been figured by authors, and called the Sea Eagle'.

But it was not until the early nineteenth century that the art of faking a basilisk reached its almost inevitable climax. Edward Donovan, writing on the subject of 'Cockatrices' in 1824, says, 'We once received a specimen of this with a declaration of its having been found alive by a fisherman in the English Channel, from whom it was immediately purchased for a few pence. This fact need not be doubted, for it was no other than a small specimen of the Angel Shark, *Squalus squatina* . . . which the fishermen call the fiddle fish, from the general similitude of its form to the figure of that instrument of music. But subsequently the legs of a cock armed with very formidable spurs had been ingeniously added, upon which it was perched like a bird on a twig of a tree, and the whole form otherwise tortured into a fantastical shape that is usually ascribed to that creature of imagination denominated a dragon'[17]. The addition of the legs of a cock seems such an obvious thing to do, bearing in mind the basilisk legend, that it is surprising a jenny haniver like this was not made before. Possibly the fabricator of this one had read something about the basilisk, had probably seen a representation of it and had attempted to make something approximating to it. As Donovan was the author of several articles on mythical and faked animals in encyclopedias, and in his own books, it is just possible that this jenny haniver was manufactured by someone acquainted with his writings. The question would still remain, why should someone want to make such an object if not for gain? Its sale for a few pence hardly suggests the achievement of that objective.

Throughout the nineteenth century, jenny hanivers and similar frauds were

A sophisticated jenny haniver with lion-like front paws, possibly modelled from wax. This illustration appeared in Traité général des Pesches *by Duhamel du Monceau, 1769-82. By courtesy of the British Museum (Natural History).*

27

circulating around fairgrounds, curio shops and similar places. Frank Buckland, for instance, mentions an 'angelfish' seen in a wandering showman's exhibition in London[18]. He concluded that it was only 'a "fiddler" fish tortured into something like a human shape'. But the reasons such objects were made were not the same as they had been in earlier times. By Buckland's day, the basilisk and similar mythical monsters had little or no relevance or meaning for anyone (although the public could still be drawn to exhibitions of mermaids and similar curiosities so long as they were cleverly advertised and presented, as we shall see in a later chapter).

The basilisk has even less relevance and meaning for us in the twentieth century than it had for our Victorian forbears, but the jenny haniver – the nearest approach there has ever been to a three-dimensional basilisk – is with us still. It was a modern jenny haniver which inspired E.W. Gudger to collect information on others and later to publish the long and fascinating article which has been so fruitful a source of information to me in the writing of this chapter. The specimen brought to him had been found in an old house at Brooklyn in 1925, its previous history being unknown. It had artificial eyes inserted in the nostrils, the appendages of the pelvic fins had been made to look something like legs and were supported by wires running through the tissues, the whole creature being vaguely reminiscent of an upright grotesque humanoid. It was certainly not a vintage jenny haniver and was presumably manufactured in the late nineteenth or early twentieth century. G.P. Whitley had showed, in his 1928 article on jenny hanivers, that they were still being manufactured in England, Normandy and Belgium and that

English seamen on the New South Wales trawlers had introduced the art of making them to Australia. Whitley illustrates one which he had received from England next to one which had been made for him by a New South Wales trawlerman. They were essentially similar. Gudger illustrates a guitar fish which resembled a very narrow and elongated humanoid. This was obtained at Miami in 1933 from a Swedish fisherman who had made it purely because he was struck by its faint resemblance to a human figure and wanted to accentuate this further. Certainly he had no idea that such things had been manufactured elsewhere, centuries earlier, and for rather different reasons. Another jenny haniver illustrated by Gudger came to his attention because of a newspaper account. This stated that a cobbler-fisherman of Allentown, Philadelphia had caught it and that it had a face which was 'slightly mongoloid and a bit weird but none the less a face'. The rest of the description and Gudger's photograph show that the fisherman, who had no more idea that such things had been manufactured before than the Swedish fisherman had, also wanted to make something approximating the shape of the human figure.

In 1968, when I first began gathering material for this book, I found that jenny hanivers were still being made. Firstly, Mr. Alwynne Wheeler of London's Natural History Museum, showed me a letter, dated 31 July 1968, which had been received from Wing Commander J.L. Sherrard. It said that a faked-up fish had been found on the shore of the Solway Firth between Silloth and Allenby. The enclosed photos showed it to be a jenny haniver of the 'humanoid' variety. Then, on 20 November 1968, an acquaintance of mine, Philip Cam-

This specimen was recently purchased in London, providing proof that jenny hanivers are still being manufactured today. It may have been imported from somewhere in the Gulf of Mexico.

bridge, sent me a photo showing an American friend of his holding in each hand a distorted 'devil fish' *(Rhinobates productus)*. These had been obtained at Guaymas, Sonora, Mexico, and had been made by local people. Finally I acquired incontestable proof that jenny hanivers were still being manufactured for sale. I bought one, in London. According to the proprietor of the shop in Soho, whence I obtained it, it was said to have come from the Gulf of Mexico. It was, he said, a very good selling line, and I know it did not take him long to sell the others he had. The photo of it, reproduced in this chapter, shows that it is another example of a 'humanoid' jenny haniver.

To satisfy the tourist trade, and perhaps for other reasons too, the manufacture of jenny hanivers resembling the human form continues to occupy the hands, and to some small extent the imaginations, of people in various parts of the world. But it cannot be pretended that these artefacts have much in common with those which were manufactured in Europe many years ago. The modern jenny haniver is a playful and not very ingenious attempt to distort a natural object into the grotesque semblance of a human being; it seems to have no deeper significance than that. The jenny haniver of yesteryear was, in part at any rate, an attempt to give tangible form to something intangible and supposedly terrible. It was also a very imaginative attempt: it was impossible to fabricate a basilisk unless your imagination, or someone else's to which you had access, was equal to the task.

I concluded, therefore, that the modern jenny haniver differs from the old one in both appearance and purpose. I concluded also that the modern one must have replaced the old some time during the early part of the last century at latest. Then, in December 1968, I was sent an extract from a published article on the basilisk which convinced me that the manufacture of the old-style jenny haniver was continued up to very recent times and with it, perhaps, there lingered a vestigial knowledge of the legend which gave birth to it. The article said that in the summer of 1939 Joost ter Pelkwijk, a Dutchman with a sound knowledge of biology, was walking along the quay of a fishing town on the Adriatic coast and came across a nearly blind old fisherman from whom he bought a jenny haniver (but ter Pelkwijk calls it a basilisk) and learnt from him the secret of its manufacture. 'The basilisk', he said, 'is made by drying a ray in the sun after having made only one pair of incisions left and right of the head. Then you fasten a string very tightly from the ventral fins, which are bent upwards, to the beak. The string presses the broad pectoral fins upwards. The sun does the rest. The cartilaginous skeleton of the fish, weakened in gin, shrivels. The beak then protrudes. The bony nostrils remain where they are and resemble eyes. The beak becomes a crown and the pectoral fins seem to be wings and reduced feet'[19]. It is interesting to note the use of the word basilisk here. Evidently ter Pelkwijk had not heard of the word jenny haniver or any appropriate Dutch equivalent. From the description it seems clear that this jenny haniver was a direct descendant of those which used to be made in the supposed likeness of 'the true basilisk'.

Did that old fisherman know about the dreaded basilisk, the monster which could kill with its breath or with a look? Was he aware that he was fashioning something which, in former times, had had sinister overtones? Probably not. But can there be any doubt that, deep down in his subconscious, there were traces of an ancient legend which, centuries earlier, had struck fear into the hearts of his ancestors?

Chapter 3
The hydra

The hydra, one of the few legendary monsters that seems to have originated with the ancient Greeks, deserves a chapter to itself even though it should really be considered as a kind of dragon. It is associated directly with the best known of all heroes of Greek mythology, Hercules. The second of the twelve labours he undertook at the bidding of Eurystheus was to destroy the hydra which lived in a swamp in the country of Lerna. This fearful monster, born of two other monsters, Typhon and Echidna, had nine heads, the middle one of which was immortal. Hercules discovered that it was pointless simply to strike off a head because the hydra's regenerative powers were such that two heads quickly sprang up to replace it. Eventually he vanquished the monster by getting his servant Iolaus to cauterize the stump as he severed each head, finally burying the immortal member under a huge rock[1].

The number of heads to each hydra varies according to the fancy of the commentators but most give it from seven to nine, the favourite number being seven.

An obvious candidate for the real-life hydra is the eight-tentacled octopus. The Mediterranean harbours specimens which may measure as much as three metres or more from tentacle tip to tentacle tip. There are numerous representations of the Herculean struggle. A Greek vase painting shows Hercules and Iolaus grappling with a 12-headed monster. On the other hand several Roman terra-cotta statues in the Campagna and Vatican museums indicate clearly the hydra's identity with a large octopus, although the number of tentacles shown is at variance with the number proper to an octopus[2]. As the hydra was not identified with an octopus until the nineteenth century it is scarcely surprising that its ugly heads should rear up malevolently from time to time in early manuscripts[3] and published books.

A hydra was said by Gessner to have been brought from Turkey to Venice in the year 1530 and afterwards sent to the King of France[4]. It was then valued at 6,000 ducats. Gessner provided an illustration, one of the most famous of all monster pictures, showing a well-groomed hydra with two large, six-clawed feet, a coiled tail and seven heads, each one bearing a crown. He was careful to point out that the illustration was the product of the artist's imagination. Topsell, not the most reliable authority on monsters but unquestionably the most entertaining, said, in 1607, 'I have also heard that in Venice in the Duke's treasury, among the rare Monuments of that City, there

It is not difficult to imagine that the eight-tentacled octopus (above left) may have formed the basis for the hydra legend. Below left: An ancient Greek vase-painting depicting an octopus-like hydra being killed by Hercules and Iolans.

is preserved a Serpent with seven heads, which, if it be true, it is the more probable that there is a Hydra, and that the Poets were not altogether deceived, that say Hercules killed such a one[5]. Unreliable though he usually is it is unlikely that Topsell would have mentioned the existence of this artefact without good cause. Presumably it was the one mentioned by Gessner. How it was manufactured and what happened to it no-one knows.

Another hydra, with more than twice as many heads but of diminutive stature, was seen in 1645 by the itinerant and ever curious John Evelyn. His famous *Diary* records a fleeting visit he paid to the Villa Ludovisi in Rome in that year where he stopped to measure 'the Hidra' which he found to be 'not a foote long, the 3 necks & 15 heads seeme to be but patch'd up with

severall pieces of serpents Skins'[6]. It is disappointing to be told that a hydra is 'not a foote long', the imagination having conjured up something more substantial. We have had to wait until modern times, for the development of the motion picture industry, to get monsters which come up to our expectations of what monsters should be.

Something much more satisfying in the way of preserved hydras was to be seen at Hamburg in the early eighteenth century. Along with Barnum's 'Feejee Mermaid' it is the best documented of all fabricated monsters and provides us with a rare scandal involving a famous naturalist. We also have a very complete description of its appearance and its history as well as a first-class illustration, making it a monster to dwell on at length here. On a day in the year 1720, Albert Seba, an

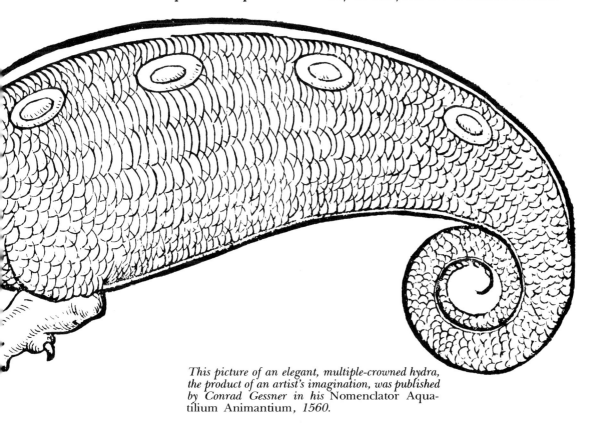

This picture of an elegant, multiple-crowned hydra, the product of an artist's imagination, was published by Conrad Gessner in his Nomenclator Aquatilium Animantium, *1560.*

33

A detail of Seba's illustration of a man-made hydra published in his
Thesaurus *in 1734.*

Amsterdam apothecary and enthusiastic collector of natural curiosities, received a visit from someone who said he had seen a strange animal in the establishment of Messrs Dreyern and Hambel, merchants of Hamburg. It resembled a serpent with seven uplifted heads each having an open mouth within which were great and small teeth. As it had only two feet and a long tail it approached nearer to a dragon in form than a serpent. Seba, whose collection of stuffed and pickled animals was famous throughout Europe, could not believe such a creature existed and dismissed the story as a fable. But the following year M.F. Eibsen, a minister of the gospel at Wustern, in the duchy of Bremen, visited him one day to see his collection. Eibsen gave Seba a similar story and also promised to obtain a drawing of the strange creature for him.

The minister's statement and the rumour that the specimen was for sale for 10,000 florins–a very large sum in those days–set Seba wondering about it once again and he asked Eibsen to send him the promised drawing. Eibsen sent it, but Seba was still not satisfied and wrote to a fellow collector of curiosities living in Hamburg, Johann Friedrich Natorp, asking him to send a drawing too. Natorp sent him one and said he was convinced that the hydra was no work of art but truly that of nature. The two drawings agreeing in all essential points and Natorp's opinion being valued, Seba himself became convinced that the monster was authentic[7].

Several years later, in 1734, he published an account of the hydra in his huge four-volume *Thesaurus* and reproduced the illustration sent him by Natorp[8]. From the description and figure we learn that the hydra was bay-brown with ash-grey shading. Its back was uneven and rugged and had a row of six large, oblong tubercles, as hard as horn, protruding from each of its sides, and under this row was another row of seven more-rounded tubercles of the same nature. The skin of the whole trunk, as well as that of the seven heads, was of a marbled chestnut colour but did not appear to be scaly. The long tail, however, was covered with rhomboidal scales. The seven necks appeared to be encircled by rings and the seven mouths were armed with teeth in the manner of a lion's. Each foot had four toes and each toe a long, pointed claw.

Further information on this fearsome creature was provided, a few years later, by Erik Ludvigsen Pontopiddan, Bishop of Bergen, whose *Natural History of Norway* is a classic source of monster lore. Pontopiddan,

after mentioning a two-headed snake in the possession of a Mr Christie, says, 'This puts me in mind of a Serpent, or young Dragon, with seven heads and necks, on a thick body, and a long pointed tail, with four legs [an obvious error], covered with scales, less than the scales of a herring. This creature is, as well as I can carry it in my eye, two German ells long [an *ell* corresponded roughly to an arm's length, which would make the hydra about 1.5 to 2.0 metres long]. This I have seen, and perhaps many thousands besides me may have seen it; and it is still to be seen at Mr Stampeel's, an eminent merchant in Hamburgh, to whose fore-fathers it was pawned for a considerable sum of money, by the Königsmark's family, who got it, among other booty, at the plundering of Prague. A painting of it is to be seen at Copenhagen, in the King's cabinet of curiosities, and which I can truly attest is perfectly done from the original. The emblematic Dragon with seven heads, which the Scripture takes notice of, has not alone an imagination, but a natural truth for its foundation; and I take this opportunity to observe it[9].

This hydra had a long history. Having had a place on the altar of a church in Prague, it was carried off, in 1648, by Königsmark. After his death, it was inherited by Count Bjelke and eventually came to Hamburg where it was kept in the collection of the Burgomaster, Johann Anderson and his brother. It was said that the Danish King Frederick IV had vainly offered 30,000 thalers for it, but that afterwards the price had fallen to 10,000 florins and 4,000 rixdalers (or about a quarter of the amount offered by Frederick IV). In 1735, the year after Seba's book appeared, negotiations were being carried on to sell it for 2,000 thalers, a mere fraction of the amount Frederick IV had been prepared to give. The vendors were desperate to dispose of it before its value dropped further.

While the negotiations for its sale were still in progress a young stranger from a foreign land came to inspect it. He took one look at it and exclaimed, 'Great God, who never put more than one clear brain in one of thy created bodies'. Seven heads was just six too many. As the young stranger was Carl Linnaeus, soon to become acknowledged as the foremost genius of systematic botany and zoology in Europe, it did not take him long to see that this monster was a thing of threads and patches, an object owing more to the skills of a taxidermist than to the caprices of nature. The heads, jaws and feet were those of weasels and the body was covered with pasted-on snake skins. Linnaeus presumed that it had probably been made by monks as a representation of the Dragon of the Apocalypse to deceive the credulous in

former times, and he was probably right. Of course the already drastically reduced price set on its seven heads plummeted to nothing as soon as the exposure was made public. Linnaeus and his friends feared that the Burgomaster would cause trouble, and on the advice of a Dr. Jaenisch, Linnaeus decided to quit Hamburg and continue on his journey. He seems to have been unnecessarily cautious because nothing more was done about the episode and the Hamburg hydra was never heard of again (although it is possible that Pontopiddan saw it some time after Linnaeus did).[10]

A month later Linnaeus was in Amsterdam and there met Seba. We know he was amazed at Seba's wonderful collection but we do not know if he made any reference to his recent adventures in Hamburg. If he did it would be pleasant to think of the old man sharing a joke which, to some extent, the younger man had pulled on him.

Chapter 4
The mermaid

As well as yearning to fly like a bird, we humans have always wanted to swim like a fish, and that may be one reason for the existence of the mermaid legend, prevalent in all ages and in almost all countries. If that legend can be said to have a single origin then it is probably the fish-tailed god Oannes (or Ea), Lord of the Waters, one of the principal Babylonian gods. He was adopted by the Babylonians, ready made and named, from the non-Semitic Accadians who worshipped him about 5000-4000 B.C. As the Babylonians believed that Oannes left the sea in the daytime and returned to it at night it is not strange that they should have imagined him as half human and half fish in appearance. Also, as the most significant part of a human is his head it is natural that Oannes should have been portrayed as human from the waist up and piscine below.

Oannes is said to have had a wife, Damkina, Queen of the Waters, and their union produced six fish-tailed sons and a daughter. The chief centre of his worship was at Eridu, which had been a port before the waters of the Persian Gulf receded. The inhabitants of that place owed all they knew to Oannes. Some authorities have even equated him with Noah, who has sometimes been represented with a fish tail (as has his wife and each of his three sons). As the biblical account of the Flood is so similar to the Chaldean account it is not too far-fetched to assume that the heroes of each are identical.

But what did he look like, this fish-tailed deity? Only fragmentary descriptions of him and the culture he animated have come down to us. These sketchy descriptions derive from a Greek history of Babylonia, written in the third century B.C. by

Above: The earliest representation of a merman is the sculpted figure of Oannes at the palace of Khorsabad. Below: A traditional representation of a mermaid: a voluptuous female form with a muscular fish-like tail. This illustration depicts Morgan of the Black Rock from The Wonder of Wonders, *an 18th-century English chap-book.*

Berossus, a Chaldean priest of Bel in Babylon. From this we learn that, in the earliest days of Babylon, 'there made its appearance from a part of the Erythraean Sea, an animal endowed with reason, who was called Oannes. The whole body of the animal was like that of a fish; and had under a fish's head another head, and also feet below, similar to those of a man, subjoined to the fish's tail'[1]. Many centuries passed and the external form of Oannes became greatly modified. In the Louvre there is a marine sculpture excavated from the palace at Khorsabad dating from the time of the Assyrian king, Sargon II, about the eighth century B.C. This shows Oannes in the more simplified form of a fishtailed human, and it is this form which approximates most closely to the present-day conception of a mermaid.

Although the origins of the mermaid legend are as ancient as the oldest legends of man himself, the mermaid seems to have arrived on the mythological scene later than the merman (for there is no evidence to prove that the wife of Oannes or his daughter had fish-like extremities; and as Oannes was a god we need not investigate the probable appearance of his mother). The mermaid may have arrived later but probably not much later, and when she did it was in the form of a human enveloped in a fishlike cloak, the guise under which Oannes first appeared. She was a Semitic moon goddess, Atergatis, or Derceto, who, as the result of an indiscretion with a handsome youth, threw herself into a lake and acquired her fish-like form. It was not long before she too acquired the simplified, more-familiar form of a fish-tailed human. The Phoenicians were probably the inventors of Atergatis—she certainly appears on their coins—but versions of her, and of Oannes, are to be found in the mythologies of India, China, Japan and of course Greece. All this means that the mermaid legend is very old and very widely diffused. Understandably, maritime nations have been much more mermaid conscious than those having little or no contact with the sea. Thus mermaid legends begin at sea or not very far from it.

By the sixteenth century the conception of a mermaid sitting on a rock, combing her long tresses with one hand and holding a mirror in the other was well established in the popular mind. This concept differs so much from the fish-tailed gods and goddesses of the ancients that it almost seems as though we are dealing with two distinct and unrelated ideas. All that has happened, however, is that the gods and goddesses have been humanised and consequently have become easier to accept. The only non-human feature remaining is the fish tail.

It is this more humanised mermaid which has taken such a firm hold on the popular imagination. The many supposed sightings of 'true mermaids' have sprung from a belief in the existence of such creatures and an inability or an unwillingness to recognise a seal, a manatee, or some other marine animal with certain vaguely anthropoid characteristics, for what it is. The persistence of the mermaid myth is easier to understand if we accept that, for a very long time, civilised men and women have *wanted* to perpetuate it.

A nineteenth-century zoologist, William Swainson, found it difficult to accept and impossible to explain an animal kingdom lacking a mermaid. 'We do not implicitly believe in the existence of mermaids', he says, 'as described and depicted by the old writers–with a comb in the one hand and a mirror in the other; but it is difficult to imagine that the numerous records of singular marine animals, unlike any of those well known, have their origin in fraud or gross ignor-

A mermaid and merman of the Nile Delta, from Aldrovandi's Historia Monstrorum, *1642.*

Above: The mermaid legend may have grown from brief sightings of such marine mammals as the manatee (above). Certainly Gessner's fanciful illustration of this animal (below) suggests this.

ance. Many of these narratives are given by eye-witnesses of the facts they vouch for–men of honesty and probity, having no object to gain by deception, and whose accounts have been confirmed by other witnesses equally trustworthy. Can it be supposed that the unfathomable depths of ocean are without their *peculiar* inhabitants, whose habits and economy rarely, if ever, bring them to the surface of the watery element? As reasonably might a Swiss mountaineer disbelieve in the existence of an ostrich, because it cannot inhabit his Alpine precipices, as that we should doubt that the rocks and caverns of the ocean are without animals destined to live in such situations, and such only[2].

Swainson, one of the best known writers on zoology of his day, had an axe to grind in wanting the mermaid to exist. He was a fervent supporter of an outlandish hypothesis, known as the Circular or Quinary Theory, which attempted to prove that the animal kingdom was arranged on a circular basis. There were many circles each comprising a series of animals or animal groups related to each other. Each circle was linked at one point to another circle by an animal or group of animals displaying characters common to at least one animal in each circle. Swainson was always looking for ways to 'complete' circles and link them to others and he wanted to connect a circle containing the seals to another circle containing monkeys but couldn't find a suitably linking animal. A swimming primate, such as man, would have been adequate but he'd set his heart on a mermaid, or something very like one, and this was very nearly enough to make him believe such a creature must exist. If this could happen to a zoologist who had, in addition to a profound knowledge of the animal kingdom, an appropriately sceptical attitude towards animal mythology, it is not surprising that less qualified persons should have been willing to believe in the mermaid.

Swainson wrote his piece on the mermaid in 1835–at the same time as Charles Darwin was working on the idea which was to revolutionise biological thought–but a few years earlier, in 1829, George Johnston, a competent all-round naturalist of Berwick-upon-Tweed, had ventured his own rather different opinions on the mermaid in a little article entitled 'The tests by which a real mermaid may be discovered'[3]. He was led to write such an article after having seen a mermaid in the museum of a large Dutch city (probably Amsterdam or Leiden, each of these cities having a museum with a resident mermaid), and because the subject of mermaids was one 'which has at various times interested the ingenious, and not a little puzzled philosophers themselves; I mean the tests by which a real mermaid may be discovered; if indeed there is such an animal at all'. He provided a sketch of the Dutch specimen, which was about a metre long and in a glass case, drawn from memory, and described it as a creature having the face, head and breast like those of an orang-outang; it was without arms and from the middle downwards resembled a fish. In answer to some questions he asked about it he was told that 'its inward conformation down to the middle resembled that of a human being; that, like an honest creature, it had its heart in the right place; that its lungs were excellent; and that it was not deficient in brains! I asked from whence it came, and was told from Japan; and I could not help replying, after I had spent some time in its examination, that, if it had been presented as an artificial instead of a natural curiosity, it would have been worthy of admiration, but that, as it was, I conceived it to be an unworthy imposition'. Johnston then raises a few objections to mermaids in general with especial reference to the incongruous way they are constructed. The possession of lungs he considers strange indeed in a creature which, if it had any close affinity with the fishes, had no use for a voice and couldn't hear anyway. If the nature of the lungs was evidence of a need for fairly frequent gulps of air why wasn't the mermaid seen more often? How, too, could a fish above a metre in length, and fairly bulky, get along with only a tail fin? And what can be said about a creature 'which has, as one may say, a broad chest and a heavy head, without any one contrivance to keep it from being, at all times, lower than any other part of its body? It might, indeed, be inferred, that so extraordinary a creature would live in an extraordinary manner; and certainly no manner could be more extraordinary, than that of living with its head downwards, and its tail in the opposite extreme! But this must be impossible under these points of view; and, I am apt to believe, that if all mermaids were tried by one or other, or all, of these tests, they would be found equally imaginary'. In conclusion George Johnston said, 'I cannot help thinking that in such cases we are not less deceived than our ancestors were, though it may be less agreeably; for their mermaids sang, and combed their sunny locks, and were, besides, extremely personable monsters, while ours are not only altogether mute, but as ugly as can well be conceived.'

Examined thus, in the light of known zoological, anatomical and physiological principles, the mermaid ought not, indeed could not, exist no matter how neatly she may have completed one of Mr. Swainson's circles. But by the same tokens would anyone have dared postulate the existence of the platypus, in some ways an even more improbable creature than the mermaid? Yet the platypus exists, so why not the mermaid? No, this is not the way to discredit a popular fallacy. Even in our own day we have seen that the considerable opposition to the existence of a monster in Loch Ness, far from diminishing a willingness to believe in it has, indeed, helped to keep the controversy alive and before the public eye. The way to discredit mermaids and monsters in Loch Ness, or anywhere else, is to say absolutely nothing; but saying nothing about such eminently discussable things as these is against human nature whereas a willingness to believe in the impossible or the improbable is not. Popular fallacies die hard and some of them have remarkable recuperative powers. None have enjoyed such a long and healthy life as the fish-tailed lady.

For reasons which are more or less obvious, the mermaid has never lacked admirers – she may be considered the first 'pin-up' girl of those who go down to the sea in ships – and this, perhaps, has helped to stimulate a willingness to believe in her existence. There are, for instance, numerous reports telling of the capture of mermaids and mermen. Henry Hudson gives a detailed description of one seen in 1608 by two of his crew during the second attempt to find a North-west Passage: 'This morning, one of our companie looking over boord saw a Mermaid, and calling up some of the companie to see her, one more came up, and by the time shee was come close to the ship's side, looking earnestly on the men: a little after, a Sea came and overturned her: From the Navill upward, her backe and breasts were like a womans (as they say that saw her) her body as big as one of us; her skin very white; and long haire hanging down behinde, of colour blacke; in her going downe they saw her tayle, which was like the tayle of a Porpesse, and speckled like a Macrell'[4].

Even during the nineteenth century there were reports of mermaid sightings and captures. A miniature specimen seen at Benbecula in the Hebrides about 1830 was killed by a stone and subsequently buried in the presence of many people[5]. Mermaids seem to have thrived in Scottish waters then, for there are numerous reports of mermaid sightings and captures, but occasionally they turned up elsewhere. One, captured in Aspinwall Bay in 1881 and brought to New Orleans, had all the experts baffled. A Boston daily newspaper reporting the incident said: 'This wonder of the deep is in a fine state of preservation. The head and body of a woman are very plainly and distinctly marked. The features of the face, eyes, nose, mouth, teeth, arms, breasts and hair are those of a human being. The hair on its head is of a pale, silky blonde, several inches in length. The arms terminate in claws closely resembling an eagle's talons instead of fingers with nails. From the waist up, the resemblance to a woman is perfect, and from the waist down, the body is exactly the same as the ordinary mullet of our waters, with its scales, fins and tail perfect. Many old fishermen and amateur anglers who have seen it, pronounce it unlike any fish they have ever seen. Scientists and savants alike are "all at sea" respecting it, and say that if the mermaid be indeed a fabulous creature, they cannot class this strange comer from the blue waters'[6]. Whether or not these accounts and the many others were all the outcome of deliberate hoaxes (and some undoubtedly were) is irrelevant here. The continued interest in the mermaid legend, which they evince, is not.

But to substantiate a legend, and if possible to make money out of it, mere words and pictures or eye-witness accounts are not enough. It is essential to have material evidence. In the nineteenth century and earlier it was essential to have a mermaid and to exhibit it. The legend, in its later form, calls for a glamorous half-woman, half-fish creation which posed apparently insuperable problems for would-be mermaid manufacturers. Ideally the mermaid needed to be – well, like a mermaid is supposed to be – good to look at. The reality, as concocted by the mermaid manufacturers, fell far short of this ideal. It is as if they knew they could not produce anything even remotely as satisfying as the legendary mermaid and abandoned the attempt in favour of a grotesque parody of it. To achieve the parody they had to resort to pastiche, as we shall now see.

The manufacture of mermaids is probably of ancient origin but we have no proof of this. The earliest indications of manufactured mermaids being in circulation date from about the sixteenth century. Samuel Purchas, a clerk in holy orders and a man of immense learning, quotes some information about a mermaid's 'skinne', seen in 1565, from the *Foure journals of Breidenbach, Baumgarten, Bellonius and Christopher Furer of Haimendors*: 'The 18th [of November 1565] we came to Thora, which Citie is on the shoare of the Red Sea of no lustrue; the Haven small, in which ships laden with Spices out of Arabia, and India resort. In this citie wee saw a mermaids skinne taken there many yeares before, which in the lower part ends Fish-fashion: of the upper part, only the Navill and Breasts remaine; the armes and head being lost'[7]. This may have been the remains of a manatee, of course, but it seems to have been exhibited as a mermaid and may have been deprived of its head to strengthen the deception.

By the eighteenth century, mermaids of a rather different kind were being exhibited in Europe. Some reached England and were reported in the popular press. One of these, said to have been taken in home waters, was the subject of an advertisement in the London *Daily Post* of January 23rd 1738. The advertisement read: 'To be Seen, next door to the Crown Tavern in Threadneedle Street, behind the Royal Exchange, at One Shilling each, the Surprising Fish or Maremaid, taken by eight Fishermen on Friday the 9th of September last, at Topsham Bar, near Exeter, and has been shewn to several Gentlemen, and those of the Faculty, in the Cities of Exeter, Bath, and Bristol, who declare never to have seen the like, so remarkable is this Curiosity amongst the Wonders of Creation. This uncommon Species of Nature represents from the Collarbone down the Body what the Antients called a Maremaid, has a Wing to each Shoulder like those of a Cherubim mentioned in History, with regular Ribs, Breasts, Thighs, and Feet, the Joints thereto having their proper Motions, and to each Thigh a Fin; the Tail resembles a Dolphin's, which turns up to the Shoulders, the forepart of the Body very smooth, but the skin of the Back rough; the back part of the Head like a Lyon, has a large Mouth, sharp Teeth, two Eyes, Spout holes, Nostrils, and a thick Neck'[8].

In several respects, this was an unusual mermaid, the wings, spout holes and feet being incongruous refinements which the mermaid legend does not call for. From the description it is not easy to discover what it was made of, particularly as we don't know how big it was. As it had been taken by eight fishermen it could have been the size of a human being, and the presence of 'regular Ribs, Breasts, Thighs, and Feet' all properly jointed suggests that the upper part was mammalian, though presumably not human. It would be incorrect, however, to assume that the human body has not been utilised by ambitious mermaid makers. In his *Literary anecdotes of the eighteenth century,* John Nichols indicates that the human body, albeit in an undeveloped condition, provided the basis for at least one mermaid. Speaking of the personal effects left behind by one, Dr. James Parsons (1705-70), a physician and antiquary who practised in London, he says: 'Amongst other curiosities is an exact delineation of a human foetus, which was the subject of an extraordinary imposture; the upper part being well made, and in good proportion,

43

BY THE KING'S ROYAL AUTHORITY.

WHEREAS many have IMAGINED that the HISTORY of

Mermaids,

mentioned by the Authors of Voyages, is fabulous, and only introduced as the *Tale of a Traveller*; there is now in Town an Opportunity, for the Nobility, Gentry, &c. to have an occular Demonstration of its Reality.

This curious and surprising Nymph, even the Queen of the Sea-Fishes, was taken in the Year 1784, in the Gulph of Stanchio, on Board of a Merchant-Man called *the Good Luck*, Captain Fortier. It is exactly three Feet in Length, and in Form like a Woman from the Head down to the lower Part of the Waist, and half a Fish from thence downwards, and is as perfect at this very Moment as when alive, standing in the same Position as when it rises at Sea, between Wind and Water, in order to make resound the neighbouring Echoes of the Archipelago with her sweet and melodious Voice.

ALSO A

UNICORN - COCK

(*alive*) a Phenomenon of the Feathered Creation, of exquisite Plumage, of fine Form, and of which Nature never before produced the like. And

A TERRIER BITCH
WITH THREE LEGS!

(*alive*), true bred, very handsome, and extraordinarily swift of Foot; was pupped with three Legs *only*, seeming not in want of the *fourth*; and what is very singular, has no Place in the Shoulder for it. The Whole to be seen at the

GREAT ROOM, IN SPRING-GARDENS,

during this and the ensuing Week, between the Hours of 9 in the Morning and 6 in the Evening.

Admittance One Shilling each.

Vivant Rex et Regina.

GLINDON, PRINTER, COVENTRY-COURT, HAY-MARKET.

the lower extremities monstrous. It was inclosed in a glass case, and shewn at the Heathcock, Charing Cross, as "a surprizing young Mermaid, taken on the coast of Acapulco." This figure the Doctor drew; and caused the show-man to be turned out of town'[9].

The late eighteenth century saw the beginning of a 'mermaid craze' which was to continue until well into the nineteenth century. There are prob-ably several reasons why this was a good period for mermaids, but the most telling of these is the perennial human interest in public exhibitions, particularly those purporting to dis-play the incredible and the marvellous. Virtually every manufactured mer-maid has become known because it has been displayed somewhere at some time or another for the delectation of the public, usually a fee-paying public. One placed on exhibition in London in 1775 was found, according to its owner, in the Aegean Sea. Edmund Burke and others eminent in scientific circles had no doubt that it was a real mermaid[10]. Then, in 1794, one was exhibited at 2 Broad Court, Bow Street, Covent Garden in London. This was supposed to have been cap-tured in the North Sea by a Captain Fortier[11]. Yet another was shown pub-licly at the 'Great Room', Spring Gar-dens, in September 1795, and a hand bill with a crude woodcut showing what it looked like was distributed[12].

London, in those days, was a show-man's paradise and mermaids often took their place in exhibitions along-side bearded ladies, two-headed chil-dren and giant fossil remains. Before long, however, mermaid owners came to realise that they could make much

A handbill advertising exhibits, including a mer-maid, at the 'Great Room', Spring Gardens, London, in 1795. Reproduced by courtesy of the Guildhall Library, London.

more money out of their bizarre wares if they paid more attention to advertis-ing and public relations. They had to pay some attention to these things anyway, because they were pushing credulity to its limits and offering to the public gaze objects which never came up to the public's expectations.

In its simplest form, mermaid adver-tising consisted of a bald announce-ment in the popular press, such as that which appeared in *The Gentleman's Magazine* for December 1820. This stated: 'One of those natural curiosities, which some people affect to believe does not exist, called a Mer-maid, has arrived on board the *Borneo*, J. C. Rose, master, now lying in the Thames, from Bencoolen, in Sumatra. It is of a perfect human form from the head to the middle, and the rest con-sists of a tail of a fish resembling the dolphin'[13]. In the same magazine for May 1821 a correspondent queried the authenticity of this mermaid. He accepted that the hands and breasts resembled those of a human but said that the face 'is far from looking like the human race, and the long hair is entirely wanted'[14]. But mermaids could produce much more detailed and, occasionally, more literary reports than these. The 1822 mermaid (as I shall call her for convenience) was virtually showered with words of praise, calumny, belief and disbelief, and it is those words, more than her sweet self, which has made her one of the most notorious of all mermaids.

The 1822 mermaid seems to have been first heard of in 1813 (almost certainly an error for 1818), someone having reported seeing her at St. Helena in that year on board the ship bringing her to England from the East Indies. Years later, the man who had seen her there said that she was impressed on his mind 'as an artificial compound of the upper part of a small ape with the lower half of a fish; and being allowed to examine it as closely as I pleased externally, my attention was directed, by the aid of a powerful glass, to ascertain the point of union between the two parts. I confess I was somewhat staggered to find that this was so neatly effected, that the precise line of junction was not satisfactorily apparent'[15]. The disparate halves of mermaids and the difficulty of detecting their place of union was to be referred to constantly throughout the nineteenth century. Following on the above anonymous report a Mr. J. Murray of Carmarthen said: 'I examined the "thing of shreds and patches" exhibited some years ago as a "mermaid" in the metropolis . . . and could distinctly perceive the *junction* of the compound, for it was certainly sewed together. I concluded it to be the upper part of the long-armed ape attached to the tail portion of a fish from the Ganges allied to the genus Salmo. The creature seemed to have been put to some cruel death to produce a horrid caricature of humanity. It was constructed in utter defiance of the laws of gravitation, and would have been in the condition of the man who ventured into the water with cork boots. Moreover, it would have required two distinct species of circulation, for a *warm*-blooded animal could never coalesce with a *cold*-blooded one'[16]. A great deal more has been written about this particular specimen, and at the risk of being tedious, the principal facts relating to it—its appearance, apparent composition and the vicissitudes it underwent —are here set down, and where possible are set down in the words of contemporary commentators.

No man-made monster can have been subjected to closer scrutiny and none can have had its wanderings so minutely chronicled. A letter, written by the Rev. M. Phillip of the London Missionary Society at Cape Town, was published in the *Philanthropic Gazette* of 31 July, 1822. In it he states: 'I have today seen a mermaid now exhibiting in this town. I have always treated the existence of this creature as fabulous, but my scepticism is now removed. As it is probable no description of this extraordinary creature has reached England, the following particulars respecting it may gratify your curiosity and amuse you. The head is almost the size of that of a baboon. It is thinly covered with black hair, hanging down and not inclined to frizzle. On the upper lip and on the chin are a few hairs. The cheek bones are prominent, the forehead low, but except in this particular, the features are much better proportioned and bear a more decided resemblance to the human countenance than that of a baboon.

'From the position of the arms, I can have no doubt, that it has clavicles, an appendage belonging to the human body which baboons are without! The canine teeth resemble those of a full-grown dog; all the others those of a human subject. The length of the animal is three feet. From the point where the human figure ceases, it resembles a fish of the salmon species and is covered with scales all over. It has six fins and a tail. The proprietor of this extraordinary animal is Captain Eades of Boston in the United States. From him I have learned, it was caught somewhere in the north of China by a fisherman who sold it for a trifle, after which it was brought to Batavia. Here it was purchased by Captain Eades for 5,000 Spanish dollars. Captain Eades is a passenger on board the American ship *Lion* now in Table Bay, and he leaves this port in about a fortnight and the *Lion* visits the Thames, so it

Two different representations of the '1822' mermaid exhibited in London in St. James' Street. A rather unflattering handbill was distributed (right) to encourage the public to view it. Reproduced by courtesy of the Guildhall Library, London.

will probably be soon exhibited in London[17].

Eagerly London awaited the arrival of this most unusual curiosity. The *Lion* came up the Thames and Captain Eades and his mermaid came ashore. The customs officials were dubious about allowing a mermaid ashore free of duty and so she was temporarily deposited in the East India baggage warehouse. While her ladyship lan-

47

guished in these unglamorous surroundings Captain Eades applied to Sir Everard Home, President of the Royal College of Surgeons, requesting him to examine it. This application to so eminent a surgeon certainly indicates that Captain Eades had implicit faith in the authenticity of his mermaid and shows him to have been a man of some honesty and no little gullibility. Sir Everard asked William Clift, Curator of the Hunterian Museum, to go and report on the specimen for him. Accordingly Mr. Clift went to the warehouse. The account of his visit is as follows. He says that he found the mermaid 'locked in a tin case, very carefully wrapped in soft materials and surrounded by a silken mattress to protect it from injury. Captain Eades permitted me to examine it very minutely, and I immediately saw it was a *palpable imposition* and soon made out the manner in which it had been prepared.

'The cranium appears evidently to belong to an orang-outang of full growth, the teeth and probably the jaws, do not belong to the cranium, but from the size and length of the canine teeth, they appear to be those of a large baboon. The scalp is thinly and partially covered with dark-coloured hair, which is glossy like that of an orang-outang. The skin covering the face has a singularly loose and shrivelled appearance and on a very close inspection, it appears to have been artificially joined to the skin of the head across the eyes and upper part of the nose. The projections in lieu of ears, are composed of folds of the same piece of skin of which the face is formed. The eyes appear to have been distended by some means, so as to have kept very nearly the natural form, and there is a faint appearance as though the cornea had been painted to represent the pupil and iris. The object has been so contrived as to leave no appearance to a cursory observer of its having been opened, but simply dried, and there are two small holes on the forehead, through which a string has been passed for its suspension while drying.

'The nails of the orang-outang being very short and their peculiar appearance well known, these have been removed and their places supplied, or else covered with pieces, either of horn or quill, but from their opaque, whitish appearance, probably the latter, but of whatever substance they are formed, they have not the character of nails. The mammae appear to have had some slight stuffing from within, and immediately below them is a deep fold, in order to hide the junction with that which forms the lower or posterior part of the figure. This consists of the entire body of a fish, apparently of the salmon genus, separated from the head immediately behind the branchiae and the pectoral fins and brought immediately below the situation of the ensiform cartilage of the orang-outang. On the posterior part of the body of the fish, the skin has been preserved as high as possible towards the head, so as to terminate in a point of very thin skin, which is placed between the scapula of the orang-outang, and has been pressed down very closely upon the spinous processes of the dorsal vertebrae while drying.

'The place of junction, and for a little distance on each side of it, has been smeared over with some ochry substance, but the whole figure has acquired a brown mummy-like appearance from drying which prevents this from being readily perceived. But, if anything were wanting to convince me that the anterior and posterior parts of the figure have been separate from each other, there is a hoop of some firm substance, similar to paper or pasteboard, which distends the body of the fish nearly all the way from the pectoral to the anal fins, but below or behind this part, the body has shrunk in from the want of the same support, leaving a distinct edge all round.

'The fins appear to correspond exactly in number and situation with those of the salmon, but if they did not, it would only have proved how very practicable a thing it was for so ingenious an artist as the person who prepared it, whether Chinese or European, to have added some by way of embellishment, as well as the tuft of black hair, which has been inserted into and projects from each nostril. This object, such as it is, measures about two feet ten inches in length, and was first exhibited in London at the Turf Coffee-house in St. James's Street at the corner of Jermyn Street on Tuesday, October 15, 1822. Admittance, one shilling[18]. An illustrated print was distributed which showed that the mermaid was the ugliest, most deformed object imaginable. This did not prevent–and may possibly have encouraged–from three to four hundred persons per day paying a shilling each to indulge their credulity.

That tireless investigator and exposer of outré deformities, Edward Donovan, also inspected Captain Eades' mermaid. He noted that it was in a bell glass 'and the aspect of the whole at once suggests the idea of an ape, emerging from the mouth of a fish much smaller than can be considered sufficiently capacious to contain it . . . Looking upon this heterogeneous object the naturalist is at once struck with the total want of knowledge as well as clumsy workmanship of the fabricator . . . No small degree of pains

he must admit has been bestowed upon the unfortunate biped, the skin of the face having been tortured into a form of peculiar extravagance . . . As to the "breasts", which we are told "are large and resemble those of a woman, and which, though now small and shrivelled, yet must have been full and prominent when the animal was living", we may also be permitted to say a few words. The comparison, it must be allowed, affords no very handsome compliment to the fair sex; much pains appears to have been taken to distend and enlarge the skin; the mammae or teats of the breast are composition, and it would not be difficult to say that the same ingredient has been serviceable in distending the dried skin of the breast, or in partially filling up the cavities of its wrinkles'.

Commenting upon the fishy portion of this mermaid Donovan points out that, in this particular, 'it presents a new anomaly in the records both of fable and of science; it is not the tail merely but the whole body of the fish after undergoing decapitation that we now behold appendant to the "Mermaid's" bust . . . therefore it will be observed, that it is not the tail merely of the fish, but the whole body of the fish with the exception of the head that constitutes the tail of our present "Mermaid": an unwieldy and inflexible posterior appendage truly for the trunk of such an active being as an ape'. Donovan concluded that the fish was a specimen of the common salmon and that the trunk of an orang-outang had been thrust or placed into it. His further interminable discussion of the mermaid's peculiarities do not concern us here, their principal purpose being to prove beyond all doubt that the creature was a composite of human manufacture. On the other hand he adds some particulars about its origins

49

and travels which are of some interest.

Donovan says that this mermaid was supposedly found on board a native vessel in the 'archipelago of the Malaccas' and was carried by a Dutch vessel to Batavia where it was sold for a price stated to be 5,000 dollars. It was said to have created an 'instinctive awe' amongst its former owners from its resemblance to the human form. Donovan was of the opinion that it was meant originally to be 'an imposition on Asiatic credulity rather than European discrimination', and this may well have been so as its former owners probably had some kind of veneration for mermaids, these creatures being close to, if not identical with, their conception of one of the transformations of Vishnu[19].

About a month after Captain Eades' mermaid was placed on public view it was reported that, in the Court of Chancery, 'Mr. Hart applied for his Lordship's injunction to restrain a Mr. Eles [Eades] from removing a certain mermaid or dried specimen from the room in which it was now exhibiting in St. James's Street, and from selling or disposing of it'. A Mr. Stephen Ellery claimed to have had a joint interest in the mermaid in 1817 and was part owner of a vessel commanded by Captain Eades. It was alleged that the Captain had obtained the money to buy the mermaid by selling the vessel and cargo, nearly all of which belonged to Mr. Ellery. When the Captain arrived in London he had taken a room for the exhibition of the mermaid and retained the profits for his own use. He threatened to remove the mermaid if any claim was made. 'Whether man, woman or mermaid', said the Lord Chancellor in this truly Gilbertian case, if the right to the property was clearly made out, it was the duty of the Court to protect it. In the event, the Lord Chancellor pronounced the injunction, surely the strangest he must ever have pronounced[20].

This was not the only mermaid to be discussed in Court. 'A person entered the office in great consternation', said *The Mirror* for 8 December 1822, 'and claimed the protection of the Magistrates in behalf of himself, his mermaid and his Sapient pig'. Apparently he had ruffled the feelings of two unpleasant characters by denying them permission to see his mermaid and pig, these gentlemen swearing that they would return on the next night to 'blow up himself, barbecue his pig and split his mermaid'. Nothing came of the threat, and the owner of these wonders even benefited slightly from the free publicity he received[21].

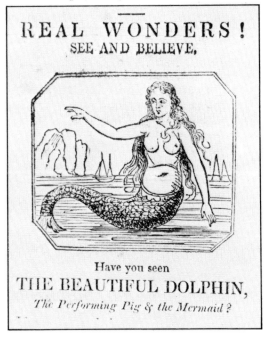

An undated broadsheet advertising a mermaid and other curiosities. The Guildhall Library, London.

In 1836 another mermaid was the subject of a suit in Chancery. This mermaid caused trouble because she was a popular exhibit in the West End of London and made a lot of money for her owners who quarrelled over profit sharing. The suit was brought to decide who owned the repulsive object which, like the majority of such objects, seems to have originated from Indonesia[22].

But it was left to that prince of hoaxers, Phineas Taylor Barnum, to

Phineas Taylor Barnum, showman and entrepreneur. The frontispiece to his autobiography, published in 1855.

make real capital out of the mermaid legend. Amusingly enough it seems as though it was the 1822 mermaid which gave him the incentive and the necessary material to exploit the legend. His 'Fejee Mermaid', as he christened it, came into his possession in 1842, as he relates himself in his autobiography. It appears that Captain Eades, who never ceased to believe in the authenticity of his mermaid, valued it highly for the rest of his life, and died possessing no other property. His son sold it to a Mr. Kimball who brought it to New York to

show to Barnum. The rest of the story is best told in Barnum's own words.

'Not trusting my own acuteness on such matters', says the great showman, 'I requested my naturalist's opinion of the *genuineness* of the animal. He replied that he could not conceive how it was manufactured; for he never knew a monkey with such peculiar teeth, arms, hands, etc., nor had he knowledge of a fish with such peculiar fins.

'"Then why do you suppose it is manufactured?" I inquired.

'"Because I don't believe in mermaids", replied the naturalist.

'"That is no reason at all", said I, "and therefore I'll believe in the mermaid, and hire it".

'This was the easiest part of the experiment. How to modify general incredulity in the existence of mermaids, so far as to awaken curiosity to see and examine this specimen, was now the all-important question. Some extraordinary means must be resorted to, and I saw no better method than to "start the ball a-rolling" at some distance from the centre of attraction. In due time a communication appeared in the *New York Herald*, dated and mailed in Montgomery, Ala., giving the news of the day, trade, the crops, political gossip, etc., and also an incidental paragraph about a certain Dr. Griffin, agent of the Lyceum of Natural History in London, recently from Pernambuco, who had in his possession a most remarkable curiosity, being nothing less than a veritable mermaid taken among the Fejee Islands, and preserved in China, where the Doctor had bought it at a high figure for the Lyceum of Natural History. A week or ten days afterwards, a letter of similar tenor, dated and mailed in Charleston, S.C., varying of course in the items of local news, was published in another New York paper'. Another letter, dated and posted in Washington appeared in yet another New York paper shortly afterwards and this time expressed the hope that the editors would beg a sight of the curiosity before Dr. Griffin took ship for England.

A few days later Mr. Lyman, an employee of Barnum's, was registered at a principal Philadelphia hotel as Dr. Griffin of Pernambuco, en route for London. Having behaved in an exemplary manner for the few days of his stay, and thereby gaining a fine reputation as a gentleman, he paid his bill and expressed his thanks to the landlord for special attention and courtesy. 'If you will step to my room', said Lyman, alias Griffin, 'I will permit you to see something that will surprise

The fascination of a mermaid. From The Life of P. T. Barnum Written by Himself, *1855.*

you'. So impressed was the landlord with the sight of the mermaid that he begged to be allowed to show it to several friends of his, among whom were several editors. Of course Lyman acceded to the request with the result that the Philadelphia press aided the New York press in awakening a wide and increasing interest in the mermaid.

'I may as well confess', says Barnum unblushingly, 'that those three communications from the South were written by myself, and forwarded to friends of mine, with instructions respectively to mail them, each on the day of its date. This fact and the corresponding post-marks did much to prevent suspicion of a hoax, and the New York editors thus unconsciously contributed to my arrangements for bringing the mermaid into public notice'. Lyman then returned to New York, and having put up at an hotel it soon became common knowledge that the mermaid was in town. Several reporters and editors examined the mermaid and numerous reports of their examinations were published, to the entire satisfaction of Phineas Taylor Barnum.

While Lyman was exciting public opinion on the mermaid at his New York hotel, Barnum was busy working towards the same end, but by rather different means. 'I was industriously at work', he says, 'in getting up wood-cuts and transparencies, as well as a pamphlet, proving the authenticity of mermaids, all in speedy anticipation of Dr. Griffin's specimen. I had three several and distinct pictures of mermaids engraved, and with a peculiar description written for each, had them inserted in 10,000 copies of the pamphlet which I had printed and quietly stored away in a back office until the time came to use them. I then called respectively on the editors of the *New York Herald,* and two of the Sunday papers, and tendered to each the free use of a mermaid cut, with a well-written description, for their papers of the ensuing Sunday. I informed each editor that I had hoped to use this cut in showing the Fejee Mermaid, but since Mr. Griffin had announced that as agent for the Lyceum of Natural

History, he could not permit it to be exhibited in America, my chance seemed dubious, and therefore he was welcome to the use of the engraving and description. The three mermaids made their appearance in the three different papers on the morning of Sunday, 17 July, 1842. Each editor supposed he was giving his readers an exclusive treat in the mermaid line, but when they came to discover that I had played the same game with the three different papers, they pronounced it a *scaly* trick'.

Together the newspaper announcements and Barnum's pamphlets created sufficient interest for an exhibition of the mermaid to be mounted. Concert Hall on Broadway was engaged and the newspapers immediately contained the following advertisement:

'THE MERMAID, AND OTHER WONDERFUL SPECIMENS OF THE ANIMAL CREATION.–The public are respectfully informed that, in accordance with numerous and urgent solicitations from scientific gentlemen in this city, Mr. J. GRIFFIN, proprietor of the Mermaid, recently arrived from Pernambuco, S.A., has consented to exhibit it to the public, *positively for one week only!* . . . etc.'. Barnum's carefully laid plans were totally successful and large numbers of people paid 25 cents each to see what Barnum himself described as 'an ugly, dried-up, black-looking, and diminutive specimen'. Afterwards the American Museum in New York showed off the specimen to even more members of the public. A flag representing a mermaid 5.4 metres in length was flown for a short time in the front of the museum but had to be taken down in deference to the feelings of Mr. Lyman who thought that this was taking things a little too far considering the small

An illustration of Barnum's 'Fejee' Mermaid which appeared in the New York Sunday Herald *on 17th July 1842.*

size of the mermaid he had been instrumental in bringing before the public. The Fejee Mermaid was on show in the museum for several weeks and the receipts show very clearly how popular she was during that time. For the four weeks immediately before the mermaid's arrival, the museum's takings amounted to $1272. During the first four weeks of the mermaid's exhibition the takings amounted to $3341.93, an increase of about two and a half times[23]. But with Barnum behind her the Fejee Mermaid could hardly fail to be a success.

Mermaids continued to make news intermittently throughout the rest of

ROYAL AQUARIUM.

MR. HARRY PHILLIPS'
LIVING
MYTHOLOGICAL
MERMAID.

First Exhibited at the **BRIGHTON AQUARIUM,** February 10th, 1886.

First Exhibited at the **BRIGHTON AQUARIUM,** February 10th, 1886.

HALF BEAUTIFUL WOMAN,
HALF FISH.

Submerged in a Glass Tank with Live Fish.

A FEW PRESS NOTICES.

" . . . The wonderful 'Mermaid,' which is sure to be the talk of London."—*Bell's Life,* October 4th, 1886.

"We may especially recommend to the notice of those who patronize the Palace the real live Mermaid, exhibited by Mr. Harry Phillips. There is no mistake this time, and we absolutely decline to credit the exhibitor, who is himself a Tyrolean and character vocalist and ventriloquist, when he tells us that it is all an illusion. We prefer to believe the other way. There, in a glass tank, with sticklebacks and gudgeon for her companions, sits the lovely creature, very beautiful as to her head, with its lovely flowing hair, and very fishy as to her tail. She looks quite bewitching, and she smiles so graciously, that the spectator at once conjures up reminiscences of the sirens, and lingers long and admiringly upon the scene. All should see the real live Mermaid."—*Era,* April 24, 1886.

"The Aquarium has recently obtained a new attraction in the person of a good looking living Mermaid. The entirely novel illusion displays a lady in a recumbent attitude and apparently at ease in all the surroundings of an ordinary Aquarium. Fish are seen swimming, and all sides of the tank are open to the inspection of visitors. The illusion, which is cleverly contrived, is the invention of Mr. Harry Phillips, and is well worth going to see."—*Brighton Gazette,* February 17th, 1886.

"Among the other attractions in the Exhibition, is that of a living Mermaid. It is located in the Conservatory. It is a combination of the real and the illusory on quite a novel plan, and will be found to well repay a visit."—*The Brighton Guardian,* February 17th, 1886.

"A new illusion on an entirely original and novel principle, is styled a 'Living Mermaid,' with sportive fish swimming about. As the tank stands on bare supports, and no part of it is surrounded by drapery, the illusion is very complete."—*The Brighton Herald,* February 20th, 1886.

"Among the attractions of the Aquarium must be included Mr. Harry Phillips' clever optical illusion, the Living Mermaid, which deserves a high place in the list of such exhibitions. The supports of the tank are raised at an height of about 5 feet from the floor and open to the wall principle of the illusion is, we understand, an entirely new one, and the 'Living Mermaid,' wh her first appearance at the Aquarium last week, has never previously been exhibited, sc novelty should account for this curiosity being inspected by large numbers of visitors *Evening News,* Feb. 18th.

ON VIEW ALL DA
ADMISSION 6d.   NO WAITING.

PURT & SONS, 19, PORCHESTER ROAD, BAYSWATER, W.

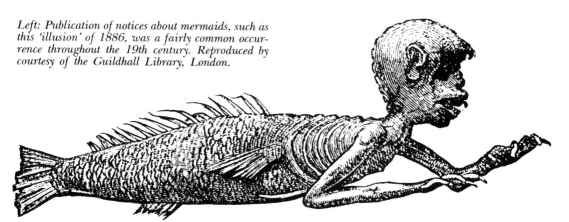

Left: Publication of notices about mermaids, such as this 'illusion' of 1886, was a fairly common occurrence throughout the 19th century. Reproduced by courtesy of the Guildhall Library, London.

An engraving of the 'very capital' mermaid seen by Frank Buckland at the oriental warehouse of Messrs. Farmer and Rogers. From Buckland's Curiosities of Natural History, *4th series, 1875.*

the nineteenth century even though all those exhibited showed a monotonous resemblance to each other. There was usually at least one on show at any given time in London giving a certain amount of innocent amusement to the public and providing useful copy for popular-science writers like Frank Buckland. Writing about one he saw at the Oriental warehouse of Messrs. Farmer and Rogers in Regent Street, Buckland says: 'The total length of her marine ladyship is 25 inches, and she is composed in the usual regulation mermaid style, viz., half fish and half quasi-human . . . The lower half of her body is made of the skin and scales of a fish of the carp family, neatly fastened on to a wooden body. The upper part of the mermaid is in the attitude of a sphinx, leaning upon its elbows and forearm. The arms are long and scraggy, and the fingers attenuated and skeleton-like. The nails are formed of little bits of ivory or bone. The head is about the size of a small orange, and the face has a laughing expression of good-nature and roguish simplicity. I cannot say much for the expression of her ladyship's mouth, which is a regular gape, like the clown's mouth at a pantomime: behind her lips

we see a double row of teeth, one rank being in advance of the other, like a regiment of volunteers drawn up in line. The hind teeth are conical, but the front ones project, like diminutive tusks. I am nearly as certain as I can be that these are the teeth of a young cat-fish – a hideous fish that one sometimes sees hanging up in the fishmongers' shops in London. Her ears are very pig-like, and certainly not elegant, and her nose decidedly snub. The coiffeur is submarine, and undoubtedly *not* Parisian: it would, in fact, be none the worse for a touch of the brush and comb . . . If I were a merman *I* should decidedly not fall in love with any mermaid who was not a *great deal* more particular in matters of hair-dressing than our friend under the glass case'.

Buckland was evidently not captivated by this mermaid. He continues: 'At the back of her head we see a series of nobs, which run down the back till they join with a bristling row of 24 spines – evidently the spines of the dorsal fin of the carp-like fish. The ribs in our mermaid are exceedingly prominent . . . To judge, however, from the appearance of our Regent Street specimen, there must have been a rinderpest and famine price of provisions in general down in these splendid submarine regions, for our poor mermaid is very thin, seems half starved and terribly shabby, and altogether has a workhouse look about her'. A very similar mermaid, brought back from Yokohama by a Captain Cuming in 1866, was illustrated by Buckland who said that it was 'almost a counterpart of that in the possession of Farmer and Rogers'[24]. Buckland's illustration represents a typical nineteenth-century mermaid and his account indicates that Japan, as well as Indonesia, had a mermaid factory.

A number of manufactured mermaids have been featured in twentieth-century newspapers and magazines and they amuse the public in the same way as they used to in less sophisticated times. Evidently the mermaids which occasionally come to light these days are not of twentieth-century manufacture but are relics, often in very dilapidated condition, of nineteenth-century artefacts. What is reputedly the mermaid shown off by Barnum is still on display in the United States although it bears little resemblance to the illustrations prepared of it in Barnum's time. There are still several specimens in private hands, most of them conforming to the type illustrated by Buckland. One has been on display in the Banff Indian Trading Post, Alberta, since the beginning of the twentieth century.

Sometimes one meets with a mermaid which does not conform to this type. One exhibited at the British Museum in 1961 was about 45 centimetres long and had glass eyes and a set of teeth carved from a single, inserted piece of ivory. Its tail was curved upwards towards the head and the body from the waist up, for a change, did not look scraggy and starved. X-ray photos showed a complicated arrangement of wires which supported the body but failed to support the credibility of this charming mermaid[25].

No less charming was the mermaid reported in the *Daily Express* for 22 June 1921. This one was then to be seen 'in Bloomsbury of all places'. The report continues: 'She sits on her tail, as all the very best mermaids do, beneath a glass case, goggling with stark, fishy eyes at the many visitors who pilgrimage to see her. The story of the mermaid is a romance. Her birthplace was the West Coast of Africa, but nobody knows how long she has been in London or who brought her here. Two doctors who examined her were completely puzzled. The figure, wizened dry like a mummy, is about 16 inches long, with a female form from the waist up, and below an excellent fish tail. The baby skull is grinning grotesquely, disclosing twenty-five tiny teeth. An inscription on the pedestal reads:—Lus. Nat. Presented by Mr. Graham, Surgeon-General at Sierra Leone'. The expression 'Lus. Nat.'—short for 'Lusus Naturae'—means 'freak of nature'. This specimen was acquired by Mr. Richard Whittington-Egan in the 1930's who allowed Rowland Ward, the well-known firm of taxidermists, to set it up more propitiously.

Whoever fashioned this mermaid was anxious to show her off in classical pose, one of her little arms being set in the act of combing her hair (a commodity she has very little of) and the other is raised as though holding a mirror. She is as tolerable a facsimile of that mythical fish-tailed beauty of the seas as any which has survived to our own day. Separated by a mere six thousand years from her earliest progenitor, Oannes, Lord of the Waters, she is also as suitable a subject as any to end this account of the mermaid.

Chapter 5
Dragons and sea serpents

The dragon is one of the oldest and one of the most shadowy of all mythical monsters. It is also one of the most widespread, being a conspicuous element in the mythologies of many eastern and western cultures. In the western world, it has nearly always been a sinister, frightening and destructive monster associated with evil, hell, heresy, superstition and other unpleasant ideas. Oriental dragons, though superficially similar in appearance to those of the west, are not malevolent, unfriendly beings. They are, on the contrary, kind and lovable, or at least are meant to be.

The works of the classic poets of Greece and Rome are infested with dragons defending the retreats of the gods and their sacred groves. The chariot of Ceres was drawn by dragons, and the garden of the Hesperides was protected by one. The Scandinavians had their dragon, a mean and vengeful creature, as was that of those early Britons who were influenced by Druidism. Frequently, occidental dragons lived in caves and guarded treasures kept therein. Often they had designs on nubile maidens and only the bravest and most righteous of men were able to thwart their evil intentions. Christian mythology is peppered with anecdotes about saints who were victorious in their encounters with dragons, St. George being the most familiar of these. The dragons of Far-Eastern mythologies symbolise the rain-giving powers of the gods of water and clouds, or merely guard the subterranean treasures of the earth in the friendliest way and therefore nobody wants to fight them.

The dragons of antiquity assumed many forms. The simplest were monsters of enormous length, legless and wingless (in later times these became known as pythons and had, therefore,

a real, if exaggerated, foundation). There were dragons with two feet but no wings, with four feet but no wings, with two feet and two wings, and with four feet and two wings. The hydra, which has a chapter to itself in this book and rightly so, is really a variant dragon of the two-footed and wingless class. Usually, dragons had a scaly skin, a forked tongue, long claws and a long tail. Occasionally, they had horned heads and a sting in the tail. Altogether they were very unpleasant to look at.

Many are the accounts of encounters with dragons but it is not until the sixteenth century that someone described one from an actual specimen. Aldrovandi, an unashamed draconophile, professed to have received a 'true dried Aethiopian dragon' in 1551. This he described as having two clawed feet, two ears and five prominent tubercles on its back, a pair of wings, a long and flexible tail,

Above: St. George slaying the Dragon, an illustration from an edition of Spenser's The Faerie Queene, *1590. Below: The demonic, horned dragon of Hell reproduced from a pen drawing which appears in a 19th-century French manuscript* La Magie noire.

sharp teeth and open nostrils. It was completely covered in dusky green scales, except on the belly and throat, these parts bearing yellowish scales. He also says that Cardan saw five winged dragons in the William Museum at Paris each of them having two feet and very slender wings[1]. A biped dragon without wings and two cubits long was said by Aldrovandi to have been killed by a countryman of his near Bonn in 1572. It ended up in Aldrovandi's museum[2].

Large dragons were obviously very acceptable but were probably difficult to make. Evidently diminutive ones were just as acceptable if well made. In Grainger's edition of Samuel Butler's *Hudibras* there is the following note concerning a very small dragon indeed: 'Mr. Smith, of Bedford, observes to me on the word dragon as follows: Mr. Jacob Bobart, botany professor of Oxford, did, about forty years ago, find a dead rat in the physic garden, which he made to resemble the common picture of dragons, by altering its head and tail, and thrusting in taper sharp sticks, which distended the skin on each side till it mimicked wings. He let it dry as hard as possible. The learned immediately pronounced it a dragon; and one of them sent an accurate description of it to Dr. Magliabechi, librarian to the Grand Duke of Tuscany; several fine copies of verses were wrote on so rare a subject; but at last Mr. Bobart owned the cheat: however it was looked upon as a master-piece of art, and as such deposited in the museum, or anatomy school, where I saw it many years after'[3]. Bobart died in 1680, so his 'cheat' was presumably still on display during the first half of the eighteenth century.

In the *Gentleman's Magazine* for 1749 there was published a letter about a much larger monster which, for con-

A young dragon, or dragonel, illustrated by Gessner in his Historiae Animalium, *1587.*

59

venience, may be referred to as a sea dragon. The letter is interesting enough to be transcribed in full: 'I send you enclosed such a representation, as I could delineate from my memory, of a sea monster, which is carried about the countries by a fisherman, who was disabled by it when taken.

'Its head and tail resemble those of an alligator; it has two large fins, which serve it both to swim and to fly: and, tho' they were so dried that I could not extend them, yet they appear, by the folds, to be shaped like those which painters have given to dragons, and other winged monsters, that serve as supporters to coats of arms. Its body is cover'd with impenetrable scales; its legs have two joints, and its feet are hoofed, like those of an ass; it has five rows of very white and sharp teeth in each jaw, and is in length about four feet, tho' it was longer when alive, it

having shrunk as it became dry.

'It was caught in a net with a mackerel, and being dragged on shore was knock'd down with a stretcher, or boathook. The net being open'd, it suddenly sprung up, and flew above 50 yards; the man who first seized it had several of his fingers bitten off, and the wound mortifying, he died: It afterwards fasten'd on the man's arm who shews it, and lacerated it so much, that the muscles are shrunk, and the hand and fingers distorted; the wound is not yet healed, and is thought to be incurable. It is said, by some, to have been described by naturalists under the name of the *Sea-Dragon.* I have not, however, seen any description that corresponds with this creature, and am inclined to think it a monster. *Your constant Reader, T.H.*'[4].

This monster, which was said to have been captured between Orford and Southwold on the coast of Suffolk, was

60

EXTRAORDINARY FISH!!
NOW EXHIBITING
AT THE
Golden Lion Inn,
COMMERCIAL PLACE, ABERDARE.

This Wonder of the Deep was caught on Wednesday last off Port Talbot Bar. It measures between 4 and 5 feet in length, and amongst other peculiarities is possessed of two legs, with hoofs similar to a calf's, four rows of teeth, &c., &c., and is well worthy of Inspection.

ADMISSION, 2d.; CHILDREN, HALF PRICE.

J. T. JONES, PRINTER, &c., "ABERDARE TIMES" OFFICE, COMMERCIAL-PLACE, ABERDARE.

also described and illustrated in an early edition of the *Encyclopedia Britannica* and this version was seen by Edward Donovan who said of it: 'A slight examination of this amazing prodigy will incontestably prove that the whole is a deception; the article described is nothing more than the skin of the angel shark, *Squalus squatina*, rudely distorted, and with very little contrivance disposed into the figure in which we see it'[5]. Donovan points out that the angel shark has several rows of teeth in each jaw, and a 120 centimetre specimen would be expected to have about five rows in each. The conformation of the body could have been arrived at, he says, by compressing the head laterally to give it a more elongated appearance, by torturing the broad lateral fins into the semblance of wings, and by the ventral fins being compressed into the shape of a pair of legs. The whole skin, thus distorted and braced up with wire or a bandage of some kind, would afterwards retain the grotesque form which its preserver had given it. Donovan added that a 'similar cheat' had been 'very lately attempted by some artful fisherman on one of the learned institutions in Ireland'.

In 1861, over forty years after Donovan wrote those words, there was exhibited in the South Wales town of Aberdare a similar monster. A contemporary handbill advertised it as the 'EXTRAORDINARY FISH! Now exhibiting at the Golden Lion Inn, Commercial Place, Aberdare'. The handbill described it as 'This wonder of the Deep was caught on Wednesday last off Port Talbot Bar. It measures between 4 and 5 feet in length, and amongst other peculiarities is possessed of two legs, with hoofs similar to a calf's, four rows of teeth, &c., &c., and is well worthy of Inspection.' Admission to see it was 2d., half price for children[6]. It is interesting to note that the 'monster' of 1749 becomes the 'Extraordinary Fish' of 1861. In little over a century a frightening and dangerous object has become a mere curiosity.

Whatever these objects were or were meant to be they make convenient stepping stones allowing us to progress smoothly from dragons of air and land to those of the sea. These are not referred to as sea dragons these days but as sea serpents. In one form or another sea serpents have been with us for a very long time and occur in most of the ancient mythologies. The leviathan referred to in the Old Testament is thought by some authorities to have been a huge sea serpent. Other huge sea monsters, serpentine in appearance, are mentioned in the writings of classical authors such as Ctesias, Aelian and Palladius. One of the illustrations in Pontoppidan's *Natural History of Norway* shows us how the sea serpent was visualised in the eighteenth century. The alleged presence of a large sea serpent in Loch Ness is based on numerous reported sightings of very recent date and there are many other sightings of large aquatic monsters at sea and on inland waters which suggest that leviathan is with us still. The Assyrian king Sargon II is said to have seen a sea serpent in the Mediterranean in the eighth century B.C. which shows that the sea serpent legend, based on sightings, has a respectably long history.

The reputed great size of sea serpents, however, has inhibited artificial construction of them, only one—and that a fossil—having been attempted.

Left: An interesting webbed-footed sea-dragon after Ambrosinus, 1642. Below: An 18th-century representation of a sea-serpent as illustrated in Pontopiddan's Natural History of Norway, *1755.*

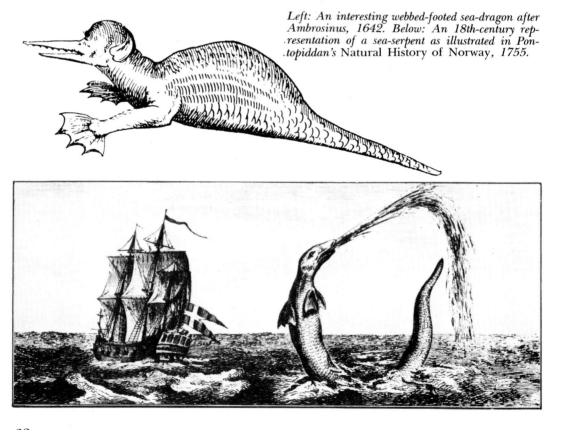

This imposture, one of the most ambitious and certainly the largest in the history of monster faking, was the work of a Dr. Albert C. Koch who, in 1845, exhibited in the Apollo Saloon on New York's Broadway a large skeleton of a fossil animal to which he gave the name *Hydrargos sillimanii*. Said to be the remains of an extinct sea serpent, it consisted of a head, a vertebral column, a few ribs occupying the thoracic portion, and parts of supposed paddles. It measured from one end to the other ·35 metres. In other words this skeleton matched up very well with the popular conception of a gigantic sea serpent. For exhibition purposes, Dr. Koch had taken great care to mount it on stilts, so that the head was in the raised position supposedly assumed by its living counterpart, the rest of the skeleton being arranged in a sinuous manner.

Koch charged visitors 25 cents each to see his remarkable fossil (named in honour of Benjamin Silliman who had recognised the existence of the sea serpent in 1827) and the exhibition was apparently well received by the public. Unfortunately for Koch one of the visitors was Professor Jeffries Wyman, a competent anatomist, who proceeded to show that the bones were not those of a large reptile. The teeth had double roots–a characteristic of mammalian teeth–and as if this was not enough he showed that the bones came from several different skeletons. This was a most embarrassing disclosure for Koch who had said that he had found all the bones in the ground together, those of the spine forming a single uninterrupted series. In his published account Wyman concluded that

This huge fossil of 'an extinct marine serpent' was exhibited by Dr. Albert Koch in 1845. Christened Hydrargos sillimannii, *this audacious fake was exposed by an anatomist, Professor Jeffries Wyman. Wyman said that most of the bones of the 114-foot-long 'serpent' belonged to an extinct marine mammal measuring only 45 feet long.*

most of the bones belonged to specimens of a fossil whale only 13 metres long. These revelations should have put paid to *Hydrargos sillimanii* immediately, but they didn't. Koch was not one of your faint-hearted impostors who slink away as soon as their impostures are uncovered. Even though Professor Silliman refused to have his name associated any longer with the heterogeneous assemblage of bones reposing in the Apollo Saloon Dr. Koch was not ruffled. He continued to exhibit the skeleton, merely changing the generic name to *Hydrarchos* and the specific name to *harlani* (named after Dr. Richard Harlan, a reputable zoologist, who had examined an enormous fossil vertebra some years previously and concluded that it belonged to a new genus of lizard-like reptiles, later shown by Richard Owen to be a primitive cetacean, *Zeuglodon*, the same fossil whale Koch transformed into his gigantic sea serpent).

In 1848, while the 35 metre-long fake was still attracting public attention, Gideon Algernon Mantell, the well known English palaeontologist and geologist, wrote to the Editor of the *Illustrated London News* to correct a statement that had appeared in a previous edition of that magazine. 'The fossil,' he said, 'mentioned at the conclusion of the admirable notice of the so-called Sea-Serpent, as having been exhibited in America under the name of *Hydrarchos sillimanii*, was constructed by the exhibitor Koch, from bones collected in various parts of Alabama, and which belonged to several individual skeletons of an extinct marine cetacean, termed *Basilosaurus* by the American naturalists, and better known in this country by that of *Zeuglodon*, a term signifying *yoked teeth*. Mr. Koch is the person who, a few years

ago, had a fine collection of fossil bones of elephants and Mastodons, out of which he made up an enormous skeleton, and exhibited it in the Egyptian Hall, Piccadilly, under the name of *Missourium*. This collection was purchased by the trustees of the British Museum, and from it were selected the bones which now constitute the matchless skeleton of a Mastodon in our National Gallery of Organic Remains.

'Not content with the interest which the fossils which he collected in various parts of the United States really possess, Mr. Koch, with the view of exciting the curiosity of the ignorant multitude, strung together all the vertebrae he could obtain of the *Basilosaurus*, and arranged them in a serpentine form; manufactured a skull and claws, and exhibited the monster as a fossil Sea-Serpent, under the name above mentioned – *Hydrarchos*. But the trick was immediately exposed by the American naturalists, and the true nature of the fossil bones pointed out'[7].

Even front-rank scientists may be carried away by their imagination when attempting to secure evidence supporting privately-held beliefs. Koch took his serpent to Dresden where it was examined by Carl Gustav Carus, a leading student of comparative anatomy in his day. In describing and illustrating it, Carus attempted to restore the cranium, only a portion of which had then been found. He restored the cranium of a reptile, a restoration which, if it was not guesswork, must have been the result of wishful thinking. Like Dr. Koch, though presumably for less mercenary reasons, Carus wanted to convince others that here was, indeed, a gigantic fossil sea serpent. To other scientists these two would seem almost to be tarred with the same deceitful and dishonest brush.

Chapter 6
The human form divine

Towards the end of the thirteenth century, the great Venetian traveller, Marco Polo, was allowed by Kublai Khan to leave his court to sail back from China to Venice. Marco's route took him through Sumatra where, in the kingdom of Basman (=Pasai), he was able to watch the manufacture of some unusual export items: pygmies. Fortunately, although he was indignant about the marketing of this kind of export, he has left us a detailed account of the making of pygmies.

'I also wish you to know,' he said, 'that the pygmies that some travellers assert they bring from India, are a lie and cheat, for I may tell you that these creatures, whom they call men, are manufactured in this island; and I will tell you how. You must know that in this island there is a kind of very small monkey, with a face like a man's. They take these monkeys, and, by means of a certain ointment, remove all their hairs except around their genitals; then they stick into their chins certain long hairs to look like a beard. Then they dry them. As the skin dries, the holes into which the hairs have been stuck, close, so that the hairs look as if they had grown there naturally. Further, as their feet, hands and certain other members are not quite the same as those of a man, they pull and shape them with their hands, and so make them similar to those of a man. Then they put these beasts out to dry, and shape them, daubing them with camphor and other things, until they look as if they had been men. But it is a great cheat since they are manufactured even as I have told you. For such tiny men as these would seem to be, have never been in India or in any other more savage country'[1].

Here then is a very early example of a manufactured human or anthropoid, albeit a diminutive one. Remarkably

Charles Waterton, Squire of Walton Hall, traveller and master taxidermist. The Mansell Collection, London.

enough a similar fake caused a minor sensation in Sumatra seven centuries later. By this time, the pygmy of Marco Polo's day had become the Orang Pendek (the name given it by Dutch settlers) or Ape Man of Sumatra. Rumours of the existence of an anthropoid creature, between 76 and 152 centimetres high, have been current in Sumatra since the beginning of the twentieth century (the fossil remains of *Pithecanthropus erectus,* the Java Ape Man, had been discovered in the 1890's and their discovery may have helped to get the orang pendek story off the ground).

Some of the numerous sightings are accompanied with such detailed information and originate from such impeccable sources that it does seem as though there could be a creature, as yet unknown to science and having anthropoid characteristics, living in the Sumatran jungle. But, as always, science and the public needed a specimen to add conviction to rumour. In May 1932 a baby orang pendek was shot, some natives having been tempted by the reward offered to anyone who brought one back dead or alive. It was 42 centimetres tall, had a very human anatomy, bare skin and grey hair on its head. It was placed in the expert hands of Dr. K.W. Dammerman who examined it closely and speedily published his findings.

The baby orang pendek turned out to be a lotong (*Trachypithecus pyrrhus* Horsfield), a kind of langur monkey. It had been shaved all over except on the top of its head, its nose had been stretched with a piece of wood, its cheekbones had been crushed, and its canine teeth had been filed to a point[2]. It is as well that the perpetrators of hoaxes like this usually lack skill in taxidermy. Possibly Sumatra was also the source of at least some of the artificial mermaids which reached Europe from time to time. It has even been suggested, erroneously, that Marco Polo was referring to them in the passage just quoted[3].

In the domain of animal imposture nothing, it seems, is sacred. But even long after the thirteenth century, Christian Europe was not the safest place to fabricate artificial humans. It was not until the more enlightened nineteenth century, therefore, that a European dared to make a facsimile of the human form, to be precise the head and shoulders of a human, out of baser materials. The European who did so was Charles Waterton, the Squire of Walton Hall and animal stuffer extraordinary.

The story of Waterton's 'Nondescript' has been told often but always as part of a biography or an autobiography. In the present context the Non-

66

A portrait of the Nondescript as it appears on the frontispiece of Waterton's Wanderings in South America, *1828.*

descript is almost as important—though scarcely so interesting–as its maker, the author of *Wanderings in South America.* In that well known book Waterton says that, during his fourth and last journey into the wilds of Guiana, he procured an animal 'which has caused not a little speculation and astonishment. In my opinion, his thick coat of hair, and great length of tail, put his species out of all question; but then his face and head cause the inspector to pause for a moment, before he ventures to pronounce his opinion of the classification. He was a large animal, and as I was pressed for daylight, and moreover, felt no inclination to have the whole weight of his body upon my back, I contented myself with his head and shoulders, which I cut off; and have brought them with me to Europe'[4]. The frontispiece to the *Wanderings* shows a drawing of

the Nondescript which makes it appear for all the world like a hirsute and bucolic gentleman. The real thing, now a conversation piece in the City Museum and Art Gallery of Wakefield, Yorkshire, is rather different and certainly does not have features 'of the Grecian cast', as Waterton described them. But its features are undoubtedly very human in appearance, so human indeed that many people thought that it must be a member of the human race.

One James Stuart Menteath wrote to J.C. Loudon, editor of the *Magazine of Natural History,* about Waterton's adventures as recounted in the *Wanderings.* 'Though crediting the narrative of his adventures', he said, 'I cannot refrain adding, that the figure in the frontispiece of the *Wanderings* has put this belief not a little to the test. Having looked at it over and over again, I cannot discover what animal it is intended to represent. In its face and head, it resembles the human; but unless it belong to a new species of Homo, or be a hybrid between Homo and Simia, I am at a loss under what class of animals to arrange it'. Menteath thought it 'not improbable, from the well known ability of Mr. Waterton, he may have moulded some poor monkey's visage into the face divine. All who have visited Walton Hall, and looked over the beautiful collection of stuffed birds, which Mr. Waterton, in the kindest manner, suffers all to see, can bear testimony to his skill as a naturalist; and also, with what Promethean art the learned proprietor can, by his magical hand, give as it were to these lifeless feathered bodies, life and being. Whichever of these suppositions be correct, many of the readers of Mr. Waterton's *Wanderings* solicit his further explanation of the frontispiece'[5].

Waterton replied in the next number of the *Magazine,* assuring Mr. Menteath that all he had related in the *Wanderings* was true. Of the Nondescript he said, 'I intentionally enveloped it in mystery, on account of the illiberality of the British Treasury'. (The Treasury, in 1821, had ruled that he had to pay a twenty per cent duty on all those animals imported into Britain by him from South America which were intended for his own or any other private collection. J.R. Lushington, secretary to the Treasury, had signed the letter to this effect which had been sent to the customs officials.) Waterton went on to say that he had spent many years trying to make improvements in taxidermy and had made great strides in this direction. He had intended to publish the details of his discoveries but decided not to do so because of the long detention of his collection at the Custom House and the tone of Lushington's letter. Instead he chose to illustrate the Nondescript on the frontispiece to the *Wanderings,* 'calculating that its appearance would give rise to much investigation by naturalists, especially by those who are connected with museums'. Having made this very unconvincing statement he then flatly denied that he had intended to 'pass off this extraordinary thing' as the head of a man or an ape. 'My sole object', he said, 'has been to leave the thing in absolute doubt; and I have no wish whatever that it should pass for any other thing than that which the reader himself may wish it to pass for. Not considering myself anywise pledged to its identity, I leave it entirely to the reader's own penetration to say what it is, or what it is not'[6].

Sydney Smith, who gave a favourable review of the *Wanderings,* had no difficulty deciding what it was. 'In this exhibition', he says, speaking of the Nondescript, 'the author is surely abusing his stuffing talents, and laughing at the public. It is clearly the head of a Master in Chancery whom we have often seen basking in the House of Commons after he has delivered his message'[7]. Over a century later Richard Aldington, who wrote a life of Waterton, was able to be more specific about the identity of the Nondescript. 'Taking everything into consideration', he said, 'I am convinced that, among other things, the Nondescript was intended as a caricature of Mr. Lushington and a Watertonian retort to his "illiberality" in 1821'[8]. Aldington also attempts to prove that Waterton's fourth journey to Guiana was made for the express purpose of obtaining the creature from which the Nondescript was manufactured. That, it seems to me, is unlikely, but perhaps I do not yet know the lengths to which a man will go to cancel out a grievance.

If it is not human, this Nondescript, what is it? The Rev. J.G. Wood, friend of the Squire and high priest of popular-science writing in late-Victorian England, tells us that this 'wonderful specimen of Waterton's skill in taxidermy is formed from the head and shoulders of the Red Howler monkey. In manipulating it, Waterton has so modelled the skin that he has discharged from the face every vestige of the original features, and has substituted those of a man, grotesque enough, but still human. As bare skin becomes black when dry, the contrast of the black face with the fiery red hair has a very striking effect and adds to the resemblance'. The facial angle of a Red Howler monkey being very different from a man's made the preparation of this grotesque head very difficult, said Wood. The preparation would have been impossible 'if the skull, or any part of it, had been

Waterton's Nondescript, fashioned from a Red Howler monkey, still intrigues visitors to the City Museum and Art Gallery in Wakefield.

allowed to remain, and the really wonderful feat could only be performed by Waterton's system of removing the whole of the bones and having drawn all the bare skin until it was no thicker than ordinary writing paper'[9].

Assuming the correctness of Aldington's conjecture the Nondescript is probably unique in the annals of taxidermy, politics and caricature. Unique it may be; subtle it is not. But then the Squire of Walton Hall was not a subtle man. Inevitably the Nondescript attracted a lot of publicity to its creator but, understandably, it did nothing to enhance his reputation. It was an elaborate but cheap joke. The most that can be said for his creation is that it is a mildly intriguing enigma. We know that the distorted features which confront visitors to the City Museum and Art Gallery of Wakefield are those of a Red Howler monkey. Whether or

not they are also those of a certain J.R. Lushington we may never know.

With one giant stride we step out of the nineteenth century and into the twentieth, for the remaining object dealt with in this chapter has not been in the public eye very long and, unlike the Nondescript, is definitely still topical and newsworthy. Waiting for us is something, or perhaps someone, to whom giant strides are commonplace, for our quarry is none other than the Yeti, or Abominable Snowman.

Although first reported in the early nineteenth century (much earlier if stories emanating from Tibet and its southern borders are to be believed) the Yeti saga didn't really catch on until the 1920's, when a sighting of one at 4575 metres by a reputable observer was reported. Other reports followed in quick succession, usually, but not always, of huge footprints in the snow. The evidence of the footprints and sightings together suggest that in the mountain fastnesses of the high Himalayas there may be a large anthropoid creature, up to 2.5 metres in height, with large feet and a hairy body. The evidence for the existence of such a creature is so compelling that, in 1958, the Government of Nepal began to take it very seriously and announced that it required a fee of 5000 rupees from anyone wishing to look for the yeti. It also forbade anyone to kill a yeti except in self-defence, claimed a right in it dead or alive and even a right to photographs that might be taken of it.

Once again, however, the world at large, and scientists in particular, needed more than sightings and rumours before accepting the existence of an unknown animal. Once again the solid evidence required was forthcoming. In 1954 the *Daily Mail* sent an expedition to look for the yeti.

The expedition didn't find a real, live flesh-and-blood specimen but it did collect a lot of evidence, positive and negative, which had not been available before. Most importantly it was able to examine three yeti 'scalps'. Most descriptions of the yeti insist that its head is tall and pointed and only sparsely covered with hair. Consequently it is no surprise to learn that each of the three 'scalps' is conical and not overloaded with hair.

The 'scalp' in the monastery at

Above: A 'scalp' of the fabled Yeti, from the monastery at Khumjung. The 'scalp' is made from the skin of a southern serow, a chamois goat, shown below. Both illustrations reproduced by courtesy of the British Museum (Natural History).

Pangboche looks like a mitre made of leather and is covered with hair 3 to 5 centimetres long on each side of a medial crest of erect hair. There is no hair on the top. As this relic is said by the monks to have been at Pangboche for over three hundred years it should not be assumed that it came from a bald yeti. The second 'scalp' examined came from the monastery at Khumjung and was similar to but hairier than the first. Each of these scalps consisted of a single piece of skin and showed no traces of stitching or glue. The third 'scalp', from Namche Bazar, was evidently a crude imitation of the other two, being made of pieces of similar hairy skin sewn together into the same mitre shape.

Several hairs removed from the three 'scalps' were studied by experts who ascertained that they belonged to the same animal species, but they were baffled by the identity of the species. Eventually Bernard Heuvelmans, the famous hunter of vanishing, lost, legendary and apocryphal animals, made a close study of the Khumjung specimen. At first he had concluded that it had every appearance of being a genuine scalp but the appearance of the hair on the object in his hand reminded him forcibly of a rare animal he had seen many years before in the Amsterdam Zoo: the southern serow, a chamois goat. In Nepal there is a race of this animal which ascends to an altitude of 4575 metres in the Himalayas, so there was a distinct possibility that the 'scalps' could have been made from the skin of Nepalese serows. This animal is so rare that Heuvelmans had difficulty finding one for comparative purposes, but finally he discovered a mounted specimen in Brussels. A comparison of its hair with that from the 'scalps' showed that all the hairs belonged to the same species.

The 'scalps' were made by taking a piece (or pieces) of skin from the neck of a Nepalese serow and stretching it over an appropriately-shaped mould. Presumably the experts had been unable to identify the source of the hairs because the animal they came from is so rare. Later it transpired that both the Khumjung and Namche Bazar 'scalps' had been faked in recent years. The Pangboche specimen, the only one having any claim to antiquity, was probably not faked deliberately but may have been worn by dancers representing the yeti. There is a series of holes along one side, presumably for attachment to the dancer's dress, some other holes near the top being probably used for attaching prayer flags[10]. It should be remembered that the Nepalese have very different attitudes over material and immaterial things to Europeans. During the Hillary Expedition of 1960-61 a Sherpa helped two of the non-Nepalese members of the expedition make a yeti 'scalp' out of goat skin. The Sherpa seemed to revere it as though it were a holy relic[11].

The snowy slopes of Central Asia's high mountains may well be the home of a large biped anthropoid (Heuvelmans is sufficiently convinced of its existence to have given it a scientific name, *Dinanthropoides nivalis* or 'terrible anthropoid of the snows'). As far as we are concerned in this book, however, the material evidence adduced to encourage belief in him is nothing more than the skin of a rare, but otherwise unremarkable, goat.

It is natural that man should seek out his origins, inevitable that he should be presented sooner or later with evidence proving his great antiquity, remarkable that the evidence should accord so well with a preconceived scientific notion, salutary that it should be shown nearly half a century later to be false. I refer, of course, to the most celebrated and most humiliating forgery of all time: Piltdown Man.

The full story of the rise and fall of this spurious ancestor of the human race is too long, and much of it too familiar or too technical to be re-told here in full, but the main features of this extraordinary episode are worth repeating. In 1913 there appeared a report in the *Quarterly Journal of the Geological Society of London* which set the scientific world agog. It recorded the discovery, by Charles Dawson, a solicitor and amateur geologist, of several cranial fragments, a portion of a mandible with molar teeth and some associated animal bones and human artefacts, which had been found together in a gravel pit in Sussex. Before long, the cranial fragments and the jaw became the most famous bone fragments in the world for they were those of the Dawn Man of Piltdown. To the scientific world, with few exceptions, and eventually to the man-in-the-street, they were evidence of man's ape-like ancestry, the remains of that previously hypothetical creature intermediate between apes and humans –the former or present existence of which, it was popularly supposed, Darwin had postulated. In the following two or three years the discovery of more bones in the area only enhanced the importance of the original discovery. The village of Piltdown became world-famous, its public house proudly displaying its new sign-board 'The Piltdown Man', its two hundred or so inhabitants rubbing shoulders with some of the world's foremost students of anthropology and palaeontology.

In addition to the principal finds a young and ultimately illustrious French priest, Teilhard de Chardin,

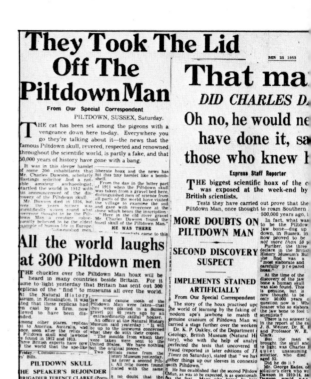

found a canine tooth belonging to the jaw. Then Dawson found the remains of yet another skull essentially similar to the first one. From the moment they were publicised these bones were controversial, but, by and large, their authenticity was allowed, and soon *Eoanthropus dawsoni*, as Arthur Smith Woodward had christened it, became entrenched in scientific and popular literature. The Dawn Man was accepted, partly because the material evidence seemed convincing, but more probably because he fulfilled evolutionary expectations. It is, after all, very tempting–if you are a certain kind of scientist–to be able to prove the correctness of a scientific prediction; and when the evidence fits in so neatly with the preconception the temptation to try to make it fit exactly is irresistible.

Crucial to the whole problem was the relationship of the jaw and its teeth

to the cranial fragments. Very skilfully Woodward had shown that these remains had belonged to one specimen and very few experts disagreed with him. Thus the Dawn Man apparently had an essentially human skull and human teeth but an essentially ape-like jaw. In other words he provided the long-hoped-for 'Missing Link' between an ancestral ape-like creature and modern man. If the cranial fragments had been accepted as the remains of one creature and the jaw as the remains of another, there would not have been an *Eoanthropus dawsoni*, at least not in the form described by Woodward. The ape-like jaw with its non-ape-like teeth would still, in all probability, have been enough for Woodward to base a description upon, but without the cranium it would have been impossible to visualise clearly the appearance of the creature it came from.

Piltdown Man was soon taken for granted even though he was strangely anomalous compared with other fossil men whose remains had been found from time to time. Sceptics there were, of course, but they were greatly outnumbered by believers, and, more to the point, they were not in a position to justify their scepticism because they did not have easy access to the remains. These were jealously guarded in a safe at the British Museum (Natural History). To examine the remains closely, it was almost necessary to be a member of the British Museum staff, preferably one employed in the Geology Department. Fortunately, a member of that Department was extremely interested in the Piltdown fragments and the anomalies they presented. He was also aware that the fluorine content of bones increases with age and that an analysis of the Piltdown fragments might throw some light on their rela-

73

tive ages. So, in 1949, Dr. K.P. Oakley analysed them and found no significant difference in age between them. The analysis, which was not as refined as it could have been (Oakley was breaking new ground in those days), merely showed that the fragments were nearer 50,000 years old than 500,000 as some believed.

At this point, Professor W.E. Le Gros Clark and his assistant Dr. J.S. Weiner at the Department of Anatomy, Oxford, came on the scene. They would often puzzle over the casts of the fragments in their Department–the British Museum had liberally distributed casts to scientific institutions all over the world–and especially over the molar teeth which showed a 'human' rather than an 'anthropoid' type of wear. Dr. Weiner found that he could make the teeth of a chimpanzee look astonishingly similar to the Piltdown molars and canine by rubbing them down and staining them. In August 1953, he suggested to Dr. Oakley that the jaw and teeth were those of a modern ape. Immediately Dr. Oakley decided to re-test the fragments. It was while the jaw bone was being drilled to obtain a sample for testing that he turned to his assistant and said, 'Do you notice anything?' –one of the less memorable utterances it is given to scientists to utter when on the threshold of an epochal discovery–to which the assistant replied, in similar vein, 'Yes, there's a smell of burning'. Only fresh bone would smell of burning when being drilled. Nothing of the sort was noticed when the cranial fragments were drilled. That, and the subsequent accurate analyses of the samples obtained, proved that the jaw and teeth were never intimately associated with the cranium and that they were of younger date. The bones were then tested for

iron, nitrogen and radio-activity, among other things, and all the tests confirmed the disparate origins of jaw, teeth and cranium. It was also found that the apparent iron-staining of the fragments was due to a bituminous earth containing iron oxide, very likely the well-known Vandyke brown beloved of artists. The teeth, like the jaw, proved to belong to a modern ape or orang utan and had been ground down artificially to simulate human teeth. The cranium, on the other hand, seems to have been part of a genuinely fossilised, pathologically thickened, human skull but one of no great antiquity, certainly no older than Neolithic.

These disclosures created quite a stir in November 1953, the newspapers producing a predictable crop of headlines such as 'Skullduggery', 'Oldest Briton turns out to be a monkey', 'Great "Missing Link" hoax rocks scientists', 'They took the lid off the Piltdown Man', and 'That man–the Great Whodunit'. The newspapers and most of their readers were at least as interested in the identity of the hoaxer and his motive as in the scientific details of the hoax itself. Not so the scientists[12, 13].

The finger of suspicion has been pointed at Dawson more than once, but has been pointed elsewhere too. We may never know who engineered the hoax, and unless we do know we won't be able to discover a motive. The scientists were–and still are–less interested in the identity and the motive of the hoaxer than in ensuring that they were not duped in the same way again. But even they have to admit that the Piltdown hoax taught them something useful. They now know that it is far more difficult to make men out of monkeys than it is to make monkeys out of men.

Chapter 7
Birds

For many years birds have provided good sport for forgers and jokesters, as well as sportsmen. Some composite birds have been taken seriously by ornithologists, and some birds have been fabricated or divested of some of their parts to bring profit or provide amusement. Several spoofs foisted upon the ornithological world in recent years have taken a purely literary form, but rightly find a place here too.

Whatever their ultimate destination, dead birds and other vertebrate animals, intended for display or study purposes, have to be carefully prepared. Usually they are stuffed and often they must be braced with wire, wood or other materials. It helps if the preparator has a little imagination and a knowledge of their actual or probable appearance in life, in addition to a command of his materials. This being so, it is scarcely surprising if, from time to time, he has abused his art for profit or amusement.

Possibly the earliest example of ornithological deception was the so-called 'legless bird of paradise'. Birds with beautiful long feathers but without wings or legs were seen by early travellers to Indonesia and some were sent to Europe. About 1420, Nicolò de Conti was in Java and saw there a 'remarkable bird resembling a wood pigeon without feet and with an oblong tail', and this may well have been a bird of paradise[1]. It became the custom of the natives to remove the wings and feet of these gorgeous creatures before selling them to travellers, or to improve the appearance of the skins for their own use. This practice originated the belief that these birds were forever in flight. They were also supposed to have their heads always turned towards the sun, to live on dew and the nectar of spice trees. These

75

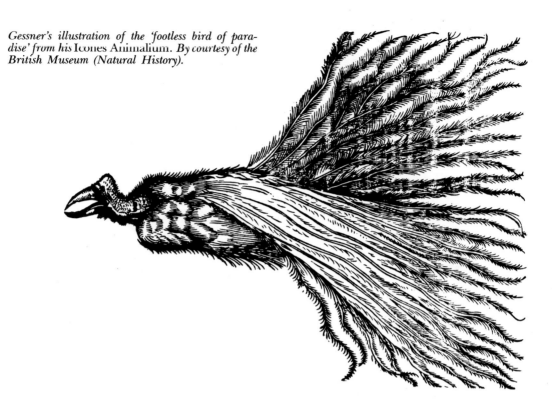

Gessner's illustration of the 'footless bird of paradise' from his Icones Animalium. *By courtesy of the British Museum (Natural History).*

birds were even said to be extra-terrestrial wanderers, perhaps from Paradise itself, hence their name. Even Linnaeus (whose botany was much sounder than his zoology) perpetuated the mythical attributes of these birds when he christened one of them *Paradisea apoda* 'the footless bird of paradise'. Gessner illustrates one of these footless and wingless birds in his *Icones Animalium,* and others like it were often brought back from the Spice Islands.

The living birds of paradise are found in parts of New Guinea and some islands off its western coast. It was during a brief visit to New Guinea in the 1820's that a Frenchman, R.P. Lesson, discovered how they were prepared for the market. First, the natives removed the bones and certain thick parts of the skin, being careful not to remove or damage the feathers. The carcase was then stretched on a frame

and wood ash rubbed into it to preserve it. Finally it was removed from the frame and dried over a fire. It is small wonder that the finished product, a riot of colourful plumage, should have given rise to the belief that these birds were, indeed, visitors from Paradise.

Birds were sometimes tampered with so that they could be offered to collectors of such things as unique examples of beautiful species. G.R. Gray, writing in 1841, warned that 'continental preparers of objects of Natural History still continue the shameful practice of endeavouring to deceive the zealous collector by false means, as in bygone days, when several such were published in splendid works, that have since been discovered to be manufactured for the purpose of obtaining large sums of money from amateurs who were struck by their magnificent appearance'[2]. At the same

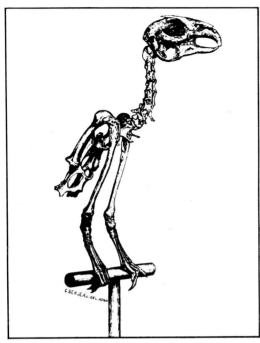

The ungainly 'skeleton of King Charles I parrot', an amusing hoax devised to fool the Victorian naturalist, Frank Buckland.

time Gray committed what modern zoologists–and probably even those of his own day–would consider an unforgivable crime: he knowingly named and described a composite bird as new to science!

A specimen which had been purchased in Paris was described by him and named *Tanysiptera nympha*, a kind of kingfisher, but in his prefatory remarks to the description Gray admitted that its underparts, wings and rump were actually parts of at least three other bird species! He continues: 'Thus far I have referred to the defective portions, which must be decidedly considered as made up from the plumage of various birds, artificially intermingled, to give the appearance of a perfect specimen. I will now pass to the more pleasing task of noticing the parts which I think are those belonging to a distinct species'[3]. In Gray's defence it should be mentioned that the

remaining parts do belong to a species which was unknown to science in 1841. This specimen is now one of the more 'colourful' items in the bird collection of the British Museum (Natural History).

Another composite bird in that collection was described, innocently, as a species new to science in 1879 by R. Bowdler Sharpe, a very experienced and conscientious ornithologist[4]. He described it as *Lalage melanothorax*, a supposedly thrush-like bird from Madras. Seven years later, however, he wrote to say that after having had another look at it he 'at once recognized that it must be an artefact! The body is that of *Lalage sykesi*, but the head and neck are those of *Buchanga atra*. That I should not have noticed this before is as surprising as the fact that I have shown the specimen to many ornithological friends, most of them intimately acquainted with the two species above mentioned, and that none of us have detected the fraud. On re-examining the specimen, as I have done many times before, it is impossible to detect where the birds have been joined together'[5]. Mr. Ian Galbraith tells me that the specimen, which is still in the British Museum (Natural History) collection, has the body of a cuckoo-shrike (*Coracina melanoptera*) and the head of a drongo (*Dicrurus macrocercus*). Undoubtedly there are similar ornithological frauds awaiting detection in other museums.

As might have been expected, Charles Waterton frequently abused the art in which he excelled. One of his numerous leg-pulls, now in the City Museum and Art Gallery of Wakefield, was the 'Noctifer'. This was 'made of the gorget and legs of a bittern and the head and legs of an eagle-owl, skilfully blended'[6]. Watertonian in spirit, but not in workmanship, was the skeleton

77

of King Charles the First's parrot, a curious object which was intended to deceive Frank Buckland who, better than anyone else in Victoria's reign, could appreciate the joke and see through it. One Christmas he was presented with a box by his 'soldier-servant' (for Buckland was one-time assistant surgeon to the 2nd Life-Guards) which was supposed to have been found bricked up in an old chimney of one of the Queen's apartments at Windsor Castle. Some of the old servants at the Castle, so the story went, had said it was the 'Skeleton of King Charles the First's favourite parrot'. With great solemnity the box was opened before him, but Buckland 'quickly discovered that a trap had been laid by some of the troopers to catch "the Doctor", for it must be acknowledged that the skeleton has a very parrot-like appearance'[7]. He found that it was simply 'the skeleton

Above: An ingenious marriage of the body of a red grouse and head of a tufted duck produces a 'Gruck'. This fake is now in the Royal Scottish Museum, Edinburgh.

Right: An even more imaginatively contrived ornithological hoax is the 'Bare-fronted Hoodwink'. This has the head of a carrion crow and the body of a plover. The wings and tail feathers are possibly those of a duck, while the 'bare front' is red wax. Both illustrations by courtesy of the Royal Scottish Museum, Edinburgh.

of a rabbit, put up in a bird-like attitude; the rabbit has been cut into two, and the flesh taken off the bones, which are coloured brown to give an appearance of antiquity; the neck bones and part of the back-bone have been left attached to the head; the hind legs have also been left attached to the hip bones, or pelvis, and the two halves of the animal then fastened ingeniously together in the outline of a bird's skeleton; the hind legs have been neatly tucked up exactly like the legs of

a bird sitting, and the bones of the rabbit's feet have been moistened and then turned round a perch to give the idea of a bird's claws. The whole thing was then set upon a perch to carry out the idea of a bird, especially a parrot'[8]. It was later discovered that an ingenious Life-Guardsman had engineered the whole deception to get a laugh out of the author of *Curiosities of Natural History* who, we may be sure, enjoyed the joke as much as anybody.

Among the series of zoological impostures in the Royal Scottish Museum at Edinburgh is a 'Gruck', a marriage of the body of a Red Grouse with the head of a Tufted Duck and a few extra feathers from another kind of duck. This was constructed by Ian Lyster, taxidermist at the museum. More imaginatively contrived is the museum's Bare-fronted Hoodwink which was put together by Willie Sterling, a former taxidermist there. This has the head of a Carrion Crow and the body of a kind of plover. The wings are possibly those of a Scaup Duck, the tail feathers are from a duck or a goose, the feet are from a wading bird of some kind and have a hind claw, and the 'bare front' is red wax. Recently the museum has added the original, or type specimen of Meiklejohn's Hoodwink, to its collection. This is a study skin comprising pieces of various unidentifiable and rather ordinary-looking birds in a somewhat worn condition, one of its two labels bearing a whole series of unsuccessful identifications. This item, which was mysteriously 'discovered' by Ian Lyster, was exhibited on April 1st, 1975 along with various photographs of ornithological field meetings caught in the act of 'just missing' a sight of the Hoodwink, and a copy of a paper about this previously unknown bird published in 1950 by M.F. Meiklejohn[9]. In his paper Meiklejohn, having studied many reports of birds 'partially seen or indeterminately heard', concluded that all were attributable to a single species to which he gave the scientific name *Dissimulatrix spuria*, or the Hoodwink.

'The existence of this species,' he says, 'has already been recognised by several authors, amongst them James Thurber, who has presented a somewhat imaginative picture of the bird perched upon a spray of Ragamuffin.' He goes on to say that someone shot several specimens of this very elusive creature on Heligoland 'but they invariably fell over steep cliffs into the sea'. In tropical forests, the Hoodwink invariably keeps to the densest vegetation (where it is extremely vociferous), and refuses to be lured into the open by the observer's imitation of a Black Mamba.

Meiklejohn points out that the Hoodwink 'is more frequently observed by beginners in ornithology than by more practised observers', and seems to have a 'marked preference for suburban bird tables'. In the field it is generally recognisable 'by *blurred appearance* and extremely rapid flight away from observer'. Its call has caused some controversy in bird-watching circles, but it has been shown that the call 'resembling the creaking of an unoiled hinge, formerly supposed to be uttered by Hoodwinks', is actually made by the creaking of an unoiled hinge. In the breeding season, curiously enough, the 'male flies round in ever-decreasing circles, evoking no response whatever from the female'. Its food preferences are little understood but 'McSporran considers that haggises are the pellets of the Hoodwink'. Its eggs, according to Meiklejohn, are 'served in British hotels –recognisable by glycerine-like consistency and frequent presence of embryo'. The Royal Scottish Museum's Bare-fronted Hoodwink differs notably from the one so capably monographed by Meiklejohn by laying eggs which, with few exceptions, are unlike those served in British hotels being entirely black or bearing large black spots on them. Meiklejohn's Hoodwink occasioned, and deserved, serious discussion on the radio.

Somewhat related to the Hoodwink is the 'Siggahfoops' which has been written up in an article in *Scottish Field*[10]. The Siggahfoops, which has a kind of inverse relationship to the ubiquitous haggis, is said to resemble the corncrake and has often been seen by moonlight in the early hours of the morning, 'but usually the reports come from observers whose reliability is suspect'. It is a peculiarly sensitive creature but 'has frequently been tempted from cover by the recitation, in a firm voice, of verse'.

Another bird which, until recently, bird watchers knew nothing about –nay, did not even suspect existed–is Hardy's Swift (*Apus durus*), the subject of yet another article, this time by the eminent ornithologist David Lack[11]. The chief reason why this bird has not been seen by the legions of bird watchers is the high altitude it frequents. Another reason is that it is nearly translucent when seen from below. Its habits are unusual, its egg-laying procedure decidedly so. When the single egg is ready to be laid 'the female attracts her mate by a musical twang, the only time that she breaks silence. He then flies up behind her, turns right over and sails upside down below her, at which moment she lays the egg. He grips the egg in his legs, then bends his mouth over it and sticks it to the bare brood-patch on his abdomen with saliva'. (It is worth noting in passing that this egg-laying procedure is not so very different from that which some early writers on natural history put forward as the procedure necessarily adopted by the endlessly-flying birds of paradise.) 'The egg is sky-blue, thus matching the heavens, and size and shape is extremely like that of a starling . . . Its transfer from male to female is the main cause of nesting losses, for the male occasionally misses it altogether, or fails to secure it to the brood-patch. The egg then falls to the ground and not infrequently appears on grass lawns, quite undamaged . . . It can readily be distinguished from the eggs of earth-bound species because, of course, it is single, and it is not surrounded by a nest or covered by a parent bird.' All very interesting, and convincing too, for (as I am reliably informed by Mr. Ian Galbraith) several amateurs have taken Hardy's Swift seriously, attributing to it the single eggs which starlings often lay on lawns.

Two other items of an ornithological flavour, both literary, may be mentioned here, the first making heavy weather of a transparently obvious hoax, the second pulling off a brilliant spoof without even trying. A privately published monograph on *Eoörnis pterovelox gobiensis* by one Augustus C. Fotheringham gives, in great detail, all that is known about a strange bird intermediate in appearance between a pelican and a pterodactyl. This creature, supposed to inhabit the Gobi Desert, is also known as the 'Woofenpoof' and has many peculiarities, not least its propensity for laying a double-yolked egg contained in a rubbery shell. The egg is laid in a nest consisting of small amethystene geodes pushed together in the sand, the egg resembling the geodes exactly as is proved by a photograph of same. There are 34 quarto pages of this kind of stuff resulting in a meticulously–rather too-meticulously–worked out hoax, the numerous cleverly devised photographs saving it from being merely a damp squib[12].

The other literary item was obviously intended to be an amusing little piece of satire but was misconstrued by some watch-dogs of ornithological literature who innocently turned it into an exquisite deception. In 1963 Frank A. Goodliffe published a description of the 'Dog-collared Sombre Blackbird' (*Clericus polydenominata*)[13]. It is worth repeating his description in full, as much for its own sake as for the added piquancy it gives to the delicious sequel.

DOG-COLLARED SOMBRE BLACKBIRD
(*Clericus polydenominata*)

Average length 60 to 72 inches (although longer and shorter specimens may be seen).

Identification: Similar to *common laity* but plumage and behaviour should serve to differentiate. Plumage black with narrow white collar–unbroken at throat. Feet black, of leathery appearance. Beak pink–often with blueish tint during winter months. When in groups are often seen with wings folded behind rump.

Distribution: Found throughout South Africa in close association with *common laity*. Not an indigenous species; believed migrant from Europe.

Habits: Usually found congregating with flocks of *common laity,* the females of which are frequently seen with plumage of vivid colours.

Nesting: This usually occurs close to old buildings with spires. They are usually very friendly and may be seen around nesting sites of *common laity* at tea-time.

Feeding: Mainly omnivorous and, in coastal waters, may sometimes be seen wading and fishing from beaches or rocks.

Call: The voice is distinctive, commencing 'Brrrrr—rethren' and continuing low and pleasant—often prolonged. Usually sings in congregations.
FRANK A. GOODLIFFE

Surprisingly enough Goodliffe's article was gravely listed in that most austere of natural history publications the *Zoological Record* (for 1964), the name *Clericus polydenominata* being recorded along with members of the family Icteridae (the Troupials or American Orioles). Thus, the Dog-collared Sombre Blackbird acquired a standing in the world of science which must have mystified and amused Frank A. Goodliffe. The joke was not played out yet, however, because in 1967 M. A. Traylor privately published a little booklet in which he tortures the unfortunate editors of the *Zoological Record* by discussing in a quasi-serious manner the validity of the name *Clericus polydenominata*, suggests that the 'bird' would be more suitably placed in the family Ploceidae (Bishop Birds), and reproduces Goodliffe's original description[14]. Hopefully the editors of the *Zoological Record* can smile as well as blush.

Chapter 8
Invertebrate fakes

Invertebrate animals are less familiar, and less attractive to most of us than vertebrates and, for these and other reasons, it might be expected that faked insects, shells and crustaceans would not be very numerous. Such fakes could only have been made to dupe a relatively small number of entomologists, conchologists and others who derive pleasure from collecting and studying lowly creatures. But that relatively small number includes some fanatics, particularly among those who collect insects. And as there are not enough naturally-produced marvels to satisfy their particular, sometimes peculiar, desires numerous attempts have been made to produce them artificially. The principal, indeed almost the only, faked invertebrates which have come to light belong, or are supposed to belong, to the two largest groups in the animal kingdom: the insects and the molluscs.

Insects. The body structure of some kinds of insects is such that it should be comparatively easy to alter their appearance artificially. Butterflies and moths, beetles, stick insects, flies, bees and wasps, to mention a few of the better known insect types, are not difficult to dismember; and their wings or wing coverings are often susceptible to touches of paint or dye. This being so, it is a little surprising that faked insects are not more numerous in collections. On the other hand it is likely that there are some, perhaps many, undetected in collections. The great popularity of butterflies and moths and the ready sale that some of the more remarkable ones find among collectors has, as may have been expected, led to the perpetration of a number of clever, and not-so-clever, forgeries. The almost complete absence of forgeries in other insect orders, however, is puzzling and disappointing.

The earliest, and in some respects the most remarkable, faked insect I have come across occurs in the *Metamorphosis Insectorum Surinamensium* of Maria Sibylle Merian. The authoress of this beautifully-illustrated book went to Surinam in 1698 and stayed there for two years collecting and painting the insects and flowers which she found there. Occasionally, she painted things that were not to be found there for she is known to have been gullible. She must have been, to have been fooled by so blatant a fake as that illustrated on the 49th plate of the second edition of her book. On this plate several lantern flies and cicadas are illustrated. These are drawn artistically and, for the most part, accurately, but the bottom illustration is neither a lantern fly nor a cicada but a composite of both insects. The body and wings are those of a cicada (*Diceroprocta tibicen* Linnaeus), but the head is that of a lantern fly (*Fulgora laternaria* Linnaeus) which, one would have thought, could never be mistaken for the head of any other insect. The presence of so bizarre a head on so commonplace a body should have been enough to enable Maria to detect the fraud; but to illustrate it on a page which also illustrates the two insects from which it was compounded–and yet be sublimely unaware of its false character–indicates that she was probably more interested in turning out an attractive work of art than in recording a scientific fact[1].

Later in the eighteenth century, Linnaeus went one better than Maria Merian. Whereas she merely illustrated a faked insect, he not only published the description of one but also immortalised it by giving it a scientific name. In 1763 he published the description of his *Papilio ecclipsis*, a butterfly said to have come from North America. In the twelfth edition of his *Systema Naturae*, he listed it immediately after *Papilio rhamni* (= *Gonepteryx rhamni*), better known as the Brimstone, a familiar European butterfly with sulphur-yellow wings each bearing a central orange spot. *P. ecclipsis* is known only from the two specimens in the Linnaean collection in the rooms of the Linnaean Society, London. It differs from the Brimstone by having blackish patches on the wings, and in the central area of the large patch on the lower edge of each hind wing there is a crescent-shaped blue marking which suggested the specific name Linnaeus gave to this insect. Close examination shows that these markings have been delicately painted on to the wings of ordinary Brimstone butterflies! In a copy of the 12th edition of the *Systema Naturae* in the Library of the National Museum of Wales at Cardiff, a marginal pencilled note against the description of *P. ecclipsis* reads: 'This Insect I have seen in Linnaeus's Cabt. & it is a painted spec. of Rhamni. J. Curtis.' This indicates that the forgery had been detected early in the nineteenth century by John Curtis, the famous illustrator of natural history books and author of numerous important works on insects. But he was not the first to detect it. Mr. P.E.S. Whalley of the Entomology Department in the British Museum (Natural History) tells me (*in litt.* 2.x.1975) that Fabricius had hinted, in a book published in 1793, that *P. ecclipsis* was really a Brimstone.

In connection with sales of aberrant butterflies and moths it has been said:

A hand-coloured engraving from Metamorphosis Insectorum Surinamensium, *1730, by Maria Sibylle Merian. On the plate are featured several lantern flies and cicadas. If you look closely you will see that one of these is a fake. If you fail to spot it, turn to page 90.*

A celebrated butterfly fake. The centre specimen is the Brimstone Papilio rhamni. *The other two specimens, however, are doctored Brimstone butterflies named by Linnaeus* Papilio ecclipsis *and placed by him in his collection.*

'No matter what subject the collector takes up, he studies first the normal, then the rare, and then proceeds to the abnormal. In fact the search for the abnormal becomes often almost a craze'[2]. In Britain butterfly and moth aberrations have been avidly collected, particularly if the species has been recorded as British. In a recently published note Mr. J.M. Chalmers-Hunt says: 'Many years ago, the late C. Granville Clutterbuck of Gloucester showed me a Common Wainscot (*Mythimna pallens* Linnaeus), in a collection he had acquired, whose wings were painted with red spots in a crude

attempt to simulate a Crimson-speckled Footman (*Utetheisa pulchella* Linnaeus)'[3]. Mr. Leslie Goodson, formerly curator of the Rothschild collection at Tring in Hertfordshire, tells me (*in litt.* 4.ix.1975) that he remembers seeing a butterfly (*Aglaia charlotta* Howarth) 'with the silver spots of the underside joined together by silver paint, fairly well done but obvious to an expert and purchased to save it getting into other sales'.

Of those butterflies which reach Britain from the European mainland, one of the most celebrated is the Camberwell Beauty (*Nymphalis antiopa* Linnaeus), a large and handsome insect with chocolate-brown wings bordered with yellowish white. Occasionally the border is much paler and may even be white. For a long time it was thought that the white-bordered form was peculiar to the British Isles and, for this reason, specimens so coloured were more desirable to British collectors and, consequently, more expensive to buy (it should be pointed out that this butterfly, whatever the coloration of its wings, has always been one of the insects most coveted by British collectors). That the white-bordered form was considered desirable enough to induce someone to fake it was proved in a most unexpected way. E.A. Cockayne, a distinguished collector and student of butterflies and moths, was examining butterflies in the collections of the British Museum (Natural History) some time during the 1920's, his object being to discover which species fluoresced under ultra-violet light. While examining a drawer containing specimens of the Camberwell Beauty he noticed that the wing borders of one white-bordered specimen fluoresced brightly, a phenomenon not shown by any other specimen of this species examined. The forger had used a white paint to effect the deception and had used it so well that the specimen (said to have been captured at Scarborough in 1872) would probably still be deceiving onlookers today if Cockayne had not noticed it. The notion that white-bordered specimens of the Camberwell Beauty are indigenous to Britain is no longer entertained, the few adult specimens which survive a British winter being so widely scattered that they do not find a mate for the spring pairing[3]. In any case the yellowish-white coloration of most specimens fades in the course of time to produce a paler border.

Butterfly wings have also been stained, bleached or dyed intentionally or accidentally, sometimes for experimental purposes, sometimes for less honorable reasons. Wings of brightly coloured butterflies which come into contact with cyanide condensation on the inside of a killing bottle may be turned a less attractive brown. About 1948 an unusual Green Hairstreak (*Thecla betulae* Linnaeus) was displayed at the annual exhibition of the South London Entomological and Natural History Society. It was exhibited as an undoubted aberration in which the normally green underside of the wings was marked symmetrically with brown. Someone at the meeting pronounced this butterfly a fake, but it seems as though the exhibitor had been genuinely fooled by an instance of accidental staining caused by cyanide condensation. Here we have a rare example of an animal being pronounced a fake where the faking was unintentional and unsuspected.

Wings of butterflies and moths can be turned a yellowish hue if treated with picric acid, and hydrochloric acid will change the red colours on the wings of butterflies such as the Red Admiral (*Vanessa atalanta* Linnaeus) and the Painted Lady (*Vanessa cardui* Linnaeus) to a duller, slightly greenish hue. Colours may be bleached out, partially or completely, and for experimental purposes specimens have been bleached and then dyed[4].

Sometimes a forgery of this kind remains undetected until someone makes a careful study of the specimen for scientific purposes. This was true of a South American moth studied recently at the British Museum (Natural History). While studying specimens of *Stenognatha* (a genus of moths in the family Arctiidae) the type specimen (i.e. the first described specimen) of *Stenognatha pyrophora* was found to be artificially coloured. The entomologists who discovered the forgery wrote: 'The type of *pyrophora* Hering appears to have been stained with a pinkish red colourant. Much, but not all, of the orange and white markings of the wings and thorax have been stained by the "artist". Close examination shows that not only are the wing scales stained, but also some of the detritus between them and there seems little doubt that a forgery has been perpetrated'[5]. They also discovered that the abdomen was not only similarly stained but belonged to a totally different species of moth! This particular insect was described as new to science in 1926, a comparatively late date for a competent entomologist to be fooled by such a blatant fake. It took half a century, nevertheless, to discover its true identity.

Evidently the appearance of a butterfly's or moth's wing is not difficult to modify by applying paint to it, by bleaching, dyeing or staining it, or by combinations of two or more of these methods. It may be because such modifications are so easily effected that would-be forgers of lepidopteran rarities have not paid too much attention to them. It would be very easy to saturate the market with convincingly unnatural Brimstone butterflies, for instance. To remove the sulphur-yellow coloration from the wings of this reasonably common butterfly, a profound knowledge of chemistry is not necessary: given a small amount of diluted ammonia and a steady hand anyone could turn out dozens of white-winged Brimstones in an evening. No, the mere adulteration of a butterfly by staining, painting, dyeing or bleaching its wings is not a sufficient challenge to the top-class butterfly forger. But to create a 'gynandromorph' . . . now that's quite another matter.

To create a gynandromorph you have to know what it is. Without becoming too technical it is enough to say that a gynandromorph is an animal which, because of abnormalities affecting the distribution of its sex-chromosomes, is of mixed sex, the male and female parts developing simultaneously side by side. In insects a 'bilateral gynandromorph' is one in which one side is male and the other female, the line of division being straight and the two halves being of opposite sex not only in colour and pattern but also in structure. Gynandromorph butterflies and moths are extremely rare and of great interest to collectors who, fascinated by the presence of dissimilar wings on a single specimen and aware of the rarity factor, have been prepared to pay a high price to get one.

Here, indeed, is a worthy challenge for the butterfly forger who takes a pride in his work. Mr. Leslie Goodson has told me the story of two 'gynandromorphs', now in the British Museum (Natural History), which are a credit to the forger's craft (*in litt.* 4.ix.1975). For some reason Mr. Goodson was suspicious of a 'gynan-

dromorph' of the Clouded Yellow (*Colias croceus* Fourcroy) reposing in the collection he was in charge of. So he 'relaxed' it, that is to say, he softened it up a little so that its members would become pliable. The wings did not just become pliable; they fell off! The forewings were those of a male and the hindwings those of a female, but the two had never been associated in nature. A second 'gynandromorph' of the same species came under Mr. Goodson's critical eye and likewise proved to be a forgery, but this one was a work of art. The male and female wings were not just stuck on to a single body, as in the first specimen; 'an example of each sex had been sliced down the middle by an extremely sharp instrument, from the head between the antennae right down to the tip of the abdomen, and the two halves stuck together'. Only a minute examination revealed the handiwork of an expert forger. Probably several of the 'bilateral gynandromorphs' in collections today would prove to be forgeries if examined closely.

Apart from faked butterflies and moths and Maria Merian's cicadiform lantern fly, the only examples of insect forgeries that I know of are some referred to briefly by J.E. Gray of the British Museum in 1858. He refers to some beetles, 'especially the larger Cerambyces [longhorn beetles]', which had been sent to the museum from China and on which the Chinese collectors had worked with a paint brush 'so as to give them quite a different appearance from the usual and natural colour of the species'[6].

Shells. Up to the end of the eighteenth century many shells now considered common were unknown or rarely seen in collections. The conchological riches of the Pacific Ocean were then imper-

Linnaeus named the shell on the left Cypraea amethystea. *He did not realise it was merely a rubbed-down specimen of a common cowry.*

fectly known and only a few shells from that vast ocean were to be seen in European collections until after the Napoleonic wars. During the eighteenth century, therefore, dealers had great difficulty obtaining sufficient quantities of attractive shells in good condition to satisfy the importunate demands of their clients. There wasn't enough high quality material to go round and what there was had been familiar to collectors for many years. Dealers were forced to make the most of what they had and sometimes they went further than they should.

Shell cleaning and repairing was carried on in Holland and at La Rochelle in France from at least the early eighteenth century and many persons were employed to improve the appearance of defective shells by working on them with files, polishing equipment, glue, paint and varnish. But to improve a shell's appearance wasn't enough. Collectors wanted new and unique specimens for their collections. Dealers did their best (or their worst) to oblige and produced many forgeries. Some collectors were easily–perhaps willingly–duped by these bogus shells. Christian Paul Meyer, an Amsterdam merchant, was visited in 1777 by the traveller H. Sander who was shown Meyer's shell collection. This was obviously very extensive as collections went in those days, but not very select, for Sander noted that many specimens had been artificially altered and coloured. Artificial specimens of the White Hammer Oyster (*Malleus albus* Lamarck), Sander noted, had been made in Holland and it was probable that all the specimens of this Indo-Pacific shell (then very rare) in Holland were false[7].

Some of the forgeries were created by simple and effective means. In 1767, for instance, a large number of 'golden limpets' were being sold in Paris to collectors for high prices. These pretty shells were really specimens of a common limpet (*Patinigera deaurata* Gmelin) found in the Falkland Islands. They had been immersed in hot cinders or fried gently in a pan, the original reddish-brown coloration being changed by this treatment to a brilliant gold. The appearance of cowry shells is also easily altered superficially by heat treatment. A specimen of the Lurid Cowry (*Cypraea lurida* Linnaeus) with two rows of large, pale spots on its surface was catalogued for sale in 1784 by J.G. de Favanne. Probably a hot iron had produced the unnatural spotting[8].

There has long been a rumour that rice-paste imitations of the Precious Wentletrap (*Epitonium scalare* Linnaeus) were once marketed by the Chinese. As it is not easy to test a suspect shell of this species without damaging it to some extent, thereby reducing its attractiveness and value, it is difficult to substantiate or refute the rumour. The fake would certainly be worth many times more than the real thing now. In good faith I once recorded the presence of a rice-paste specimen in the collection of a London shell dealer[9]. Ever since then I have had my doubts about it and now I find

it hard to believe that such things ever were made, the exquisite lines and sheer delicacy of the originals seeming to be beyond the artistry of a human being to reproduce in rice paste.

It is possible to change the markings of a cowry shell by abrading the upper shell layers and exposing a differently coloured and patterned lower layer. Linnaeus once described a cowry under the name *Cypraea amethystea,* the specific name implying that the shell has a bluish-violet colour, which it has, or at least the one in the Linnaean collection has. But the Linnaean specimen is nothing more than a rubbed down specimen of the common Arabic Cowry (*Cypraea arabica* Linnaeus) which is not bluish-violet at all in its natural state. Tourists visiting the Fiji Islands in our own day are sometimes offered shells of the 'Tapa Cowry', a supposedly rare species for which a high price is asked. These are merely rubbed down shells of the common Humpback Cowry (*Cypraea mauritiana* Linnaeus)[10].

Mr. Tom Pain of London has shown me a shell in his collection which shows that it is possible to alter a shell's appearance by removing a small amount of its thin, outermost skin (or periostracum). The specimen is a shell of an apple snail (*Pila orbata* Perry), brought from India about 1910, which appears to have thin, well-defined spiral bands of a paler colour than the rest of the shell. Thin lines of the green periostracum have been scraped away with a pointed instrument revealing the paler coloured shell below.

Continued from page 84: The insect shown at the bottom of the plate, resting on a flower, is a composite. The wings of a cicada are superimposed on the body of a lantern fly. Maria Merian was not a trained naturalist but was fascinated by exotic plants and insects. It is possible that she drew the fake without realising its true identity. By courtesy of the British Museum (Natural History).

Right: A modern jenny haniver bought by the author from a London dealer in 1970. It was said to have come from the Gulf of Mexico.

The hydra as illustrated by Seba in his Thesaurus, *1734. It was exposed as a fake by Linnaeus during the following year.*

Photo overleaf: The Bloomsbury Mermaid became a celebrity when a feature was written about her in the Daily Express *for 22nd June 1921 (see page 56). It is now owned by Mr. Richard Whittington-Egan.*

93

Top: The mermaid which is reputed to be the one exhibited by Phineas Taylor Barnum in 1842.

Below: A case containing two miniature 'Roman' dogs, a sparrow decorated with canary feathers and a *redstart, owned by a former hotel proprietor in Wales. The two dogs were said to be the last of a miniature breed living among the ancient ruins of Rome. It is thought that they were probably very young spaniel puppies.*

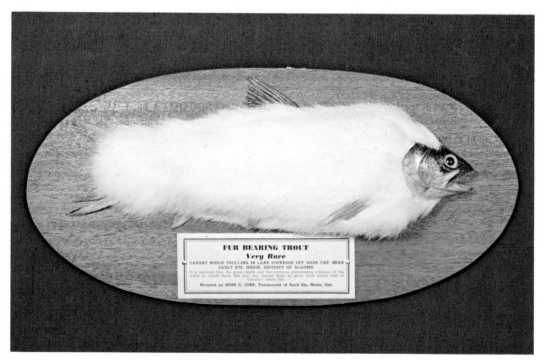

The Fur-bearing Trout. By courtesy of the Royal Scottish Museum, Edinburgh.

The White-Russian Shore Muddler. By courtesy of the Natural History Museum, Göteburg, Sweden.

96

Chapter 9
Beringer's lying stones

The case of the 'lying stones of Beringer' is one of the most remarkable and bizarre episodes in the history of geology. Played out in an academic atmosphere, it soon transcended academic boundaries and eventually became enshrined in semi-popular literature. Any scientific hoax which ends up in the court room is bound to be intriguing; and when scandal is added to credulity it becomes of interest to scientist and non-scientist alike.

Dr. Johann Bartholomew Adam Beringer, a German virtuoso and physician of wide attainments, was well known in medical and non-medical circles in and around Würzburg. During the early eighteenth century he developed an interest in the study of 'oryctics'–things dug out of the ground –and in particular those objects known in his day as 'formed stones' and in ours as fossils. It was this interest which resulted in a cunning attempt to ruin his reputation.

Up to 1725, Beringer's cabinet had contained nothing out of the ordinary in the way of fossils and probably his collection differed in no significant way from similar collections of the kind formed by contemporary collectors. But on the last day of May 1725, or shortly after, three very remarkable formed stones were brought to him. One of these bore a likeness of the sun and its rays, the other two having the likeness of worms on them. They had just been dug up, so he was informed, on Mount Eivelstadt, a hill near Würzburg. Subsequently many more stones were obtained from the same hill, each bearing in bold relief the forms of animals and plants or astronomical bodies and hieroglyphs, etc. Beringer was captivated by these incredible objects and saw to it that any stones remaining in the hill came his way. He had in his employ three youths, Christian Zänger and the brothers Niklaus and Valentin Hehn, who were paid to bring him any interesting formed stones they found. Once it was learnt that Mount Eivelstadt was the only source of these wonderful stones the three youths concentrated their searches upon its slopes, at least the Hehn brothers did, for as we shall now see, Christian Zänger did not need to.

It appears that Beringer had enemies in the University of Würzburg who were prepared to go to great lengths to accomplish his downfall. These included the academicians J. Ignatz Roderick, Professor of Geography, Algebra, and Analysis, and the Honorable Georg von Eckhart, Privy Councillor and Librarian to the Court and to the University. Von Eckhart was the better scholar of the two and had been engaged on a history of the Duchy of Würzburg for a long time before becoming involved with the 'Lügensteine' ('lying stones'). A third figure, Baron von Hof, had a hand in the affair, but nothing is known about him beyond his having a liking for being carried about in a sedan chair. It was probably Roderick, an unsavoury and unscrupulous character, who masterminded the hoax.

Roderick and his accomplices conceived the idea of hand-carving formed stones and planting them somewhere close at hand so that they could be dug up, and by devious means brought to the notice of Beringer whose interest in such things was well known to them. Evidently Beringer was a credulous individual, and it was his credulity which they wanted to exploit. To effect their unacademic ends it was essential that they brought into their confidence one of the youths employed by Beringer and, by offering suitable bribes, get him to work for them as well. They

singled out the seventeen-year-old Christian Zänger. This young fellow, who seems to have been motivated by a love of money, agreed to do what they wanted. Roderick hand-carved the stones, which were made of a soft shell-limestone, and either gave them to Zänger to be taken to Beringer direct or saw that they were hidden under rocks at various places on Mount Eivelstadt where they could be found without too much difficulty by the Hehn brothers. Zänger also polished some of the stones, so he must be considered almost as guilty as the principals, perhaps more so considering that he was still being employed by Beringer.

Soon Beringer had a large collection of these stones, over two hundred of them, and they were so unlike any other formed stones that he felt compelled to look for a new and convincing explanation of their origin. Thus he came to write the book which ensured that his name had a permanent place, though not a very enviable one, in the history of geology and palaeontology. The *Lithographiae Wirceburgensis* was published in 1726. In it Beringer examines all the theories which had been promulgated to account for the occurrence of formed stones; and he advanced his own opinion on the origin of the lying stones (he did not call them lying stones, of course, but referred to them as iconoliths or idiomorphic stones). His conclusion about the origin of the Würzburg finds is expressed quite clearly: 'No intelligent person could entertain the slightest suspicion that our iconoliths were petrified by the sea waters–whether in the general flood, or drawn from the ocean by some other channel. However, by reason of the contrast, which we have intimated in this chapter, between our controverted figured stones, and genuine diluvial and maritime specimens found on the same mountain, certain dabblers and other mere amateurs in the field of Lithography [his term for palaeontology] have underhandedly and falsely taken occasion to insinuate that, while the others are true relics of the Flood, ours are the suppositious product of recent artificiality. Thanks to their vicious raillery, their false rumours and gossip, they have forced me—though I shrink from the task—to refute and confound them all in good time'[1].

Many of the 'iconoliths' are illustrated in the book and a more ludicrous collection of 'fossilized' objects it would be difficult to imagine: soft-bodied animals such as slugs and snails, spiders and worms; birds complete with feathers and an occasional egg; fishes and frogs; beetles and centipedes; flowering plants, including one with a bee apparently fossilized just before it had alighted on it; astronomical symbols such as stars with cometary tails; and mysterious-looking letters and hieroglyphs of Hebraic affinity. Each stone was about 10 to 20 centimetres across and the objects are depicted on them in bold relief. It is unbelievable that anyone as intelligent as Beringer should have been fooled for one moment by such obvious artefacts, but he was, initially anyway. Shortly after the publication of his book, however, he began to have doubts about his beloved stones. Even before the book was published the hoaxers, deciding that they had succeeded too well in their design and concerned lest their own reputation should suffer should the truth be revealed, began spreading a rumour that the stones were fakes. They even sold Beringer some stones and then told him that they were hand-made. But Beringer was so infatuated with the stones he already possessed, with his preconceived notion of their authenticity and with his book and the new ideas expressed in it, that he would not be persuaded that all the stones were artefacts.

It is not known for certain what did persuade him eventually. One story (and there are many stories about Beringer and his lying stones) says that he came across a stone on which was spelled out his own name. Another says that the Bishop of the Church at Würzburg made him see reason. Whatever, or whoever, brought him to his senses he seems to have acted quickly to try to salvage his reputation. First he recalled every copy of the book he could lay his hands on—leaving in circulation just a sufficient number to make the *Lithographiae Wirceburgensis* one of the rarest and most sought after of all geological treatises—in a hopeless attempt to prevent the outside world having a good laugh at his expense. Then he instituted proceedings which were opened in April 1726.

It is from the surviving records of these proceedings, which only came to light in 1935, that the truth about this remarkable hoax has been obtained. Previously it had been thought that some of his students had played a joke on him. It has also been said that the episode ruined Beringer financially and shortened his life. The facts suggest that the hoaxers suffered more than the hoaxed. Nothing more was heard of Zänger; von Eckhart died four years after the trial, leaving a mass of unpublished material, his history of the Duchy of Würzburg remaining incomplete because he was refused access to the archives of the University; and Roderick left Würzburg, or was thrown out of it, and was in disgrace for the rest of his days. Beringer, on the other hand, lived for

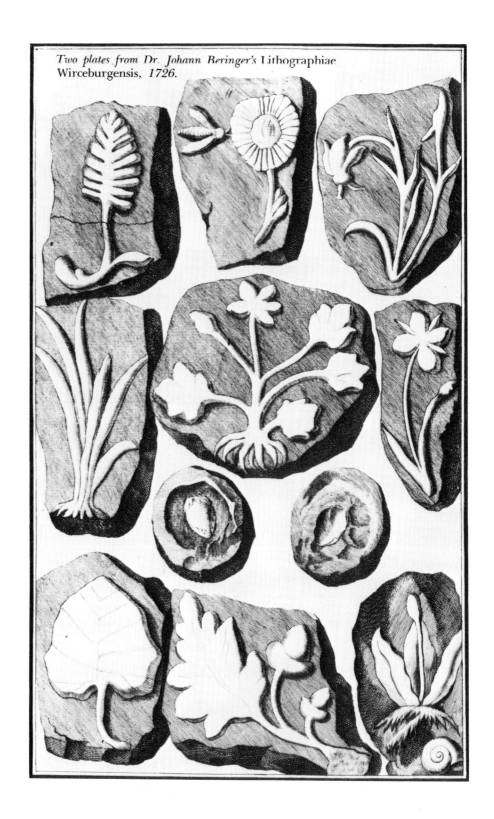

Two plates from Dr. Johann Beringer's Lithographiae Wirceburgensis, 1726.

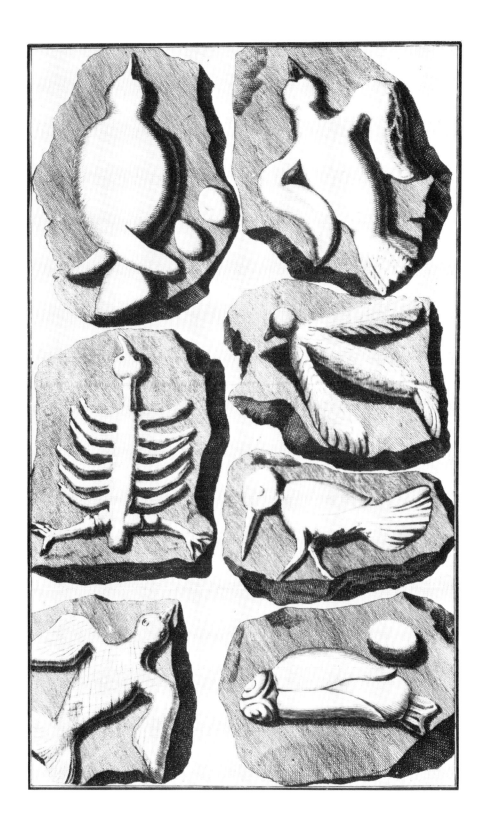

fourteen years after the trial and wrote at least two more books, which were well received.

Why anyone should have wanted to devise such an elaborate and time-consuming hoax is not entirely clear. If, as has been suggested, the conspirators were motivated by revenge and envy[2], it must be assumed that Beringer gave them something substantial to be vengeful and envious about, but we have nothing to go on apart from Zänger's statement in court that the conspirators had discussed how they could bring an accusation against Beringer 'because he was so arrogant and despised them all'[3].

A passage in a contemporary satirical commentary, said to have been circulated about Würzburg at the time of the trial, suggests that Beringer was inclined to sling his weight about and to be pontifical. Roderick and his accomplices may not have been alone in wanting to take the wind out of his sails. 'He who is wont to stone others with his words', says our anonymous commentator, 'now like a stony field, utters stones. A living stone is he, endowed with body, spirit and soul. Himself become stony in a shower of stones, he, in his turn, showers stones. From the very heavens he has stoned us, this peerless Doctor J.B.A.B. . . . But, as stone is the direct child of water, so have these imaginary stones of the celebrated J.B.A.B. passed into water. The stone mines are at last exhausted'[4].

But the lying stones have not passed into water; some of them are still preserved at Würzburg and elsewhere[5], mute witnesses to a most exquisite if slightly cruel joke.

Two of Beringer's 'lying stones' now in the University Museum, Oxford. They are carved in soft calcareous mudstone. By courtesy of the Curator of the Geological Collections, University Museum, Oxford.

c.m.

102

Chapter 10
Pseudo-fossils

The 'fossil sea-serpent' of Dr. Koch and Beringer's 'lying stones', discussed in earlier chapters, are certainly the most remarkable pseudo-fossils which human ingenuity has assembled or manufactured. But other examples are known, in particular the so-called 'snakestones' and 'Dudley locusts'.

Snakestones have nothing to do with snakes, being the fossil remains of molluscan shells, known today as ammonites and found principally in deposits of Mesozoic age. They were called snakestones because they resemble coiled and ribbed snakes without heads. Around Whitby in Yorkshire ammonites are abundant. 'Legend supposes that the fossils were once living serpents which were common in that area until the seventh century A.D. when the Saxon abbess St. Hilda turned them into stone in order to clear a site for the building of her convent. The heads of the serpents were assumed to have been destroyed on their death . . . The absence of heads in the Whitby snakestones is sometimes attributed to a further curse by St. Cuthbert, another local saint. In order to perpetuate the legend and to effect sales of specimens, local collectors and dealers in fossils frequently "restored" the snakestones by carving heads on them'[1].

Snakestones, complete with heads, have been sold in the Whitby area for centuries and one of the most famous examples, now in the British Museum (Natural History), is the original (or type) specimen of *Dactylioceras commune* Sowerby. There is a similar snakestone legend at Keynsham where large ammonites are found. A fine example of one of these snakestones is in the National Museum of Wales at Cardiff.

The 'Dudley locust', similarly, is not an insect but is the fossilized remnant

of an extinct invertebrate animal resembling a large wood-louse and correctly known as a trilobite. There are trilobites in rocks of Palaeozoic age in many parts of the world but, as at Dudley, they seldom occur complete, and in their incomplete state are less appealing and less desirable to collectors. Consequently, the more complete the specimen the more a collector is inclined to pay for it. 'Unscrupulous quarrymen often "repaired" fragmentary trilobites, and skilfully carved segments between detached heads and tails, or added new heads to headless bodies. The end-products were often quite bizarre, combining parts of quite different trilobites. Quarrymen working at the large, world-famous limestone quarries at Dudley, Worcestershire, had a ready market for the elegant "Dudley locust" or "Dudley insect", so common there when the quarries were working. This particular trilobite always has 13 segments on the thorax, but one example was known with a considerably greater number, which for a time perplexed palaeontologists. It was not until the lacquer began to peel off the specimen that it was realized that the whole thorax had been skilfully carved by some dexterous quarryman, who was doubtless rewarded for his labours by a high price'[2]. The National Museum of Wales has some good examples of doctored trilobites from Dudley.

Fossils from chalk deposits in Eng-

Above: An example of the 'Dudley Locust', a composite trilobite measuring 28 mm. The head is of Dalmanites myops König. The thorax and tail belong to a different trilobite, Acaste downingiae Murchison. The area round the tail has been filled in with matrix to simulate the natural limestone. Below: Another doctored trilobite, measuring 25 mm, this time consisting of only one species, Acaste downingiae Murchison. The head has been artificially added to what was a headless thorax and tail. Both these specimens are from Dudley.

'Snakestones' are the fossil remains of molluscan shells which are known as ammonites. Sometimes, as with this large specimen, heads were carved on them to make them further resemble snakes.

land have been faked for sale to museums and collectors. 'Commonly, the hoaxer mixes up a matrix of crushed chalk or lime, and some type of cement and inserts into it a Recent specimen and then offers it for sale as a perfectly preserved Cretaceous fossil with colour markings'[3]. Fossil sea urchins are among fakes of this nature and recently one was detected, in a museum collection, which had 'false teeth'. *Conulus subrotundus* Mantell, a fossil echinoid from the Turonian Middle Chalk in the south of England, is a species that, in its adult condition at any rate, does not have the 'teeth' which, in some living sea urchins, may be seen protruding through a hole at the base of the *test* or hard outer covering. In 1911, however, H.L. Hawkins described a specimen of this fossil having 'teeth' visible through the basal hole. On the basis of this discovery it was assumed that specimens of

 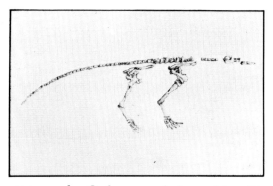

Left: Rev. Green's fossil 'mouse' skeleton from Ostend, Norfolk, fabricated from the bones of a vole and a mole. Right: A plate illustrating a 'fossil saurian' (made from the bones of a mole) from The History, Antiquities and Geology of Bacton in Norfolk *(1842) by the Rev. Charles Green. By courtesy of the British Museum (Natural History).*

this and related fossils have 'teeth' when adult. When Porter Kier came to re-examine Hawkins's specimen, however, he found that someone had excavated a cavity and inserted in it four teeth from a Recent sea urchin mixed with some cement. The quality of the preservation of the teeth proved that they were from a Recent specimen[4].

Dr. Koch's 'fossil sea-serpent' showed what can be done with a miscellaneous collection of bones, and although no other faked skeleton of comparable size has been constructed there have been other attempts, on a much smaller scale, to pass off as genuine a skeleton formed of fossilized bones of various animals. There are two or three diminutive fossil skeletons in the British Museum (Natural History), Palaeontology Department, which were acquired from the Rev. Charles Green in 1842. This gentleman collected fossils from the Pleistocene deposits along the north Norfolk coast, mainly at Bacton and Ostend. His collection included five blocks of plaster, or some other composition, in which are imbedded the articulated skeletons of certain small mammals. Only one of them, identifiable as a species of vole, comprises bones which were probably associated together naturally. The other four, skeletons of rodents, are made up from a variety of small bones.

The most elaborate of these composite skeletons has the teeth of a vole and parts of the radius appear to be those of a mole. The rest of the bones cannot be identified with certainty but it can be seen that the 'vertebrae', except those of the tail, are not vertebrae at all, the ribs are actually toe-bones, and the pelvis is composed of part of a small femur and two other unidentifiable bone fragments. On the back of the block in which this assemblage is imbedded someone has affixed a label which reads, 'A wicked deception'. It appears that these remains were passed off at one time as the skeletons of 'saurian reptiles', and that would explain the label. Whether or not the Rev. Green, by all accounts a sincere man and a good geologist, was responsible for the artefacts and the extravagant claim no-one knows, but in his book on the history, antiquities and geology of Bacton there is an illustration of a 'saurian', recognizable as a mole skeleton put together in a most unnatural manner[5]. This suggests that this man of God turned scientific dabbler may perhaps have strayed momentarily from the path of righteousness.

106

Chapter 11
The Vegetable Lamb of Tartary

In the fourteenth century Sir John Mandeville wrote an extraordinary book–in extraordinary language–about his travels 'in many diverse contreis, te se mervailes and customes of countreis, and diversiteis of folkys, and diverse shap of men and of beistis'. He says that somewhere beyond Cathay, 'there growethe a maner of Fruyt, as though it weren Gowrdes: and whan their ben rype men kutton hem ato, and men fynden with inne a lytylle Best, in Flesche, in Bon and Blode, as though it were a lytylle Lomb with outen Wolle'[1].

It would be impossible to find someone more credulous than Mandeville, and as a purveyor of tall stories about mythical creatures he is without equal (although as he wrote his book in French, based most of it on other men's narratives, and never saw it through the press he is not responsible for the peculiar orthography, the fan-

ciful illustrations or for many of the statements in the English version). But there were many other adherents to and embroiderers of the Vegetable Lamb story who did their best to out-Mandeville Mandeville.

Baron von Heberstein, writing in the middle of the sixteenth century, gives the following account in his *Rerum Muscovitarum Commentarii* (1549): 'In the neighbourhood of the Caspian Sea . . . is found a wonderful and almost incredible curiosity, of which Demetrius Danielovich, a person in high authority, gave me the following account; namely, that his father, who was once sent on an embassy by the Duke of Muscovy to the Tartar King . . . saw and remarked, amongst other things, a certain seed like that of a melon, but rather rounder and longer, from which, when it was set in the earth, grew a plant resembling a lamb, and attaining to a height of about two

Above: The Tartarian Lamb, dating from 1698 and formerly in the collection of Sir Hans Sloane. By courtesy of the British Museum (Natural History). Below: The Vegetable Lamb of Tartary, supposedly a living lamb attached by its navel to a plant stem. From an illustration published in Ashton's Curious Creatures in Zoology, *1890.*

and a half feet, and which was called in the language of the country "Borametz", or "the Little Lamb". It had a head, eyes, ears, and all the other parts of the body, as a newly-born lamb . . . an exceedingly soft wool, which was frequently used for the manufacturing of head-coverings . . . Further, he told me that this plant, if plant it should be called, had blood, but not true flesh: that, in the place of flesh, it had a substance similar to the flesh of the crab . . . It was rooted by the navel in the middle of the belly, and devoured the surrounding herbage and grass, and lived as long as that lasted; but when there was no more within its reach the stem withered, and the lamb died. It was of so excellent a flavour that it was the favourite food of wolves and other rapacious animals[2].

Of course such strange notions did not seem so absurd in those far-off days and the Vegetable Lamb was not

An impression of the fern, Cibotium barometz *Linnaeus, as it appears in nature. From an original drawing by the author.*

109

finally exposed as a half-mythical and half-botanical object until the end of the seventeenth century. In 1698, Hans Sloane, at that time Secretary of the Royal Society of London, laid before the members of the Society a curious object which had been sent to him by a Mr. Buckley from India, where it was commonly known as the 'Tartarian Lamb'. Sloane correctly identified the object (which actually came from China) as part of an arborescent fern. This fern (*Cibotium barometz* Linnaeus), in its living state, can be the size of a small tree up to 4.5 metres in height and has a woolly rhizome from which sprout upwards the long, stout stems. These stems can be trimmed a little way above the surface of the rhizome so that they simulate stiff legs and horns, the whole object then vaguely resembling a small woolly lamb. The fable was thought to be explained at last.

But this does not seem to be the whole story. There is some reason to believe that the fable arose from early travellers' accounts of the cotton plant. References in classical writings also suggest this. Herodotus wrote about trees which have fruit covered with fleece excelling that of sheep in beauty and excellence; and Theophrastus wrote of 'wool-bearing trees' which have 'gourds the size of a quince, which burst when ripe and display balls of wool'[3]. Mandeville's Vegetable Lamb could have been the cotton plant or the long-stemmed fern. A Jewish legend long pre-dating Mandeville's time tells of a creature growing from a rooted plant to which it is attached at the navel by a large stem. The creature, resembling a human in several of its features, eats all the herbage around it and kills all animals that approach within the tether of the stem. Probably the Vegetable Lamb is a composite myth in which a Chinese fern, the cotton plant, a Jewish legend and a succession of credulous commentators each play a part.

Whatever its origins the most tangible evidence of the Vegetable Lamb's existence is the rhizome and doctored stems of a Chinese fern. As the Vegetable Lamb of fact is so much less interesting than that of legend it might have been thought that both have been ignored and forgotten by the modern world. This is only partly true. The legend may have dissipated almost entirely but the material evidence of it still has a certain appeal as an item of merchandise, as much for its curious self as for its association with the legend. Probably Mr. Buckley bought his specimen or bartered for it, and he did so, no doubt, because it fascinated him for these reasons. Vegetable Lambs seem to have retained their appeal. As recently as 1955 it was reported that they were still being made in north and central Taiwan, large numbers of them being offered for sale to tourists near the temples. In these Taiwan examples eyes made of the seeds of a plant of the Vervain family are added to accentuate the animal resemblance.[4]

Chapter 12
Monster miscellany

Some of the objects which have come to light in this survey of animal fakes and frauds are so unlike any other objects or are of so heterogeneous a construction that they are difficult to classify or to discuss in previous chapters. For these reasons they are given a chapter to themselves. As may be expected most of them are composite creations, but a novel element is a fake which was exhibited alive, and the item which ends the chapter, and the book, is a masterpiece of literary spoofery.

Pygmy Bison. In 1829 someone signing himself 'V.' sent in to a natural history journal in London a 'Notice of an imposture entitled a Pygmy Bison, or American Ox'[1]. It was a very good imposture 'well calculated to deceive those little conversant with Nature'. It was said to have belonged to a Count Bournon and was owned by Mr. Murray, 'a dealer in curiosities, &c., from

Hastings, who valued it at forty guineas, as it was supposed to be unique of its kind, being but about 7 or 8 in high, and every way proportionate and symmetrical, and at the same time quite perfect in horns, coat and every other part which distinguishes the fully developed *male* Bison'.

'V.' goes on to say that as the calf of a bison would lack a mane and horns, etc. it is obviously an imposture, but may still be worth the sum demanded, as a most perfect model of an adult bison, 'and as the summit of the art of deception'. On close examination it appeared to him 'to have been grounded on a well-formed model of wood, very tightly covered, in the first instance, by the skin of a pug-dog of corresponding size, the long hair about the head, hunch, and belly being added with consummate skill from the skin of a young bear, while the horns and hoofs were formed out of the

Above: An illustration of an 'imposture entitled a Pygmy Bison or American Ox' which appeared in the Magazine of Natural History, *Vol. 2, in 1829. Below: One of the 'Roman dogs' seen by the author in 1971. It measures 8-10 centimetres long.*

black horn of the buffalo, all, however, so admirably put together, and the *tout ensemble* so elegant, as to stamp the artist as the first of his calling'.

Roman Dogs. About the middle of the nineteenth century there was a craze in Britain for miniature or 'toy' dogs. The owners of these tiny dogs seem to have been very fond of them because instead of giving them a doggy burial they often had them set up by a taxidermist. Several of these miniature mounted dogs are extant but some are more diminutive than others and are sometimes no more than 10 centimetres long.

In 1971 I was shown a case containing a pair of these very small toy dogs. The owner, who came from a village in west Wales, insisted that they were 'Roman dogs' and explained to me that they were the last representatives of a breed which lived exclusively among the ruins of that city. Both were mounted in a glass-fronted showcase along with stuffed birds, mounted butterflies and dried flowers–a very Victorian arrangement–and both were set up in life-like attitudes even though they were only 8 to 10 centimetres long, and they wore decorative paper collars.

The Horniman Museum in south London has three mounted toy dogs of comparable size, but these were received there as 'Black and tan dogs'. The British Museum (Natural History) has one which is called a 'Toy Manchester dog'. This is about ten centimetres long, was bred in 1870 and was about 13 weeks old when it died or was despatched. Dr. J. Jewell, an authority on dogs working at the British Museum, tells me that these mounted dogs are often brought into the museum and are mostly very young 'Black and tan terriers'. The 'Roman dogs' she thinks could be spaniel pups. Obviously such tiny dogs could not have been old enough to be treated as pets and were probably marketed, ready-mounted, as curiosities. Even the house-sparrow mounted in the case with the 'Roman dogs' is partly bogus, its breast plumage being adulterated with canary feathers.

Winged Cat. In the early 1960's an information sheet was distributed from an address off New Bond Street, London, advertising 'The Famous Winged Cat'. This cat, it said, was preserved in a glass-fronted case, was named 'Thomas Bessy' because its sex was unknown, and had wings appearing from each of its sides. Apparently the wings started to grow when the cat was very young. A circus owner saw it and arranged for it to be removed, and

the animal's master tried to claim it back having heard that it was being exhibited for commercial gain. The circus owner maintained that it was his but the resulting lawsuit, which took place some time during the nineteenth century, established the right of the cat's original owner. The circus owner packed Thomas Bessy off in a box with some food but it was dead on arrival, the result, it is said, of its food being poisoned. The distressed owner of the cat arranged for its preservation, and that is how it came to be stuffed and enclosed in a mahogany and glass case.

According to the information sheet the case with its winged occupant inside had been lying around in an attic ever since Thomas Bessy's master died 'and there it still remains awaiting an enterprising purchaser'. It also said that 'various newspaper articles highlighting the extraordinary trial are available'. I was quite prepared to be the enterprising purchaser of such a remarkable prodigy of nature but my enthusiastic letter was never answered and Thomas Bessy, for all I know, is still gathering dust in an attic.

The Cambridge Centaur. I have not been lucky enough to fall in with an authentic example of the half-human, half-equine centaur of the ancient Greeks, but I have some information on the skeleton of a near cousin of it. Mr. Geoffrey Hopkins of the Sub-Department of Veterinary Anatomy at the University of Cambridge has intimate knowledge of a so-called centaur skeleton which serves as the mascot for the Cambridge University Veterinary Society.

The Cambridge Centaur is rather small as centaurs go, being only 60 centimetres long and 60 centimetres high, and it is not easy to accept the upper half as human or the lower as

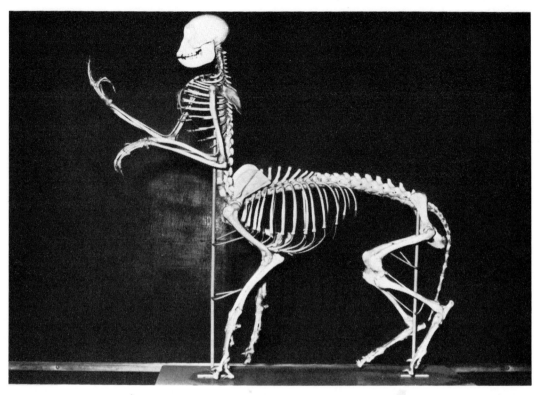

The Cambridge Centaur. By courtesy of the Cambridge University Veterinary Society.

horse (although the gesture of the upraised forearm has a decidedly human connotation). But this is not surprising as its upper half is made from the upper half of a macaque monkey, the lower half being the skeleton of a small dog minus its head. There can be no doubt about the truth of these statements because Mr. Hopkins tells me that he constructed the Cambridge Centaur himself in 1962.

The Jackalope. In the last few years visitors to Yellowstone National Park, Wyoming, and perhaps other parts of North America, have bought and distributed postcards displaying a photograph of a Jackalope. The card I have seen describes this creature as a 'nearly extinct antlered species of rabbit' and says it is found 'almost exclusively on the high plains of Wyoming'. Miss Daphne Hills of the Mammal Section in the British Museum (Natural History) tells me (*in litt.* 6.x.1975) that 'the name Jackalope is certainly an American invention, a combination of Jackrabbit (*Lepus* sp.), a kind of hare, and Antelope (the pronghorn) and these are the two animals most frequently used'. She also tells me that a Frenchwoman wrote to her recently about a Scottish specimen in a shop window at Braemar. Miss Hills thinks this was probably a hare with deer antlers attached.

But it seems as though neither the Scots nor–apart from the name–the Americans invented the Jackalope. Henry Tegner discovered that it probably originated in Central Europe many years ago. Commenting on a

114

Jackalope exhibited in a small Canadian town recently (it was a 'horned cotton-tailed rabbit' as far as he was concerned) he mentioned a discovery he had made in one of the Seine-side open-air bookstalls in Paris. There he found a series of old German prints 'beautifully painted by an artist called Haid and dated 1794'. The series included pictures of a number of antlered hares. 'The antlers of these non-existent creatures,' he says, 'appeared to resemble those of immature roebucks'[2]. Whether or not the Scottish and American Jackalopes have connections with these German examples I have not been able to discover.

The Fur-bearing Trout. Some years ago a lady brought to the Royal Scottish Museum in Edinburgh a trout covered with a fine coat of white fur. It was pleasingly mounted on a wooden shield and was labelled as follows:

FUR BEARING TROUT
Very Rare

Caught while trolling in lake Superior off Gros Cap, near Sault Ste. Marie, district of Algoma. It is believed that the great depth and the extreme penetrating coldness of the water in which these fish live has caused them to grow their dense coat of (usually) white fur. Mounted by ROSS C. JOBE, Taxidermist of Sault Ste. Marie Ont.

Visiting the museum to find out more about her unique fish, the lady was told that it was undoubtedly a trout (either brown or brook) and that its fine white coat was undoubtedly from a rabbit, whereupon she immediately presented the fish to the museum. She had bought this fake in good faith which indicates that the *idea* of a fur-bearing trout did not seem outlandish to her.

The jackalope is reputed to be an antlered species of rabbit which is nearly extinct. It is found on the plains of Wyoming and can mimic human sounds.

Night Lizard and Snake. When J.F. Gray referred to the hand-painted longhorn beetles received at the British Museum from China, he said that, at the same time, some reptiles had been received 'on which the Chinese collectors had been exercising their ingenuity in hopes of adding to their value'[3]. These included 'a stuffed specimen of a Night Lizard (*Geeko reevesi*) which had a square tuft of hair from some mammal stuck on the back of its neck'. There was also a snake 'which had the claw of a mammal surrounded with fur inserted on each side of its neck just behind the head, so as to make it appear as if it had rudimentary feet armed with large claws'. Speaking of the whole consignment, Gray commented: 'I may add that the work was so coarsely executed as to be discov-

115

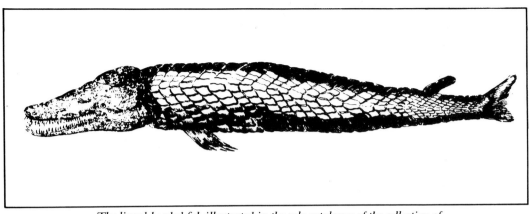

The lizard-headed fish illustrated in the sale catalogue of the collection of the Comte de la Tour d'Auvergne in 1784. By courtesy of the British Museum (Natural History).

ered on the most cursory examination of the specimens, and could only have been intended to deceive the most ignorant collectors'.

Lizard-headed Fish. Only a most ignorant collector could have been fooled by Lot 2132 at the sale of the collection of the Comte de la Tour d'Auvergne which took place at Paris in 1784. The entry in the sale-catalogue for Lot 2132 reads (my translation): 'An uncommon Lizard-headed Fish, named the Mississippi Pike, or the Armoured Snout; it has something of the form of an eel, covered with transverse bands of quadrangular, very thick scales: its head like that of the Sturgeon ends in a very elongated muzzle or snout, the jaw of which is embellished with teeth. It is four and a quarter feet long'[4]. The accompanying illustration shows that the Mississippi Pike has the body of a fish, most likely that of a sturgeon, and the head of a baby alligator. For the privilege of owning this unique creature Monsieur Gaillard paid six francs.

The Sea Spider. In J.C. Loudon's *Magazine of natural history* for 1829 there was published a letter from 'M.C.G.' about a strange creature, said to have been caught in a fishing net near Margate, which had since been exhibited under the name of a 'Tarantula Sea Spider'[5]. It resembled a spider in many respects but in others differed materially from one, its eight legs, for instance, resembling the tentacles of a cuttle-fish. 'It has but two eyes', says M.C.G., 'which, when alive, were green, and are placed on the back of the thorax. It has no head, and is destitute of palpi. The mouth is beneath the abdomen, and inside of it is a spiral tongue nearly half a yard long, the extremity of which is armed with a pair of forceps. The *spinner* is very large, out of which the exhibitor took a web, but unluckily had thrown it away ... The colour of the insect is that of a pickled tongue, which, probably, may be accounted for by the pickle that had been used to preserve it, namely, of bark, alum, and salt. You may form some idea of its size when I add, it weighed $5\frac{1}{4}$ lbs. Many wonderful stories are told of it when alive; such as that it ran with the velocity of a race horse, and changed colour every instant. The form of it is oval, and the abdomen terminates with a horny spike, nearly 3 in. in length, which,

116

when alive, was invisible. Mr. Murray, the owner of it, intends to exhibit it in London, in about a month, and he may be heard of at the Bazaar in Portman Street North. Pray what is it?'

Whatever it was it must surely have been grotesque to look at and no other specimen like it has ever been reported. But one Sea Spider was one too many for the watchful 'V.', the same gentleman who reported on the Pygmy Bison (see p. 112) which, curiously enough, had also been owned by Mr. Murray. He speedily wrote to Mr. Loudon. 'Had you inserted my article on the Pygmy Bison four months ago,' he said, 'you might have saved many individuals the mortification of being humbugged by another attempt of the same individual to appropriate some of their cash to his own use, by such unfair means as the exhibition of his *Tarantula*, or Sea Spider'.[6] Mr. Murray had a good eye for monsters but, unfortunately for him, so did 'V.'

Buckland's Nondescript. Frank Buckland came across several man-made monsters through his contacts with dealers in antiques and curiosities in London and elsewhere. One or two, including specimens of the mermaid, came into his possession, but he never acquired anything stranger than his 'Nondescript' (a totally different kind of artefact to Waterton's of the same name). Buckland bought it from a 'china curiosity-dealer' in Leicester Square who, in his turn, had bought it at a sale from an old gentleman who prized it highly and who in his lifetime valued it at £100. It was about as big as a three-months-old baby but was far from human in appearance.

Buckland describes this monstrosity in some detail: 'He has wings on the top of his shoulder like the old army aigulettes, and there are claws on the tips and on the extreme ends of each wing: these wings are so artfully contrived that one would believe they could be opened out and unfurled like a bat's wing at any moment the creature that carried it wished to take a fly either for business or amusement. The arms are amazingly human-like, and look as though the dried skin had shrunk fast on to the bone; the legs also represent a similar appearance. The hands and feet are demon-like, and of a long, scraggy, merciless appearance, and each finger and toe is armed with a formidable-looking claw. The ribs project frightfully, as though the nondescript had lately been in reduced circumstances, and had been living for some time *à la malcontent*. The head is about as big as a very large apple. The ears project outward and downward, like those of an African elephant. The face is wrinkled and deformed; the nose like a pig's snout; the eyes like those of a codfish'. He added that the teeth were just like those in a mermaid he had seen elsewhere in London–double rows in each jaw, with protruding fangs in front–and its hideous countenance was surmounted by a 'rough shock of fine wool-like hair'.

'Before this specimen came into my possession', Buckland continues, 'I was unable to examine it closely, as it was considered too valuable to be taken out from under the glass case. The moment, however, it came into my hands, I set to work to find out its composition. Everybody said there must be bones in the arms and legs and ribs. I soon tested this with a surgical exploring needle, but found no bone, nor anything like a bone, but simply soft wood, probably cedar. I made several incisions in the Nondescript's body, and found that the main portion of his composition was (like the legs) a

Frank Buckland's Nondescript, from an illustration in his Curiosities of Natural History, *1875.*

light wood. The skin, as well as the wings, are made of a species of papier-mâché, most artfully put on in wrinkles, and admirably coloured and shaded to give the appearance of the dried body of some creature that had once existed either on land or sea –had been slain–and then preserved as a curiosity[7]. The illustration accompanying Buckland's description shows what a truly nightmarish object his Nondescript was. Against it even the mermaids he had seen must have looked glamorous.

The White-Russian Shore-muddler.
This is the English name of a remarkable animal confection which was put together recently, at the instigation of the Director of Göteborg Museum, for the express purpose of increasing the attendance at his museum. The 'Vit-rysk Strandmuddlare', to give it its Swedish name, was made in 1960 and is exhibited on April 1st each year, to the great delight and amusement of the public. The head and most of the fore-parts are from a baby wild pig (although the 'tusks' are from an alligator and the eyes resemble those of a predatory bird), the tail and rear parts belong to a squirrel and the hind feet are from a water fowl. These dissimilar constituents are made up very neatly indeed, and the Director, Dr. Bengt Hubendick, tells me (*in litt.* 25.i.1968) that the museum has benefited considerably from the annual display of its strangest inmate. The scientific name, *Lirpa lirpa* Münchausen, should be taken as seriously as 'Zscicvzoskaija', the locality it is supposed to have come from.

The Pig-Faced Lady.
Throughout this book I have purposely left out human freaks, countless bizarre examples of which have been recorded. And the nature of my subject matter, it is reasonable to assume, would preclude any mention of living creatures. But the Pig-faced Lady, though exhibited alive and addressed as 'Miss Stevens', was not a human freak but an animal fake. Consequently it has a claim to be included here.

It was in 1829 or thereabouts that the Pig-faced Lady was first noticed, a small note in the *Magazine of natural history* for that year telling of a 'female bear, shaven and dressed as a woman', which was exhibited in a caravan somewhere in London 'as a monstrosity of the human species from the deserts of Arabia. The animal is placed in an armchair'[8]. Much fuller details were given many years later in the autobiography of the circus showman 'Lord' George Sanger who, as a small boy, saw the Pig-faced Lady exhibited, almost for the last time, in a booth at the great Hyde Park Fair which took place on the occasion of Queen Victoria's coronation. 'Madame Stevens was really a fine brown bear', says Sanger, 'the paws and face of which were kept closely shaved, the white skin under the fur having a close resemblance to that of a human being. Over the paws were fitted white gloves, with well-stuffed fingers, so that the pig-faced lady seemed to have nice plump white arms above them.

'The bear was strapped in a chair at the back of the caravan, clothed in female dress, shawl, cap, the poke bonnet of the time, etc. In front was a table at which the seeming lady sat, her paws being laid upon it, and all the rest of the body from the arms of the chair downwards hidden by drapery. Under the table was concealed a boy with a short stick to make the pig-faced lady talk. When all was ready, and the booth full of spectators, the showman would commence his patter thus, as he pulled aside the curtains: "I call your attention, ladies and gentlemen, to the greatest wonder of the world! Behold and marvel! Madame Stevens, the pig-faced lady, who is now in her eighteenth year. I believe that is correct, Miss?" (Here the hidden boy would prod the bear, who gave a grunt.) "As you see, ladies and gentlemen, the young lady understands what is said perfectly, though the peculiar formation of her jaws has deprived her of the power of uttering human speech in return".'

After a series of questions, all of which were answered by grunts, a plate was passed around for contributions. Miss Stevens expressed her pleasure at receiving these gifts by giving a loud growl, the boy with the stick having prodded her harder than usual. 'This show and others of its class', says Sanger, 'were stopped by the authorities at the following Camberwell fair, and the pig-faced lady became only a memory, lots of people, to their dying day, believing that such a person really existed'[9].

The Snouters. I have saved till last the story of the Snouters and would willingly have excluded them from this book, not because they are not suitable but because they are supremely so. It is only because the joke is already out that I am prepared to talk about the Snouters now, and I do so very reluctantly.

In 1957 a small book was published in Germany under the title *Bau und Leben der Rhinogradentia*, the work of one Harald Stümpke[10]. Even if one could not read German it was obvious from the exquisite illustrations, by Gerolf Steiner, that this was no ordinary book and the creatures it dealt with no ordinary creatures. Snouters, or Rhinogrades, are the members of an order of mammals, previously unknown to science, which inhabited the Hy-yi-yi Islands in the Pacific Ocean, an archipelago which remained undiscovered until 1941 when a Swede escaping from the Japanese was wrecked on Hiduddify, the largest of the islands. I say 'inhabited' because the Snouters no longer exist, the whole archipelago having sunk beneath the sea because of tectonic disturbances set up by a secret atomic explosion. Fortunately, before this catastrophe took place, Harald Stümpke had visited the islands and had prepared an account of the structure and habits of the Snouters he had studied there. Unfortunately he had returned to the islands to undertake further studies on them and was there when the archipelago vanished into the sea. Nothing more was heard of him, and he would now

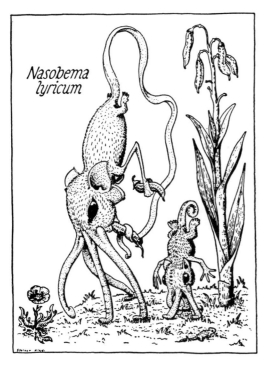

The Great Morgenstern's-Nasobame, Nasobema lyricum. *This snouter has four equal snouts on which it walks.*

The Greyish-Golden Honeytail Snouter, Dulcicauda griseaurella. *Glands on the tail secrete a fruity, sticky juice to attract its insect prey.*

have been forgotten entirely had he not left behind his manuscript account of the Snouters. By the greatest good fortune he had been able to supply the artist with specimens so that the book, when it finally appeared, was well illustrated. For some strange reason, however, Stümpke took the illustrated material back to the islands with him so that this too went under the sea.

In appearance the Snouters are characterised by their generally small size and the extraordinary development of their nasal region. In some of the more primitive species the 'nasarium', as it is called technically, is single, well developed and either flexible or fixed to a substrate so that the creature lives head downwards and kicks its legs in the air. In the more advanced Snouters the nasarium is wonderfully developed and may, as in *Nasobema lyricum* (the Hónatata of the natives of Hi-yi-yi), be used for locomotion. Stümpke points out that the presence of four fairly long snouts of equal size on a short, fat head is a typical polyrrhine condition. He also says that a polyrrhine Snouter is able to walk on its nasarium because the snouts are rendered quite rigid by the strong turgor of its *corpora spongiosa* and because highly branched air passages ramify through them the filling of which is regulated by the *ampullae choanales.*

This shows you what a lot Stümpke knew about zoology, physiology and Snouters. But even he must have been bewildered by the Miraculous Flower-faced Snouter (*Corbulonasus longicauda*) which congregated in flowery meadows on one of the islands. Instead of walking on its nasarium it was fixed in the ground by its very long, vertical tail, its short and broad, petal-like

The Miraculous Flower-faced Snouter, Cor-bulonasus longicauda. Each one has a petal-like snout which emits a fragrance to attract insects.

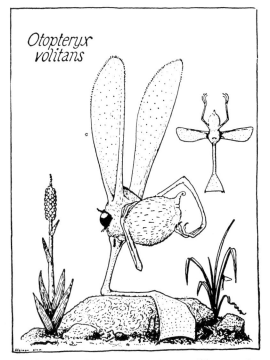

The Earwing, Otopteryx volitans. This snouter uses its muscular ears to produce rapid backward flight, steering with its well-developed autonasium.

snouts being set close about the mouth where they were employed as traps for unwary insects. Unlike other Snouters they emitted strong oral fragrances which also helped to attract insects. Because these Snouters were fixed to one spot they were able to mate only when it was windy, the desirous males taking firm hold of the females when they came into contact with each other.

All this and much more of the same kind of stuff, brilliantly worked out and, so I am led to believe, convincing enough to have fooled one or two reviewers, had sufficient appeal to ensure that Stümpke's book was translated into French and then into English. It was not until the English version came out, however, that readers could see at a glance what the Snouters were, or rather, what they were not. On the dust jacket appeared extracts from reviews which had

appeared in the American Press. The *Hartford Courant,* among others, had let the cat out of the bag. It said: 'You cannot extinguish the snouters . . . They have already migrated . . . from the land of Spoof into the safe and lasting land of Affection. You're not dealing with lemmings here, you know. Tiny characters with faces like flowers that stand on their tails most of their lives, or fly about with a whisk of their ears, or use their miraculous noses for locomotion, are far too delightful to be allowed to vanish'. How much better if the reviewer had written in the spirit of the reviewed! But it would have taken a Harald Stümpke (alias Gerolf Steiner, zoology professor at the University of Heidelberg) to see that. Here, perhaps, is the beauty and the tragedy of even the best hoaxes: they're fun while they last —but they can't last long.

References

Chapter 1

The following books, containing illustrated accounts of mythical creatures or information on their place in ancient mythologies, have been consulted for this chapter.

1 E.&J.Lehner. *A Fantastic Bestiary* (1969).
2 J.Ashton. *Curious Creatures in Zoology* (1890).
3 C.Clair. *Unnatural History* (1968).
4 F.Guirand (ed.). *Larousse Encyclopedia of Mythology* (1962).

Chapter 2

1 R.Carrington. *Mermaids and Mastodons* (1957), p.62.
2 G.P.Whitley. Jenny hanivers. *Australian Magazine*, vol.3 (1928), pp.262-4.
3 E.W.Gudger. Jenny hanivers, dragons and basilisks in the old natural history books and in modern times. *Scientific Monthly* (for June 1934), pp.511-23.
4 W.Ley. *The Lungfish, the Dodo, & the Unicorn* (1952), p.67.
5 W.Ley, *ibid.*, pp.61-3.
6 C.Gesner. *Historia Animalium. Pars 4. De piscium & aquatilium natura* (1558), p.945. Translation as published by Gudger (1934).
7 F.M.Misson. *A New Voyage to Italy* (1699), vol.1, pp.134-5.
8 P.Belon. *De Aquatilibus. Libri duo* (1553), p.97. See also Gudger (1934, p.515)
9 U.Aldrovandi. *De Piscibus. Libri V* (1613), p.437.
10 E.W.Gudger, *ibid.*, p.517.
11 J.H.Lochner von Hummelstein. *Rariora musei Besleriani* (1716), pl.15.
12 H.L.Duhamel du Monceau. *Traité général des pesches* (1769-82), vol.3, sect.ix, pl.7, fig.2.
13 P.Buonanni. *Museum Kircherianum* (1709).
14 J.Tradescant. *Museum Tradescantianum* (1656), p.6.
15 R.Blunt. *The Lure of Old Chelsea* (1922), p.124.
16 G.Humphrey. *Museum Calonnianum* (1797), p.71, item 1293.
17 E.Donovan. Footnote to article on *Simia satyrus* and plate 57 in: *Naturalist's Repository*, vol.2 (1824).
18 F.Buckland. *Curiosities of Natural History. Second series* (1877), p.227.
19 J. ter Pelkwijk. De basilisk. *Toeristen Kampionen* (for 2 March 1940). I have not seen this article. Peter van der Feen of Domburg, Holland, gave me the reference in 1968 and translated part of it for my use. I have slightly edited the translation without altering its sense.

Chapter 3

1 E.H.Blakeney. *A Smaller Classical Dictionary* (1920), p.253.
2 F.W.Lane. *Kingdom of the Octopus* (1957), p.181.

3 F.D.Klingender. St. Francis and the birds of the Apocalypse. *Journal of the Warburg and Courtauld Institute*, vol.16 (1953), pp.13-23, 5 pls. Plate 3b shows a picture in a 13th-century manuscript in Trinity College, Cambridge, of the so-called Hydra of the Apocalypse.
4 C.Gesner. *Nomenclator Aquatilium Animantium. Icones animalium* (1560), p.362.
5 E.Topsell. *Historie of Foure-footed Beastes* (1607), p.202.
6 E.S. de Beer (ed.). *The Diary of John Evelyn* (1955), vol.2, p.391.
7 W.J.Broderip. *Zoological Recreations*, 4th edition (1860), p.371.
8 A.Seba. *Locupletissimum rerum naturalium thesauri accurata descriptio, etc.*, vol.1 (1734), pp.158-9, pl.110, fig.1.
9 E.L.Pontopiddan. *The Natural History of Norway*. English translation (from the Danish edition of 1752-3), (1755), pp. 37-8.
10 B.D.Jackson. *Linnaeus* (1923), pp.138-9.

Chapter 4

1 This quotation, as well as the rest of the information concerning Oannes and his female counterpart, Atergatis, is taken from the excellent book by G.Benwell & A.Waugh, *Sea Enchantress: the Tale of the Mermaid and her Kin* (1961), chapter 2.
2 P.H.Gosse. *The Romance of Natural History. Second Series.* (1861), p.127 (quoting W.Swainson's *A Treatise on the Geography and Classification of Animals* (1835), p.249.
3 'Conchilla' (i.e. J.G.Johnston). The tests by which a real mermaid may be discovered. *Annals and Magazine of Natural History*, vol.1 (1829), pp.106-8.
4 Quoted in G.Benwell &A.Waugh, *ibid.*, p.95.
5 Benwell & Waugh, *ibid.*, p.117.
6 Benwell & Waugh, *ibid.*, p.119-20.
7 Benwell & Waugh, *ibid.*, p.88.
8 F.E.Hulme. *Natural History Lore and Legend* (1895), p.90.
9 J.Nichols. *Literary Anecdotes of the 18th Century* (1812), vol.5, p.487.
10 Benwell & Waugh, *ibid.*, p.123.
11 Benwell & Waugh, *ibid.*, p.123.
12 A copy of this handbill is in the Guildhall Library Print Room, London.
13 Benwell & Waugh, *ibid.*, p.124.
14 Benwell & Waugh, *ibid.*, p.124.
15 Anon. Mermaids. *Magazine of Natural History* (1830), vol.3, p.188.
16 J.Murray. Mermaid. *Magazine of Natural History* (1830), vol.3, p.447.
17 C.J.S.Thompson. *The Mystery and Lore of Monsters* (1930), pp.111-12.
18 C.J.S.Thompson, *ibid.*, pp.112-14.
19 E.Donovan. *Naturalist's Repository* (1824), vol.2, article on *Simia satyrus*, Rufous Orang Outang, or Wild Man of the Woods. Unpaginated text to Plate LVII.

20 Thompson, *ibid.*, pp.114-15.
21 Benwell & Waugh, *ibid.*, pp.124-5.
22 Benwell & Waugh, *ibid.*, p.125.
23 P.T.Barnum. *The Life of P.T.Barnum Written by Himself* (1855), pp.231-42.
24 F.T.Buckland. *Curiosities of Natural History. Fourth Series.* (1875), pp.134-7.
25 J.Hutchins. *Discovering Mermaids and Sea Monsters* (1968), p.31. This publication includes a photo showing the external appearance of the mermaid compared with an X-ray photo of the same object.

Chapter 5

1 C.Gould. *Mythical Monsters* (1886), pp.202-4.
2 C.Gould, *ibid.*, p.233.
3 Quoted in E.Donovan. *Rees's Cyclopedia* (1819), vol. 12, article 'Draco' (unpaginated).
4 *Gentleman's Magazine*, vol.19 (for 1749), p.506, and fig.C on illustrative plate.
5 E.Donovan, *ibid.*, article 'Draco' (unpaginated).
6 A copy of this handbill is in the National Museum of Wales, Cardiff. It is dated Sept. 13th, 1861.
7 A.C.Oudemans. *The Great Sea-serpent* (1892), pp.30-4.

Chapter 6

1 *The Travels of Marco Polo*, translated from the text of L.F.Benedetto by A.Ricci (1931), pp.283-4.
2 Details of the baby orang pendek examined in 1932 are in K.W.Dammerman. Die nieuw ontdekte Orang Pendek. *De tropische Natuur*, vol. 21, pp.123-31 (1932). Further details of the orang pendek are given by B.Heuvelmans. *On the Track of Unknown Animals* (1962), pp.108-26.
3 E.W.Gudger. Jenny hanivers, dragons and basilisks in the old natural history books and in modern times. *Scientific Monthly*, June 1934, p.512.
4 C.Waterton. *Wanderings in South America* (2nd edition) (1828), pp.306-7.
5 J.S.Menteath. *Magazine of Natural History*, vol.6, p.283 (1833).
6 C.Waterton. The Nondescript. *Magazine of Natural History*, vol.6, p.381-3 (1833).
7 Quoted in R.Aldington. *The Strange Life of Charles Waterton 1782-1865* (1949), p.113.
8 R.Aldington. *ibid.*, p.114.
9 Quoted in P.Gosse. *The Squire of Walton Hall* (1940), p.138.
10 B.Heuvelmans, *ibid.*, pp.127-82.
11 J.Napier. *Bigfoot* (1972), p.56.
12 J.S.Weiner. *The Piltdown Forgery* (1955).
13 S.Cole. *Counterfeit* (1955), chapters 10 and 11. I have tried to distil and interweave the accounts of the Piltdown hoax given by Weiner and Cole and have added very little to them. The unravelling of the case was much more complex than my abbreviated version suggests.

Chapter 7

1 C.Clair. *Unnatural History* (1968), p.118.

2 G.R.Gray. Remarks on a specimen of kingfisher, supposed to form a new species of the *Tanysiptera*. *Annals and Magazine of Natural History*, vol.6, pp.237-8 (1841).
3 G.R.Gray, *ibid.*
4 R.B.Sharpe. *Catalogue of . . . Birds in the . . . British Museum* vol.4, p.91 (1879).
5 R.B.Sharpe. Notes on some birds from Perak. *Proceedings of the Zoological Society of London* (for 1886), pp.350-4 (1886).
6 R.Aldington. *The Strange Life of Charles Waterton* (1949), p.131.
7 F.T.Buckland. *Log-book of a Fisherman and Zoologist* (c.1875), p.131.
8 F.T.Buckland, *ibid.*, pp.25-7.
9 M.F.Meiklejohn. Notes on the Hoodwink (*Dissimulatrix spuria*). *Bird Notes*, vol.24, pp. 89-92 (1950).
10 R.L. Spotting the Siggahfoops. *Scottish Field*, vol. 115, p.18 (1968).
11 D.Lack. An undiscovered species of swift. *Bird Notes*, vol.30, pp.258-60 (1963).
12 A.C.Fotheringham. *Eoörnis pterovelox gobiensis* (1928).
13 F.A.Goodliffe. Dog-collared Sombre Blackbird (*Clericus polydenominata*). *Bokmakierie*, vol.15, p.9 (1963).
14 M.A.Traylor. The nomenclatural standing of *Clericus polydenominata* (1967).

Chapter 8

1 M.S.Merian. *Metamorphosis Insectorum Surinamensium*, 2nd edn (1730), pl.49.
2 E.G.Allingham. *A Romance of the Rostrum* (1924), p.138.
3 J.M.Chalmers-Hunt. Faked insects. *Entomologist's Record & Journal of Variation*, vol.87, p.231 (1975).
4 E.B.Ford. *Butterflies* (1945), p.56. See also the illustrations at the bottom of pl.40. Each of the two butterflies illustrated is marked on the wings with dots of cellulose paint to facilitate studies in connection with population estimates.
5 M.A.Lane & A.Watson. A revision of the genus *Stenognatha* Felder (Lepidoptera: Arctiidae: Pericopinae). *Journal of Natural History*, vol.9, pp.107-17 (1975).
6 J.E.Gray. On a new genus of the Mytilidae, and on some distorted forms which occur among bivalve shells. *Proceedings of the Zoological Society of London* for 1858, pp.90-2 (1858).
7 S.P.Dance. *Shell Collecting: an Illustrated History* (1966), p.83.
8 S.P.Dance, *ibid.*, p.81.
9 S.P.Dance. *Rare Shells* (1969), p.87.
10 S.P.Dance. *Shells and Shell Collecting* (1972), p.87.

Chapter 9

1 M.E.Jahn & D.J.Woolf. *The Lying Stones of Dr. Johann Bartholomew Adam Beringer being his Lithographiae Wirceburgensis* (1963), p.71. My information on Beringer and the lying stones is nearly all taken from this work.
2 Jahn & Woolf, *ibid.*, p.128.
3 Jahn & Woolf, *ibid.*, p.137.
4 M.E.Jahn. A further note on Dr. Johann

Bartholomew Adam Beringer. *Journal of the Society for the Bibliography of Natural History*, vol.4 (1963), p.160-1.

5 Most of them are in the Institute of Mineralogy and Geology at Würzburg, but there are some in the University of Bonn, two in the University Museum at Oxford, and there may be some elsewhere. For further information see J.M. Edmonds & H.P.Powell. Beringer 'Lügensteine' at Oxford. *Proceedings of the Geologists' Association*, vol.85, pp.549-54 (1974).

Chapter 10

1 M.G.Bassett. 'Formed stones', folklore and fossils. *Amgueddfa*, No.7, pp.2-17 (1971).
2 R.M.Owens. In search of Welsh trilobites. *Amgueddfa*, No.9, pp.24-37 (1971).
3 P.M.Kier. A Cretaceous echinoid with false teeth. *Palaeontology*, vol.12, pp.488-93, pls.93, 94.
4 P.M.Kier, *ibid.*
5 C.Green. *The History, Antiquities, and Geology of Bacton, in Norfolk* (1842), unnumbered plate opposite p.66.

Chapter 11

1 Quoted in A.W.Exell. Barometz: the Vegetable Lamb of Scythia. *Natural History Magazine*, vol.3, pp.194-200 (1932).
2 Quoted in A.W.Exell, *ibid.*

3 Quoted in A.W.Exell, *ibid.*
4 A.F.Tryon. The Vegetable Lamb of Tartary. *Missouri Botanical Garden Bulletin*, vol.43, pp.25-8 (1955).

Chapter 12

1 'V.'. Notice of an imposture entitled a Pygmy Bison, or American Ox. *Magazine of Natural History*, vol.2, pp.218-19 (1829).
2 H.Tegner. Man made the unicorn. *The Countryman*, Summer 1975 issue, pp.182-4.
3 J.E.Gray. On a new genus of the Mytilidae, and on some distorted forms which occur among bivalve shells. *Proceedings of the Zoological Society of London* (for 1858), pp.90-2 (1858).
4 J.G. de Favanne. *Catalogue systématique . . . du magnifique cabinet . . . C[omte] de [la Tour d'Auvergne]* (1784), p.476 and pl.9, bottom fig.
5 M.C.G. A sea spider. *Magazine of Natural History*, vol.2, p.211 (1829).
6 'V.'. The Pygmy Bison. *Magazine of Natural History*, vol.2, p.301 (1829).
7 F.T.Buckland. *Curiosities of Natural History, Fourth Series* (1875), pp.140-2.
8 J.R.Zoological imposture. *Magazine of Natural History*, vol.1, p.189 (1829).
9 'Lord' George Sanger. *Seventy Years a Showman* (1927), pp.115-17.
10 H.Stümpke. *Bau und Leben der Rhinogradentia* (1957) (French translation 1962; English translation 1967).

Photocredits

Bibliography

Aldington, R. 1949. *The Strange Life of Charles Waterton 1782-1865.* Evans Brothers Ltd. London.

Aldrovandi, U. 1613. *De Piscibus. Libri V.* Bononiae.

Allingham, E.G. 1924. *A Romance of the Rostrum.* H.F.&G.Witherby. London.

Anon. 1830. Mermaids. *Magazine of Natural History*, vol.3, p.188.

Ashton, J. 1890. *Curious Creatures in Zoology.* John C.Nimmo. London.

Barnum, P.T. 1855. *The Life of P.T.Barnum Written by Himself.* Redfield. New York.

Bassett, M.G. 1971. 'Formed stones', folklore and fossils. *Amgueddfa*, No.7, pp.2-17.

Beer, E.S. de (ed.). 1955. *The Diary of John Evelyn.* 6 vols. Clarendon Press. Oxford.

Belon, P. 1553. *De Aquatilibus. Libri duo.* Paris.

Benwell, G. & Waugh, A. 1961. *Sea Enchantress; the Tale of the Mermaid and her Kin.* Hutchinson & Co. Ltd. London.

Blakeney, E.H. 1920. *A Smaller Classical Dictionary.* 4th edn. J.M.Dent & Sons Ltd. London.

Blunt, R. 1922. *The Lure of Old Chelsea.* Mills & Boon Ltd. London.

Broderip, W.J. 1860. *Zoological Recreations.* 4th edn. Richard Griffin & Co. London & Glasgow.

Buckland, F.T. c.1875. *Log-book of a Fisherman and Zoologist.* Chapman & Hall. London. 1875-77. *Curiosities of Natural History.* 4 vols. Richard Bentley & Son. London. There were numerous issues of this popular book and Buckland added new material from time to time. The following issues are referred to in this work: Series I (1877); Series II (1877); Series III (1875); Series IV (1875).

Buonanni, P. 1709. *Museum Kircherianum.* Rome.

Carrington, R. 1957. *Mermaids and Mastodons.* Chatto & Windus. London.

Clair, C. 1968. *Unnatural History.* Abelard-Schuman. London, New York & Toronto.

Cole, S. 1955. *Counterfeit.* John Murray. London.

'Conchilla' (i.e. J.G.Johnston). 1829. The tests by which a real mermaid may be discovered. *Annals and Magazine of Natural History*, vol.1, pp.106-8.

Dammerman, K.W. 1932. Die nieuw ontdekte Orang Pendek. *De tropische natuur*, vol.21, pp.123-31.

Dance, S.P. 1966. *Shell Collecting: an Illustrated History.* Faber & Faber. London. 1969. *Rare Shells.* Faber & Faber. London. 1972. *Shells and Shell Collecting.* Paul Hamlyn. London.

Donovan, E. 1819. Article 'Draco' in: *Rees's Cyclopedia*, vol.12. 1823-34. *Naturalist's Repository.* 5 vols. London.

Duhamel du Monceau, H.L. (& La Marre, L.H.). 1769-82. *Traité général des pesches, et histoire de poissons qu'elles fournissent.* 4 vols. Paris.

Edmonds, J.M. & Powell, H.P. 1974. Beringer 'Lügensteine' at Oxford. *Proceedings of the Geologist's Association*, vol.85, pp.549-54.

Exell, A.W. 1932. Barometz: the Vegetable Lamb of Scythia. *Natural History Magazine*, vol.3, pp.194-200.

Favanne, J.G. de. 1784. *Catalogue systématique et raisonné, ou description du magnifique cabinet appartenant ci-devant á M. le C[omte] de [la Tour d'Auvergne].* Paris.

Ford, E.B. 1945. *Butterflies.* Collins (New Naturalist). London.

Fotheringham, A.C. *Eoörnis pterovelox gobiensis.* The Buighleigh Press (privately published). London.

Gesner, C. 1558. *Historia Animalium. Pars 4. De piscium & aquatilium animantium natura.* Tiguri. 1560. *Nomenclator aquatilium animantium. Icones animalium.* Tiguri.

Goodliffe, F.A. 1963. Dog-collared Sombre Blackbird *(Clericus polydenominata).* Bokmakierie, vol.15, p.9.

Gosse, P. 1940. *The Squire of Walton Hall, the Life of Charles Waterton.* Cassell. London.

Gosse, P.H. 1861. *The Romance of Natural History. Second Series.* James Nisbet & Co. London.

Gould, C. 1886. *Mythical monsters.* W.H.Allen. London.

Gray, G.R. 1841. Remarks on a specimen of kingfisher, supposed to form a new species of the *Tanysiptera. Annals and Magazine of Natural History*, vol.6, pp.237-8.

Gray, J.E. 1858. On a new genus of the Mytilidae, and on some distorted forms which occur among bivalve shells. *Proceedings of the Zoological Society of London* (for 1858), pp.90-2.

Green, C. 1842. *The History, Antiquities, and Geology of Bacton, in Norfolk.* Norwich.

Gudger, E.W. 1934. Jenny hanivers, dragons and basilisks in the old natural history books and in modern times. *Scientific Monthly* (for June 1934), pp.511-23.

Guirand, F. (ed.). *Larousse Encyclopedia of Mythology.* English translation by R.Aldington & D.Ames. Paul Hamlyn. London.

Heuvelmans, B. 1962. *On the Track of Unknown Animals.* 2nd edn. Rupert Hart-Davis. London.

Hulme, F.E. 1895. *Natural History Lore and Legend.* Quaritch. London.

Humphrey, G. 1797. *Museum Calonnianum.* London.

Hutchins, J. 1968. *Discovering Mermaids and Sea Monsters.* Shire Publications. Tring.

J.R. 1829. Zoological imposture. *Magazine of Natural History*, vol.1, p.189.

Jackson, B.D. 1923. *Linnaeus.* H.F.&G.Witherby. London.

Jahn, M.E. 1963. A further note on Dr. Johann Bartholomew Adam Beringer. *Journal of the Society for the Bibliography of Natural History*, vol.4, pp.160-1. & Woolf, D.J. 1963. *The Lying Stones of Dr. Johann Bartholomew Adam Beringer being his Lithographiae Wirceburgensis.* University of California Press. Berkeley & Los Angeles.

Kier, P.M. 1969. A Cretaceous echinoid with false teeth. *Palaeontology*, vol.12, pp.488-96.

Klingender, F.D. 1953. St. Francis and the birds of the Apocalypse. *Journal of the Warburg and Courtauld Institute*, vol.16, pp.13-23.

Lack, D. 1963. An undiscovered species of swift. *Bird Notes*, vol.30, pp.258-60.

Lane, F.W. 1957. *Kingdom of the Octopus.* Jarrolds. London.

Lane, M.A. & Watson, A. 1975. A revision of the genus *Stenognatha* Felder (Lepidoptera: Arctiidae: Pericopinae). *Journal of Natural History*, vol.9, pp.107-17.

Lehner, E.&J. 1969. *A Fantastic Bestiary. Beasts and Monsters in Myth and Folklore.* Tudor Publishing Co. New York.

Ley, W. 1952. *The Lungfish, the Dodo, & the Unicorn.* New edn. The Viking Press. New York.

Lochner von Hummelstein, J.H. 1716. *Rariora musei Besleriani.* Nuremberg.

M.C.G. 1829. A sea spider. *Magazine of Natural History*, vol.2, p.211.

Marco Polo. 1931. *The Travels of Marco Polo.* Translated from the text of L.F.Benedetto by Professor Aldo Ricci, with Introduction and Index by Sir E.Dennison Ross. Routledge & Kegan Paul Ltd. London.

Meiklejohn, M.F. 1950. Notes on the Hoodwink *(Dissimulatrix spuria). Bird Notes*, vol.24, pp.89-92.

Menteath, J.S. 1833. Mr. Waterton solicited to explain the Frontispiece to his Wanderings in South America. *Magazine of Natural History*, vol.6, pp.282-3.

Merian, M.S. 1730. *Metamorphosis Insectorum Surinamensium.* 2nd edn. Amsterdam.

Misson, F.M. 1699. *A New Voyage to Italy.* 2 vols. London.

Murray, J. 1830. Mermaid. *Magazine of Natural History*, vol.3, p.447.

Napier, J. Bigfoot. *The Yeti and Sasquatch in Myth and Reality.* Jonathan Cape. London.

Nichols, J. 1812. *Literary Anecdotes of the 18th Century.* 9 vols. London.

Oudemans, A.C. 1892. *The Great Sea-serpent.* E.J.Brill. Leiden. Luzac & Co. London.

Owens, R.M. 1971. In search of Welsh trilobites. *Amgueddfa*, No.9, pp.24-37.

Pelkwijk, J.ter. 1940. De basilisk. *Toeristen kampionen* (for 2 March 1940).

Pontopiddan, E.L. 1755. *The Natural History of Norway.* (English translation from the Danish original of 1752-3.) London.

R.L. 1968. Spotting the Siggahfoops. *Scottish Field*, vol.115, p.18.

Sanger, 'Lord' G. 1927. *Seventy Years a Showman.*

J.M.Dent & Sons Ltd. London & Toronto.

Seba, A. (et al.) 1734-65. *Locupletissimum rerum naturalium thesauri accurata descriptio, etc.* 4 vols. Amsterdam.

Sharpe, R.B. 1879. *Catalogue of the Passeriformes, or Perching birds, in the collection of the British Museum*, vol.4. London.
1886. Notes on some birds from Perak. *Proceedings of the Zoological Society of London* (for 1886), pp.350-4.

Stümpke, H. (alias Steiner, G.). 1957. *Bau und Leben der Rhinogradentia.* Gustav Fischer Verlag. Stuttgart. (French translation, by R.Weill (1962), as *Anatomie et biologie des Rhinogrades; un nouvel ordre des Mammifères*, Masson, Paris; English translation, by L.Chadwick (1967), as *The Snouters: Form and Life of the Rhinogrades*, American Museum of Natural History, The Natural History Press, New York.)

T.H. 1749. [Letter concerning a sea monster]. *Gentleman's Magazine*, vol.19, p.506.

Tegner, H. 1975. Man made the unicorn. *The Countryman* (for Summer 1975), pp. 182-4.

Thompson, C.J.S. 1930. *The Mystery and Lore of Monsters.* Williams & Norgate. London.

Topsell, E. 1607. *Historie of Foure-footed Beastes.* London.

Tradescant, J. 1656. *Musaeum Tradescantianum.* London.

Traylor, M.A. 1967. *The Nomenclatural Standing of Clericus polydenominata.* The Vanishing Press (privately published). Gurnee, Illinois.

Tryon, A.F. 1955. The Vegetable Lamb of Tartary. *Missouri Botanical Garden Bulletin*, vol.43, pp.25-8.

'V.'. 1829. Notice of an imposture entitled a Pygmy Bison, or American Ox. *Magazine of Natural History*, vol.2, pp.218-19.
1829. The Pygmy Bison. *Magazine of Natural History*, vol.21, p.301.

Waterton, C. 1828. *Wanderings in South America.* 2nd edn. B.Fellowes. London.
1833. The Nondescript. *Magazine of Natural History*, vol.6, pp.381-3.

Weiner, J.S. 1955. *The Piltdown Forgery.* University Press, Oxford.

Whitley, G.P. 1928. Jenny hanivers. *Australian Magazine*, vol.3, pp.262-4.

Index